THE DARK HEART OF ITALY

The Dark Heart of Italy

TOBIAS JONES

faber and faber

First published in 2003
by Faber and Faber Limited
3 Queen Square London WC1N 3AU

Typeset by Faber and Faber Ltd
Printed in England by Clays Ltd, St Ives plc

A CIP record for this book
is available from the British Library
ISBN 0–571–20582–8

4 6 8 10 9 7 5 3

For Francesca Lenzi

Contents

Acknowledgements

Parts of this book first appeared in the *London Review of Books* and in *Prospect*. I am very grateful to the respective editors, Mary-Kay Wilmers and David Goodhart, and their colleagues.

I am enormously indebted to my Italian family. Heartfelt thanks to Raul Lenzi and Daniela Calebich for the open invitation to *La Torre*, for feeding me for four years and for constantly showing me all that's best about their country. Much respect to all the Sisters Calebich, to the Diena family – Paolo, Laura and Matteo – and to Enrico Basaglia. Without the *moschettieri* from the summer of 1998 I would never have stayed here: 'L'Albe', 'Il Davo' and 'Il Gallo' have been very, very *grandi*.

I have had the immense fortune, over many years, of picking the large brains of Professors Diego Saglia, Jeremy Elston, Hugh Jones and Niall Ferguson. The sharing of their wisdom in times of need has been invaluable. My *avvocato*, Filippo Ziveri, has accompanied me on various journeys, and has always been very generous and judicious. I've also been exceptionally lucky to share the company, contacts and Catholicism of Glenn Alessi, an outsider with the inside track.

The following have all helped me out when it really counted: Rebecca Nicolson, Lucia Sbravati, Carlo Torinesi, Pino Colombi, Betta Salvini, Giovanni Granatiero, Philippa Woolf, Norah Wallace, Marco Mazzoli, Mette Rudvin, John Foot, Giuseppe Lavagetto, Robert Frew, Marcello Ziveri, Andrew Wigley, Caterina Pavese, Mario Casartelli, John 'Killer' Carnegie, Gloria Saccò, Mauro Levati, Stefano Mercurio, Letizia Di Chiara, Stephen Flemington, Livio Lacchini, Stephanie Tann, Mario Salvini, Ciccio Perucci, the Caramaschi family and Giovanni Camattini. Respect also to Dickon and Debbie, Sparky and Rich, Matthew and Nicola, Alex and Amelia, Rob and Nobuko, Frances O'Sullivan Wallace, Clare Ranger and the rest. Stephen Anderman and Richard Hepwood both know I have a debt with them, and they both know why.

I have benefitted from extraordinary back-up from Britain. My agent, Georgina Capel at Capel & Land, has kept me fed and clothed. I'm hugely grateful to her and to Robert Caskie and Philippa Brewster. I will always be indebted to Walter Donohue at Faber. Writing on Italy has often been excruciating and Walter has kept me balanced in many ways other than just the financial. Thanks also to Jon Riley and everyone else at Faber for their faith and patience.

Above all else, I'm indebted to my family back in Britain. The generosity of my parents, Bob and Jane, and of my siblings, David and Vandana and Paul, defies description. Thanks to them, and to all the other Joneses, Wallaces, and Ramrakhas.

Unless otherwise stated, I take responsibility for the translations of Italian texts. Any errors, of translation or otherwise, are obviously entirely mine.

Preface

'Travellers, without exception,' wrote Stendhal in 1824, 'are wont to confine their descriptions of Italy to the realm of the inanimate; their portraits concern only the monuments, the sites, the sublime manifestations of nature in that happy land . . .' Even today, that is still very much the case. People only talk or write about Italy because they are obsessed by the age, the beauty and the hedonism of the country, by the Roman ruins, the Renaissance art, by a favourite *duomo* or *palazzo*. Visitors flock towards cathedrals and canals. They are overawed by the great, historical cities, Venice or Florence, and by the stunning countryside of Tuscany and Umbria. Holiday-makers head for the beautiful beaches, there to enjoy pizzas and ice-cream and Chianti. The drooling Grand Tourists' path to those 'sites' and 'sublime manifestations' is so well-trodden that I decided to take a different route, to write about the 'animate' Italy, about its livelier and stranger sides.

Someone once wrote that 'history begins when memory ends'. This book is on the cusp between the two. I moved to Italy at a time when the country was engaged in a strange sort of collective historical debate, as people tried to remember or forget what had gone on in Italy only a few years or decades before. The 'Slaughter Commission' was, after thirteen years of investigations, beginning to reach conclusions about some of the country's intermittent terrorist 'slaughters' (which were one part of the country's *anni di piombo*, its 'years of lead', from the late 1960s until the early 1980s). Simultaneously a series of acutely politicised trials were drawing controversial conclusions about that era of political terrorism. It was a unique opportunity to watch 'terrorists' – politicians, academics or militarists – defending and explaining themselves and their pasts. Extravagant accusations were made, indignant defences mounted. As one of the defendants, Adriano Sofri, wrote:

I had to overcome a resistance to fighting an old battleground I had abandoned a long time ago. I couldn't defend myself as I am today, with my more rounded thoughts . . . my good manners and my old books. I had to defend the person I was then, sharp-tongued, vituperative, constantly on the move. I was faced with the alternative of confounding time and identifying absolutely with the person I was, or denouncing that person and losing my relationship to my own past . . .

As I attended the trials and interviewed the protagonists, it often felt as if I were watching the country's history through a kaleidoscope, as every few weeks the lens was twisted and the colours spilt into new and disconcertingly different arrangements.

Meanwhile the historiography of Italy's 'revolution', its 'Clean Hands' initiative against corruption during the early 1990s, was being hurriedly rewritten. 'Corruption', according to the 'restoration' rhetoric, wasn't really in business and politics, but rather embedded deep within the Italian judiciary. Suddenly the revolution (which caused the ignominious end of the First Republic, and heralded the beginning of the Second) was being portrayed not as a noble clean-up of public life, but as a bloody coup d'état hatched by 'Jacobin judges'.

Many of the threads from those historical debates, and the scandals which surrounded them, seemed to lead in the direction of one man: Silvio Berlusconi (since May 2001 the Italian Prime Minister). Each time there was a big news story – a scandal or success story, or usually a strange combination of the two – Berlusconi or members of his political coalition seemed somehow involved. As I watched the nation's historical debate (the furious arguments between 'Fascists' and 'Communists', between 'corrupt' businessmen and 'corrupt' judges) I realised that what was at stake wasn't simply an interpretation of Italy's tragic past. Rather, political careers were on the line. The debate, I realised, was so furious precisely because many of the players were on the brink of political power and were keen to present themselves as part of the 'New Italy' rather than stalwarts of the old one. Berlusconi and his bizarre coalition were particularly compromised: their winning electoral line had always been that they were naïve newcomers to Italian politics and public life, whilst in reality they slowly began to appear very familiar players from the past. As one observer remarked, Berlusconi began to appear nothing more than the butterfly that had, since the early 1990s, emerged from the Christian Democratic caterpillar: more colourful, nimbler, but essentially the same beast.

Thus I began writing about Berlusconi almost by accident. I had wanted to write about the country's recent history, about all those aspects of Italy ignored by tourists. And yet, each time I wrote about the history, contemporary politics imposed itself. I tried writing about other things – about the nuances of the language, about the football, the television, the Catholicism – and Berlusconi and his coalition reappeared. Thus, Berlusconi's career became the thread that links the following chapters because he is, I realised, the 'owner' of Italy. As the words of one famous song comment, he seems to own everything from *Padre Nostro* (Our Father) to *Cosa Nostra* (the Mafia). Living in Italy it's impossible to move without, inadvertently, coming up against his influence. If you watch football matches, or television, try to buy a house or a book or a newspaper, rent a video, or else simply shop in a supermarket, the chances are you're somehow filling the coffers of *Il Cavaliere* (last estimated to be worth $14 billion). When you lie on any beach during the summer months, one of his planes is likely to fly overhead with a banner trailing behind: 'Liberty' it reads, or '*Forza Italia!*'

Berlusconi is, without doubt, the most unconventional and controversial political leader on the world stage. The consistent accusation against his government (from both Italy and abroad) is that it's made up of 'black shirts' and 'white collars': that is, of former Fascists and white-collar criminals. Moral indignation is the standard response, because from every angle the government really does seem contrary to normal, democratic discourse. But the indignation does little to explain the phenomenon of *Forza*

Italia. It doesn't begin to explain who Berlusconi is, nor does it explain why he is loved by, and has been elected by, millions of Italians. Italy and its *Presidente* are two sides of the same democratic coin, and I've spent four years travelling in Italy trying to understand 'both sides', both the country and its *Cavaliere*. I'm aware that I have often conflated the two, identifying Berlusconi entirely with Italy, and I'm aware that the result can tend (depending on political opinion) to portray unfairly a beautiful country in an ugly light. I have taken that approach because the electoral landslide of 2001 showed just how intimate is the marriage between the two. It would have been perverse to divorce Berlusconi from his electorate, or vice versa.

Of the following chapters, '*Parole, Parole, Parole*' is a long glossary, a description of learning the language and all its implications. 'The Mother of All Slaughters' examines the work of the parliamentary 'Slaughter Commission' and the tortuous, politicised trial with which it overlapped. 'Penalties and Impunity' is an induction into the murky waters of Italian football and media ownership. 'The Sofri Case' is a prison interview with the country's most famous 'murderer'. 'The Means of Seduction' is about Italian aesthetics; about the country's visual culture, from the heights of its cinema to the depths of its televisual 'videocracy'. 'Clean Hands' is an account of Italy's confusing 'revolution' which launched Berlusconi into politics in the first place. 'Miracles and Mysteries' admires and addresses the monolithic culture of Italian Catholicism, and traces the wafer-thin line between the Vatican and Italian politics. Thereafter, the chapters are more purely political, analysing Berlusconi's election victory ('An Italian Story') and the consequences of it ('Concrete Problems'). The final chapter, '*I Morti*', is about the growing resistance to the regime, and draws a few conclusions about my four years in Italy.

I have used the first person throughout; 'not', as Stendhal wrote, 'for egotism, but because there's no other way to tell the story.'

The Dark Heart of Italy

1

Parole, Parole, Parole

This sort of sadness has always prevailed among intelligent Italians, but most of them, to evade suicide or madness, have taken to every known means of escape . . . a passion for women, for food . . . above all, for fine-sounding words.

    Ignazio Silone

I arrived in Parma knowing only a few Italian words culled from classical music and menus (*adagio*, *allegro*, *prosciutto* and so on), and I found myself in the infantile position of trying to understand my surroundings at the same time as I was learning how to describe them. At the beginning, unable to comprehend what was being said, I only heard the noise of the language, which sounds like coins fired out of a machine gun: quick clinks, long, long words made up of short, rhythmic syllables. Conversations are also visual: words are underlined by hands which work overtime, the fingers moving into strange shapes as if the speaker were working on some invisible origami creation in his palms.

When you do begin to understand the words, you quickly appreciate the beauty of the language. Every worthy person or object or place is given an evocative nickname. Football players, the princes of society, are called 'the swan' (the tall Marco Van Basten) or 'the little pendulum' (the Brazilian Cafu who races up and down Roma's right-wing). Venice is *La Serenissima*. The south of the country is *il Mezzogiorno*, the 'midday'. The motorway that leads there is called the *Autostrada del Sole*, the 'motorway of the sun'. The little pleasures of daily life have suggestive names. The frothy milk and cocoa powder of a *cappuccino* is so called because it resembles the brown hood of a Capuchin friar. The more elegant the concept, the more beautiful the word. A bow-tie is a *farfalla*, a butterfly. Cuff-links are *gemelli*, twins. A hair-dryer is called a *fon* because the warm wind which blows over north Italy from the Austrian Alps is called the *föhn*. Even words relating to sexual matters seem more imaginative and better-phrased: to key, to sweep, to saw and, my favourite, to trombone.

Another difference is simply the decibel level. Italians, I didn't need to be told, are loud. The *palazzo* in which I live is a square medieval building. It is now divided into flats, each with windows and crumbling balconies onto our little courtyard. It's hard to explain the implications of that simple architecture. I had always seen Italian paintings of sun-drenched courtyards, lined with laundry and loggia, but never quite realised what they're like to live in. It's not that there's particularly a sense of community – most of the flats are now legal offices, since the courtroom is only a few hundred metres away; there's a restaurant on one side, a gymnasium on another. It's that you live in very close proximity to your neighbours and, above all, to their noise. Instead of answering the modern speaker-phones which double as door-bells, most lean out of the open windows and shout to their friends four floors below. The whole *palazzo*, naturally, hears the conversation. I frequently hear arguments from the lawyers' offices. There's pop music permanently blaring out of the gym, and twice a week an aggressive aerobics instructor rolls up to bark instructions which can be heard at the other end of the building. At precisely five every evening the lady in the flat opposite mine, on the west wing of the building, starts singing her arpeggios and arias. The noise, always mingled with the roar of a nearby moped, takes some getting used to but, after a while, other countries begin to seem eerily quiet, even dull.

The next, obvious difference to English is that conversations sometimes sound like excerpts from intelligent discussions in a museum. It's hard to explain, but the past seems ever-present; not just in the endless ancient buildings, but also in conversation. Even in cheery chats in the pub, people start heated arguments about some incident from the *seicento* (the seventeenth century), or begin discussing the merits of some baron or artist from the Middle Ages. It is never done boastfully, but rather casually, as if they were gossiping about a neighbour. Conversation in Parma often revolves around food or opera, since the city is the epicentre of Italian cuisine and opera (it is home to Parma ham and Parmesan cheese, the birthplace of Giuseppe Verdi and Arturo Toscanini). And yet, even those conversations are unpretentious. Listen to the old men in the squares who swig wine and play cards all day, and you sense that same easy familiarity with subjects which would, in England, appear effete: *prosciutto*, opera, grapes and so on. And they're discussed in the most earthy terms: 'I swear it, my balls rolled out of the auditorium when I heard the orchestra . . .'

The blissful creativity of the language is most obvious in the insults and arguments. The humbling effects of one-liners and put-downs are incredible, and in the course of time I received my fair share: 'Holy pig!' screamed one old woman as I inadvertently blocked her exit from a parking space, 'if you screw like you park don't be surprised when you become a cuckold!' All that verbal jousting is hard to take at first, but once you can respond in kind, arguing becomes a normal, enjoyable pastime, a refreshing burst of sincerity.

Those, at least, were my early impressions: the happy noise and creativity of the language, the carefree chaos. Gradually, though, something very different became obvious. Having read E.M. Forster and D.H. Lawrence, I had always imagined Italy as a place where reserve and reticence fall away, and where the polite hypocrisies of Britain could be thrown off. For those Edwardian writers, Italy was a country so vivacious and sensuous that it became a theatre for sexual awakening and carnal knowledge. It's what Lawrence called the Italians' 'blood-knowledge':

My great religion is a belief in the blood, the flesh, as being wiser than the intellect. We can go wrong in our minds. But what our blood feels and believes and says, is always true . . . That is why I like to live in Italy. The people are so unconscious. They only feel and want: they don't know.[1]

The more words I learnt, though, and the more I understood their origins, the more the country seemed, not chaotic, but incredibly hierarchical and formal. Even *ciao* was a greeting, I discovered, derived from the word *schiavo*, slave. The cheery *ciao*, Italians' most famous word, originally implied subservience and order, as in 'I am your slave'. (In the Veneto, when you go into a shop, you're often greeted with *comandi*, which is again rigidly hierarchical: saying *comandi* is a plea by the shop assistant to 'be commanded'.) In Italy one endlessly has to obtain 'permission': all foreigners – even those from the EU – have to have a *permesso*, a permit, to stay in the country; it's also the word used when crossing the threshold of someone else's house: 'permission to enter?'

The next word which recurred again and again was vaguely related: *sistemare*, which means to order or sort out. A situation was invariably *sistemato*, 'systemised', be it a bill, a problem, a relationship. It can also mean a murderous 'sorting out', as in *lui è stato sistemato*, 'he's been sorted'. The rigidity, the search for orderliness, was everywhere. 'All's well' is *tutt'a posto*: 'everything in its place'. Randomness is a recent, imported concept (the English is used, as in the verb *randomizzare*). Rules are, at least on the surface, very important in Italy. Since eccentricity is frowned upon, one of the most frequently heard phrases is *non si fa*, 'it's not the done thing' (which invariably refers to dietary habits or dress codes, where the rules are most rigid). Rather than excitingly chaotic, Italians began to appear incredibly conservative and obedient.

I had moved to Italy because I was in love, and I thought a relationship would be, if not 'casual', then at least outside cast-iron conformity. But that, too, came as a rude shock. It was an example of systemisation that I had never expected. About three or four months after I had arrived in Parma, friends (from southern Italy, where things are even more formal) started talking about someone called my *fidanzata*. Until that time they had usually referred to the person in question as my *ragazza*, my 'girl'. Then, almost overnight, this new word was apparently more apt. I went to the dictionary and found *fidanzata* translated as 'betrothed'. Strange, I thought, I'm sure I would have remembered if I had proposed to her, or even discussed an engagement with her family or our friends.

'No, no,' I said, wagging my finger in imitation of their usual admonition, 'she's my *ragazza*.' The amused faces were unforgettable. They slapped me on the back, enjoying having to explain exactly why I was now 'betrothed'. 'And you've done it all so quickly,' laughed Ciccio.

Thus, after a few months, I saw that the country wasn't happily chaotic, but rather systemised and rigidly hierarchical. Any approach towards authority had to involve a startling degree of grovelling. *Garbo*, I was told, was a quality that even an Englishman would need to work on. It means 'courtesy', or else the ability to smooth over contradiction, betrayal or rudeness. The other quality required of an Italian speaker, and especially a journalist, is *salamelecco*, which implies obsequiousness and flattery (from the Arabic *salaam aleikum*). As I spent weeks and then months in police stations and post offices, trying to get the correct permission to live or work in Italy, I realised that it wasn't enough to bluster in and demand the correct form. One had to deploy a contorted, formal language full of *svolazzi* (embellishments), or else the sunglassed officer reviewing my case might be offended and want to flex his bureaucratic muscles. To request interviews I had to write sentences of such sycophancy it was almost embarrassing: '. . . given one's noted fame as a political thinker, and notwithstanding the busy timetable which one has, I would be honoured if one felt able to consent to a courteous interview . . .'

Then, the more I watched and understood TV, I realised that credibility in Italian is often based upon pomposity. Nowhere else are words so often spoken just for their idyllic sound, rather than their meaning. To be *logorroico*, incredibly wordy, is esteemed more than anything that's actually being said. Invariably, the only way to get a conversational look-in is to interrupt. The only way to be taken seriously (especially as a journalist) is to hold forth with contorted clauses and forget any pretence of concision. There is one song that, for me, became Italy's alternative anthem (partly because it's so often aired, and also because it's so appropriate): Mina's *Parole, Parole, Parole* ('words, words, words'). It's beautifully sung with resignation at all the yakking, all the inconsequential talk.

The stereotype of German speakers in Britain, that they're brutally to the point, is exactly what Italians think of English speakers, and especially journalists. 'You can't be so direct,' said my 'betrothed', correcting my idiosyncratic style of writing Italian; 'you need to dress it up a bit'. So each time I wrote a letter (usually a letter of complaint to Telecom Italia) I had to have my prose turned into an august essay as if written by a rather cocky, over-erudite schoolboy. Every letter is opened by the word *egregio*, which in English implies flagrant or foolish ('egregious'), but in Italian is an honorific as in *Egregio Signor Jones*. And honorifics are the all-important sweeteners of the language – every graduate is called 'doctor', a simple football manager a 'technical commissioner', a weather forecaster has to be at least a Lieutenant-Colonel (duly decked out in medals for services to meteorology).

I used to read four or five newspapers a day to brush up on my slowly improving Italian. At the end of hours of diligent reading, with a door-step dictionary at my elbow, I knew nothing more about current affairs than I had before breakfast. I had been informed about absolutely nothing. It wasn't a case of incomprehension but of bewilderment. There were so many words, pages and pages of comment and opinion and surveys, which said absolutely nothing. Everything had to be qualified and contradicted. It was, I was told, a famous rhetorical device called *anacoluto* ('anacoluthon', inconsistency of grammar or argument). The classic advice to rookie journalists in England (that your piece will cut from the bottom up, so your first sentence has to contain the most important information, the second sentence the next important thing and so on) is entirely reversed in Italy. The last sentence, if you're lucky, will tell you what the article you've waded through thinks it's all about.

All of which does, strangely, have an important bearing on political discourse. That smoke screen of words means that no one can ever penetrate to the core of an issue, or ever understand fully what's going on. More importantly, the country appears serenely *alla mano*, which is to say entirely unpretentious: probably noisy, vivacious, never pulling its linguistic punches. But when confronted by any incarnation of authority, that directness gave way to deference, chaos gave way to conformity. I had seen friends who were, in their homes, the epitome of the carefree; when they had to go to the post office, though, they would put aside a whole morning to practise the long, imploring speeches they would have to use.

Whilst I was trying to learn Italian, everybody else was desperate to speak English. It became very obvious that the chicest thing to do in Italian is to drop in English words – rather like showing *savoir-faire* in English. Almost all the advertising slogans, on TV or on billboards, are in English. Many DJs speak half in English, or have American interns who do various chat-shows. Sometimes the news on radio stations is read in both languages. Despite the fact that Italy's fashion industry is superior to any other, if you walk down any street you will see dozens of Italians wearing clothes covered in English writing, often superimposed on a Union Jack or the Stars-and-Stripes. It's called *esterofilia*, a liking for all things foreign.

Even football, which like food and classical music is one of the bastions of Italian pride, has been thoroughly anglicised, such as 'Corner *di Totti, Delvecchio sta* dribblando, crossa, *però Montella è* offside'; a football manager is also *Il Mister* (pronounced to rhyme with 'easter'). The importations are often hilariously inaccurate. The many billboards advertising sex-shops on the ring-roads around cities advertise what are called *sexy shops*. I've often tried – and always failed – to explain why it's quite so funny: it would mean that the actual bricks and mortar of the shop are provocative, 'you know, maybe in a G-string'. Victimisation in the workplace is called *mobbing*. A morning suit is called *il tight*. A tuxedo is *lo smoking*. *Petting*, it's as well to know, doesn't mean petting in the English sense, but a type of foreplay that is at the extremely advanced stages. *Flirting* means flirting. *Slip* means slip only in the Y-front sense, not as in 'slip-up'. Politicians, too, are keen to show that they're cosmopolitan and drop in all sorts of English words, even entitling their rallies *Security Day*, or their conferences *I Care*.

Sometimes the importation of English is nothing other than *snobismo*, a bit of easy showing-off when an Italian phrase could just as well have been used. Other times, though, there are fissures in the Italian, conceptual cracks where there is no alternative to an English notion. Soon after I arrived, I spent an enjoyable night sampling a friend's grandmother's home-made *nocino* – walnut liqueur. (Anything *della nonna*, of the granny, be it a restaurant dessert or a fiery liqueur, implies family and therefore *bontà*, goodness.) The following morning I discovered that hangover simply has no equivalent in Italian. (Drinking habits are infinitely more civilised than in Britain, and even when they're not, it's a transgression to which no one's going to admit.) There's no word to express condescending or patronising, which are I suppose the flip-sides of subservience. 'Self-control' is also absent in Italian, so the English is used.

The *esterofilia*, the liking for all things foreign, extends to names. Friends despair of my taste, but my favourite Italian actor is 'Bud Spencer', a bullish, former Olympic swimmer whose real name is Carlo Pedersoli. During the 1970s he went to America with 'Terence Hill' to make B-movies which pretended to be American, but which starred Italians mouthing English; the films were then dubbed into Italian for Italian audiences. Slapstick but touching, these films deliberately put a bit of hamburger beef into the spaghetti western, thus catering for the yearning for all things American. Christian names often follow the lead. I had found a job teaching at Parma University and in my classes, next to Maria Immacolata (Mary Immaculate) and Gian Battista (John the Baptist) there was a William, a Tommy and a Gladys. Other favourites are Jessica, JR (thanks to Dallas) or Deborah. Italy's most famous televisual personalities are called 'Gerry' or 'Mike'.

More surprising was that Russia has also been – especially for those from 'red' Parma or the Communist bastion of Reggio

Emilia – the inspiration for non-Italian names. Amongst people my age (those born during the *anni di piombo*, the 'years of lead') Yuri is certainly more common than Tobia, and much less laughed at. (The first of many nicknames I was given was *Zio Tobia*, Uncle Tobias, which is the Italian for that famous farmer 'Old MacDonald'.)

The difficulties of learning the language were compounded by the fact that Italian still hasn't entirely percolated into Italy's city states. Until the advent of radio and then TV, few people actually spoke correct Italian as their first language. Children of Italians who emigrated in the first half of the twentieth century often return to Italy thinking that they know Italian, only to discover that their parents only spoke and taught them their dialect. The results are still obvious today. When I asked students to translate an English word into Italian, I was normally offered a dozen alternatives, and long arguments ensued amongst the Sicilian, Venetian and Lombard students as to what was the proper Italian.

TV and radio are dominated by quiz shows that ask contestants what a fairly ordinary Italian word means; or else question them about some long-forgotten piece of grammar. I would occasionally ask a simple linguistic question at the dinner table (the 'remote past', say, of a particular verb) only to be offered three or four alternatives, before everyone started laughing and admitted they weren't quite sure.

It was, I was informed, a problem of the *piazza*. *Piazza*, which I had always assumed meant simply 'square', had other connotations, as in 'the team had better start playing better soon because Reggio has a *piazza calda* ('a hot square', which is to say volatile fans or a politically engaged population). The *piazza* is the 'city', its symbolic centre where people (for political or footballing reasons) 'descend' to celebrate or protest. The *piazza* is the soul of local pride, a concept that is close to *campanilismo* (the affection for one's own bell-tower). It's also, sometimes, the place of resistance to outside, even Italian national, influence. If Italians spend much time deriding Italy, doing the same to their (truly) beautiful home town is unthinkable. There's a provincialism (in the proudest, least pejorative, sense) in Italy that is unthinkable elsewhere. The word for country – *paese* – even doubles as the word for town, suggesting that solidarity exists as much on a local as it does on a national level. City states are still city states, with their own cuisine, culture and dialect.

It became very obvious that 'Italy' and 'Italian' are notions that have been somewhat superimposed on city states, and which still haven't been entirely accepted or absorbed. The country is really what Carlo Levi called 'thousands of countries', in which inhabitants enjoy the best of both worlds: the cosiness of provincialism mixed with urbane cosmopolitanism. The result is the most beautiful aspect of Italian life. People invariably live and work where they were born, rather than flocking to some far-off capital. Cousins and uncles and grandparents live in the same town, and very often under the same roof. (Although the following figures are from 1988–89, they have changed little in the last decade: 15.2% of married Italian children live either in the same house or the same *palazzo* as their mother. 50.3% live in the same *comune*. Only 13.2% live further than 50 kilometres from the maternal nest.)

A more serious drawback of the proud provincialism is that any notion of the 'state' is pejorative. The word *stato*, referring to the state at a national level, is almost always used as a criticism. The *stato* is the cause of all complaints and grudges. There is, as is well known, no patriotism in Italy. Nobody feels much affection for anything national (the only exception being the *Azzurri*, the national football team). The unification of Italy is so recent that many people still feel that the Italian flag is only an 'heraldic symbol . . . crude and out-of-place – the red shameless and the green absurd.'[2] Every Italian I met spoke about their country, at the national level, as exactly the opposite of what I had been told in Britain: instead of a land of pastoral bliss, Italians told me, with disparaging sneers, that their country was 'a mess', a 'nightmare', and most often 'a brothel'. Italy, they said, was a 'banana republic', or, since the advent of Berlusconi, a 'banana monarchy'. Everyone was very welcoming, but there was always, after a few hours, a warning. No one could understand why I had left Britain. A few told me to go back as soon as possible. They all, without exception, said Italy was *bella*, before explaining to me why it's not at all what it seems.

There was an obvious, inexplicable inferiority complex about being Italian. The first time I went to browse through a bookshop, there were a host of indignant titles on display: *Italy, The Country We Don't Like, The Italian Disaster, The Abnormal Country*. Watching TV, I realised that a large percentage of the Italian film industry seemed to rely on the 'indignant' genre. Endless films have honest men taking on the dark, unknown forces of Italy and meeting their inevitable, early death: *An Everyday Hero, The Honest Man, A Good Man*.

The discrepancy between my drooling friends in Britain and the dismay of locals was even more evident when reading Italian classics. There was one metaphor that was always used to describe Italy: 'whore', 'harlot', 'brothel'. For Dante, Italy was an 'inn of woe, slavish and base . . . a brothel's space'. For Boccaccio it was the 'woman of the world', once regal but now fallen (*fuggita è ogni virtù*). Italy was, for Machiavelli, a woman disfigured and nude: 'without head, without order, beaten, undressed, lacerated, coarse . . .' So much for the sunny, celestial land I had, having read Shelley and Byron, been expecting: 'a plane of light between two heavens of azure', or a place 'whose ever-golden fields' were 'ploughed by the sunbeams solely'.

I tried to find the origin of the use of 'whore' as a metaphor, and found that it was coined because of the perception that Italy had, as it were, been through so many hands. Bourbons, Hapsburgs, rival popes and other external dynasties had so regularly conquered and 'possessed' her that a weary, common expression became *O Francia o Spagna, basta ch' a magna* – it didn't matter who the political 'pimp' was, as long as there was food to eat. Since Italy wasn't united until 1861, it remained for centuries a sort of bargaining chip in the balance of European power. Long before imperialism reached the East and West Indies, Italy was a colonised country, becoming rather like India would for the British: a 'jewel' in the imperial crown, esteemed for its age and cultural inheritance. There were, of course, indigenous dukedoms and independent republics on the peninsula, but they remained squeezed between strongholds of Hapsburgs and Bourbons in the 'race for Italy'. (Even the mythological conception of Italy was thanks to outside influence: Saturn, ousted from Olympus by his son Jupiter, became the first of Latium's many foreign rulers.) The result is that even now the metaphor of prostitution is endlessly invoked and reiterated. It's become like Albion for the English: an intuitive image of what, for Italians, Italy has been (with the difference that it is invariably a negative image, and one which hints at the uncertainty about what 'Italy' really is, or who it belongs to).

Another reason the metaphor is used is the fact that the word for brothel (*casino*) also means 'mess' or 'confusion'. The very modus operandi of Italy is confusion. That's how Italy's power and secrecy works. Any investigator simply gets tied up in knots with all the facts and words and documents; with the convictions and contradictions. The result is that their investigations invariably end up with such an unbelievable story that, even if it's true, people are already bewildered beyond the point of no return. By far the most common expression heard to describe Italy is *bel casino*, which is rather like Laurel and Hardy's 'fine mess'. It means a 'beautiful confusion' or (originally) a 'beautiful brothel'.

I quickly understood the reason for the Italians' dismay about their state. Italy isn't a religious country: it's a clerical one. The usual fourth estate, the critical media, doesn't exist, and has been replaced by another power, slower, more ponderous and invariably faceless: bureaucracy. Its clerics are the modern incarnations of priests. They are the people who classify and authorise, the people whose signature or stamp is vital to survival. Like priests, they're the intermediaries who usher you along the yellow-brick road towards the blessed paradise of 'legitimacy'.

Here post offices and banks are like large, emptied churches.

They're sacred, communal places with the same shafts of oblique sunlight falling from high windows. There's a sense of people meekly approaching authority as they queue like communicants. Waiting, though, not to receive the eucharist, but to impart large portions of their earnings to one faceless monopoly or another. (One of the favourite events around mid-August is 'liberation day', the day of the calendar year in which you stop earning money that goes to the state, and start earning for yourself.) Hours pass and you get closer to the counter, closer to your brush with institutionalised usury. Then, because nothing – except driving – is done with anything resembling speed, and because the queueing system is unorthodox, you will find yourself further back than you were an hour ago. I used to get infuriated in such situations when I first arrived, but now I rather enjoy them. I've realised that, as the British go to the pub, so the Italians go to the post office. You meet and make friends, read a paper or just pass the time.

Bureaucracy means 'office power' (*bureau-kratos*), and nowhere are offices as powerful as in Italy. One recent study suggested that two weeks of every working year are lost by Italians in queues and bureaucratic procedures.[3] The calculation went that since Italians need, on average, 25 visits to various offices each year, the equivalent of almost 7,000 minutes each year are spent queuing. That would be a normal year; if you want to apply for a job, it's best to put aside a week or ten days in order to gather the correct documents, pay for them to be stamped and so on. It's like trying to catch confetti: having to race from one office to another, filling in forms and requests, trying to grasp pieces of paper which always just elude your grasp. As much as 2,000 billion lire is spent annually by Italians just to certify their status (car owner, divorced, resident at a particular address etc). It's not just expensive: it's exceptionally slow. It's been nicknamed the *lentocrazia*, the 'slowocracy'.

For many reasons the importance of Italy's bureaucracy is in its politicisation. The civil service has often been so slow to implement laws and legislation that they are superseded before they're in place.

Funds offered by government often, in the past, never arrived, and so became *residui passivi* (funds beyond their application date) which were duly returned to the treasury. Time-wasting, the greatest skill of a politicised civil servant, became in the post-war period an art-form, whereby civil servants could delay reforms by their obstinate slowness. Endless left-wing historians have written of the clerical class as a shadow parliament: hostile to change, servile only to its insider clients. The bureaucracy is also acutely politicised by the fact that clerical jobs are so precious that thousands, millions, of Italians compete in competitions for a *poltrona*, an 'armchair'. The jobs are particularly precious because they offer contracts for *tempo indeterminato*, for 'time immemorial'. Thus politicians are lobbied by ambitious parents who long for their child to enjoy the comfortable, cosy world of a clerical job. It's an example of another key-word of Italian politics: *clientelismo*, the culture of looking after your friends and family, and thereby keeping outsiders and unknowns out of the loop. I'm told the whole set-up is much more meritocratic than it was a few years ago, especially in the north, but it's still unlikely that you'll ever get a job without the contacts; you need to know the right local politician, or have the backing of – a phrase you frequently hear – a *famiglia importante*.

If you're outside the clerical class, though, you begin to understand the contempt Italians feel for their own state. You have to be painfully deferential to the clerics, you have to plead or lobby for the simplest things in the most wordy, sycophantic way. Or else, you can employ a *faccendiere*, a 'fixer', to smooth your way through the offices. After about a year in Italy, I was queueing at the post office, furious because I was having to pay the state monopoly Telecom Italia vast amounts of money for two phone lines which hadn't existed for months. I met one of my middle-aged students, 'Lucky' Luciano, and started grumbling to him. He laughed and shook his head as if that were nothing. He was, he said, still waiting for a 28 million lire refund from the state because he had paid too much tax back in the 1980s. Most of his friends had dodged the tax because they knew it was about to be revoked; he, having been honest, had paid a hefty price. Then, someone next to us in the queue began listing her woes, which went back to a rip-off she had suffered at the hands of the state during the 1970s. Within minutes, three parallel queues were all complaining, each person coming out with a horror story of governmental avarice and bureaucratic incompetence.

To attempt to reason, of course, is as futile as Canute defying the tide. 'We're not citizens,' the mother of my 'betrothed' told me, 'but subjects.' The distance between government and its people, and the them-and-us mentality it breeds, is central to any understanding of Italy. Everyone feels so badly treated, everything is so legalistic, that people feel justified in being a little lawless. 'Impotence in front of a blocked political system, incapable of change . . . the negation of democratic logic',[4] was even offered in the 1970s as one of the central reasons for Italian terrorism. Italians, the argument went, felt it a 'metaphysical curse' to be Italian, to be subjected to those grinding, inefficient but very powerful 'offices'.

The political consequences of the Italians' disdain for the Italian state is that the sense of community and of the common weal is minimal. The distancing from anything *statale* breeds individualism and an unusual attitude towards law-abiding. I have never lived in a country where so many people thought the state so criminal, and where, therefore, breaking that state's laws was so often, and indulgently, smiled upon. Few other countries have citizens with such an 'each to his own' mentality, or so much *menefreghismo*, 'I don't carism' (signalled with the back of the fingers thrown forward from the throat to the chin). It often seems as if everyone is trying to beat the system instead of trying to uphold it. *Fatta la legge trovato l'inganno* goes a common proverb: no sooner is a law made than someone will find a way round it.

Thus *furbo*, cunning, is the adjective most usually used by Italians to describe, with both admiration and dismay, their fellow countrymen: *Italiani, furba gente* ('cunning people' . . . the hand signal is the thumb nail scratching the cheek, implying someone who's 'cut' or 'cunning'). It can also mean sly, someone who gets by or gets ahead by being smart. A *furbo* watches his money, and probably casts a wistful eye on his neighbours'; he doesn't worry unduly about the rules. It's a very attractive trait (unless the cunning is at your own expense). Its opposite, *ingenuità*, implies gullibility. It's much better, of course, to be *furbo*, mildly dodgy, than *ingenuo*, naive (which originally implied virtue, because an *ingenuo* was one 'born free' rather than into slavery).

In Italy there's a morality that is unlike anything I have ever come across before. It's best summed up by Jacob Burckhardt in his *The Civilization of the Renaissance in Italy*:

Machiavelli . . . said openly 'We Italians are irreligious and corrupt above others.' Another man would have perhaps said, 'We are individually highly developed; we have outgrown the limits of morality and religion which were natural to us in our undeveloped state, and we despise outward law, because our rulers are illegitimate, and their judges and officers wicked men.' Machiavelli adds, 'because the Church and her representatives set us the worst example' . . . [5]

Therein lies the irony. Wrong-doing is invariably excused by the fact that political or church leaders are thought to be up to much worse things, and a little tax-dodging or bribery by us lesser beings really isn't that important. Which, of course, continues the vicious circle: everyone's up to something, and you're stupid if you're not too. Judgements are, in fact, rarely moral. Linguistically, as in so much else, the country is based upon aesthetics rather than ethics. The judgement words most used are not good or bad, but rather beautiful (*bello*) or ugly (*brutto*). *Bello* is an adjective trotted out with such regularity that it entirely obscures a concept like 'good'; it can then be trumped by *troppo bello*, when something is overwhelmingly 'too beautiful'. Thus immorality is less frowned upon than inelegance; to be beautiful, or to be somewhere beautiful or with someone beautiful, is more of an achievement than righteousness. That obsession with outward appearance is at the root of the word *figura*, which implies the 'figure' you've achieved . . . not only physically, but in the sense of creating an attractive or ugly impression. *Fare una figura*, to make a bad impression, is an error not necessarily of morals, but of presentation.

Strangely, the immorality is also intimately related to the Catholic church. There's a confessionalism in which it doesn't matter what you do, whether you're good or bad, as long as you remain 'in the ranks', as long as you profess your intention to get better. Italian Catholicism is all-embracing (the origin of the word, *katholikos*, implies exactly that): everyone is included, which means that everyone's forgiven, pardoned. There's nothing that a humble nod towards the purple cassocks or judicial 'togas' can't resolve. Politicians may be criminals, everyone may even acknowledge as much, but it doesn't matter: everything is white-washed. History, personal or political, is quickly forgotten.

Another type of *figura*, this time financial, is an integral part of that presentation. Whereas in Britain talking about or overtly displaying money is rather vulgar, in Italy it's the opposite. No one must appear poor. If in Britain politicians yearn to present themselves as ordinary human beings, in Italy they try and show how superhuman and super-wealthy they are. For the European elections in 1999, Silvio Berlusconi hired a cruise ship, at his own expense, to campaign around the peninsula. His enormous personal wealth was an asset, not a handicap: people admire him for the money he's made, and even for the *furbo* way in which he might have come by that money. Not to be outdone, his rival Massimo D'Alema, the then Prime Minister and former Communist, would be pictured on his yacht, keen to prove that he, too, wasn't short of a *quattrino*, a penny. *Ricchezza* and *bellezza*, wealth and beauty, are the foundations for any decent *figura*. Personal probity seems to be a side-issue.

The upside of this famous Italian 'a-legality' or 'a-morality' is that, compared to slavish Britain, no one really feels obliged to do anything they don't really want to. Only dress and dining codes are rigorously obeyed; any other rules – red lights or speed limits or no-smoking signs – are only suggestions. Slowing for pedestrians on zebra-crossings or wearing seatbelts are optional. There is also a completely different work ethic. Maybe it's because it's harder to be hurried and industrious in the heat, or else because the beaches and lakes and ski-resorts are all so close. Italy has more bank holidays (rather, saints' days and feast days) than any other country in Europe. These wonderful, entirely unexpected days off are sometimes announced, if national, on TV; otherwise you have to know that Saint Hilary is Parma's patron saint, and therefore the 13 January you will never, for as long you're within the city's missing walls, work on that day. They're also called *ponti*, 'bridges', which arch over the week and give you an opportunity to go to the sea from Thursday until maybe Tuesday. Invariably, one of the unions calls a crafty strike the day before, or immediately after, the 'bridge', so that their grateful card-carriers can get a better tan.

There's such a lack of guilt about taking time off, there's such a ridiculing of workaholics (another nickname I was given was *Il Calvinista*), that I often felt my working week had barely begun before another blessed saint offered me a quick break, and the opportunity for a pleasant family lunch in the mountains. I also noticed, during the skiing season, that my favourite barman had left a note outside his bar, hand-written on cardboard. 'Closed because of illness. I've gone to recuperate in the Dolomites. I will be better on Monday 18.'

The more I enjoyed the leisurely beauty, the *bellezza*, of Italy, the more sophisticated it seemed. The purpose, I was told, of beauty in Italy, quite apart from simply being beautiful, is that it's a form of fancy dress: an opportunity to seduce or sedate observers. Italy was a country, I read, 'peerless in the art of illusionism'. *Bisogna far buon viso a cattivo gioco* goes a proverb: appearances are important, and it's therefore 'necessary to disguise a bad game with a good face'. It's a bit like stiff upper lip, but subtly different: it implies not stoicism, but 'presentation'. Everything is dressed up, beautified and embellished. One Italian writer once described that peacock-syndrome, in which everything becomes part of a great show and subtle disguise:

. . . dull and insignificant moments in life must be made decorous and agreeable with suitable decorations and rituals. Ugly things must be hidden, unpleasant and tragic facts swept under the carpet whenever possible. Everything must be made to sparkle, a simple meal, an ordinary transaction, a dreary speech, a cowardly capitulation must be embellished and ennobled with euphemisms, adornments and pathos . . . show is as important as, many times more important than, reality.[6]

There were two occasions on which I began to realise how disguised everything was, or at least was thought to be. One Sunday afternoon I was sitting on the terrace of a house in the Apennines. A friend put on the coffee, which came to the boil like an aircraft, arriving from nowhere with a growl and receding with a hiss and a vapour trail. 'You see,' said the friend, smiling, 'this says everything about the differences between English and Italian.' He was pointing at the icing sugar on his croissant. 'You call that icing sugar, right? We call it "veil sugar". Apart from the fact that our term,' he was nodding, smiling because he knew he was right, 'is infinitely more elegant than yours, it's also much more subtle. "Icing on the cake" implies ostentation, right? Ours is a veil, romantic, beautiful, concealing something within . . .'

   Then, a little later, I was in Parma's football stadium watching a match. Everyone was sitting on their personalised blue-and-yellow cushions, until the ref made a bad decision and they were on their feet, insinuating that he was being cheated on by his wife: *Arbitro cornuto! Arbitro cornuto!* ('The referee's a cuckold! The referee's a cuckold!') It's an amusing and apt insult (in Britain the referee is just an onanist): apart from the fact that it sounds Shakespearean when translated into English, it implies that even the black shirt of authority, controlling the game, doesn't know quite what's going on (be it in the match itself or in his marital bed).

Receiving street directions in Parma is rather like leafing through a calendar at random: go down 22 July, turn left, and then right onto 20th March. All over the city there are plaques, memorials and statues of partisans from the Resistance, guns in hand, who are sculpted to look suspiciously as if they've been shot in the back. On street corners, copies of the Socialist or Communist papers are pinned up on public boards. Often you see graffiti imploring 'Barricade Yourselves!', though I'm never sure whether it's politicking or just an advert for a nearby restaurant, 'The Barricades'.

Before living in Italy I had never really heard the words 'Fascist' and 'Communist' used. In England, such political labels are only used as critical hyperbole, or for historical debates about the early part of the last century. Here, although they are thinner on the ground than a few years ago, there are still many politicians who earnestly and proudly describe themselves as 'Fascists', 'post-Fascists' or 'Communists'. Even the flags of the political parties maintain insignia relevant to their Fascist or Communist origins, and graffiti artists follow suit. In Parma, hammers-and-sickles are standard fare; elsewhere, especially in Rome, there are swastikas or celtic crosses. 'There must be a reason,' an Italian academic wrote recently, 'why it was Italy which was the fatherland of Fascism and of the largest Communist party in the western world, why the two most important secular religions of the twentieth century had their greatest success in Italy.'[7] His explanation was that Italian politics is quasi-religious, expressing the 'hopes and fears' of its people. Whatever the reason, Fascism and Communism are bedded in the Italian soul, and their collision was the cause of the country's *guerra civile*, its 'civil war'.

Civil war is a concept that has been increasingly (and controversially) used to describe phases of Italian history since 1943. Two books published on the war between Italian Fascists and partisans between 1943 and 1945 are called *La Guerra Civile*, and *La Storia della Guerra Civile*. Recently, though, it's come to be used also for the period of political terrorism from the late 1960s to the early 1980s: 'a low intensity civil war'. Those years were called Italy's *anni di piombo*, its 'years of lead': there were almost 15,000 terrorist attacks, and 491 people were killed. I was told it was one of the enduring features of Italian history, a sort of on-going, costly conflict between civilians. The country has always been divided into two warring halves. Dante, having experienced another Italian civil war – the Guelph/Ghibelline conflict – wrote of Italy that:

... the living cannot, without shame
Of war reside in you, and man wounds man
Though guarded by one wall, one moat, the same.[8]

The more I became interested in those 'civil' and 'civilian' wars, in the Fascists and Communists who were aligned one against the other, the more I came across another elegant phrase: the *muro di gomma*, the impenetrable 'rubber wall' off which all investigations bounce. Any research, I was told, would be futile. Nothing ever comes out into the open. There may be *intrecci* and *trame*, threads and tracks, which criss-cross the peninsula, linking politicians to the Mafia or terrorist groups, but they are all buried by *omissis* (omission) and *omertà* (the silence of the *mafioso*). Investigations go on for years, sometimes decades. When someone is finally brought to court it seems almost de rigueur that if they've been condemned in *Primo Grado* ('first grade'), they will be absolved in *Secondo Grado* or else in *cassazione* (the Supreme Court). No one is ever entirely guilty, no one ever simply innocent. It's part of the rewiring process of living in Italy that you can never say, even about the most crooked criminal, that they are factually, legally guilty: there's always the qualifier that they're 'both innocent and guilty'. Sooner or later the accusation will be dropped anyway, because the deadline for a judicial decision has been superseded.

Thus when I talk politics with Italian friends, they are always astonished by, and envious of, the way in which British politicians are held accountable. 'He just took money to help a friend get a passport, and for that he's in the political wilderness? Incredible.' 'You mean he lied in court to protect his wife from the knowledge of his infidelity, and he's gone to prison?' After one recent British political scandal, one newspaper wrote on its front page that 'if the same were to happen in Italy, there would be no parliamentarians left ...' The amazement of Italians is two-fold: first astonishment that such paltry infringements represent political wrong-doing and, second, incredulity and envy that powerful men (they are only ever men) can be held to account for their actions, can ever be given a conclusive, 'guilty' stamp.

Thus, surrounding any crime or political event, there is always confusion, suspicion and 'the bacillus of secrecy'. So much so that *dietrologia* has become a sort of national pastime. It means literally 'behindology', or the attempt to trump even the most fanciful and contorted conspiracy theory. *Dietrologia* is the 'critical analysis of events in an effort to detect, behind the apparent causes, true and hidden designs.'[9] *La Stampa* has called it 'the science of imagination, the culture of suspicion, the philosophy of mistrust, the technique of the double, triple, quadruple hypothesis'. It's an indispensable sport for a society in which appearance very rarely begets reality. Stendhal wrote about it in *The Charterhouse of Parma*: 'Italian hearts are much more tormented than ours by the suspicions and the wild ideas which a burning imagination presents to them . . .' As a result of the conspiracy theorising, probably the largest genre in publishing is the *misteri d'Italia* industry. There are whole publishing houses and film production companies that survive solely by revisiting the epic mysteries of Italian post-war history.

And the more I read, the more Italy's recent history seems dark and intriguing. Leonardo Sciascia and his literary mentor, Luigi Pirandello, both wrote of their native Sicily and Italy as places of illusionism and secrecy, where nothing can ever be understood. For Sciascia, Italy was so plagued by sophistry and deceit that it had become 'a country without truth . . . there's not a criminal episode which, having some relationship with politics, has had a rational explanation or just punishment'. Many history books on modern Italy open with a resigned apology at the outset, suggesting that the whole thing is unfathomable. It's the same story with Pirandello's plays, which mock anyone's attempt to work out quite what was going on in the world. Players become puppets, pushed and pulled by unseen forces. Everything is so confusing that searching for evidence, the famous 'document', becomes entirely futile:

Granted, this document you talk about might serve your purpose – that is, to relieve you of this stupid curiosity of yours. But you don't have it, and so here you are, damned to the marvellous torment of finding here before your eyes on the one hand a world of fantasy and on the other a world of reality, and you are unable to distinguish one from the other.[10]

It was this side of Italy which, I slowly realised, was at the root of those worried warnings I had received when I arrived. Nothing, I was repeatedly assured, would ever become clear. 'If you're a journalist, forget it,' they seemed to be saying. 'You can guess at what has been going on, but no one will ever get close to the truth.' One Italian historian, for example, has written of Italy's post-war history as something 'partly submerged, dark, not revealed because perhaps not revealable, not mentionable, as if it were the history of a grim divinity'.[11]

I realised that it was, as Pirandello wrote, impossible to distinguish fantasy from reality. The words history and story are the same in Italian (*storia*). Unless it's defined, or given a definite article, *storia* could be a tale from true life or simply make-believe. You wouldn't know unless you asked. Even if you do, it's often hard to believe. The deeper I delved, the more Italy's post-war history seemed a sort of magic realism, full of symbolism and surreal touches: 'Italy,' wrote Pier Paolo Pasolini, 'is a ridiculous and sinister country. Its powers are comic masks, vaguely stained with blood . . .'[12] Even today, given the levels of intrigue and drama, real life crimes are always called *gialli* (literally 'yellows', or 'thrillers'). Newscasters often excitedly introduce news of a murder or kidnapping as *un giallo incredibile*. That's probably why, despite the huge success of Giuseppe Tomasi di Lampedusa's *The Leopard*, there are barely any other (comparatively recent) historical novels in Italy: the factual, true-life version simply couldn't be bettered. The best writers on Italy in the post-war period have been well aware of that 'thrilling' side to Italian life in which the divide between fact and fiction appears paper-thin. Leonardo Sciascia wrote about the 'untouchable, literary perfection' of one tragic Italian 'thriller';[13] Umberto Eco wrote about the same event: 'this would be a joke if the novel were not written with blood'[14] One British historian, commenting on another post-war *giallo*, wrote that it seemed 'to come straight from a best-selling novel'.[15]

As I began trying to distinguish histories from stories, there was one image of voluptuous secrecy that stuck in my mind: 'Italy is really like a great, mythological artichoke . . . A single flower, green and purple, where each leaf hides another, each layer covers another layer, jealously hidden. He who knows how to take off the outside leaves will discover unimaginable things, in a difficult voyage in time and space.'[16] Despite the warnings, I decided to make that difficult voyage, to travel in time and space across the country.

2

'The Mother of All Slaughters'

See, in these silences where things
give over and seem close to betraying
their final secret,
at times we feel we're about
to discover an error in Nature,
the dead point of the world, the link that won't hold,
the thread to untangle that will finally lead
to the midst of truth.
  Eugenio Montale

The first year I spent in Italy was idyllic. Any sense of melancholy melted away under so much clear, blue sky, and everything seemed more serene and civilised than in Britain. I was earning money in the least arduous way, writing random articles for editors in London: I would be sent to taste the wine on the steep vineyards of the Ligurian coast, or else dispatched to review the pastel colours of restored frescos in Florence. If I were ever short of money, I could sit and chat to a friend in English for a while, and they would duly pay for my ski pass in the Alps. At the end of each week, I would sit down and drink a tiny coffee in Parma's main square, getting just enough of a rush to realise how incredibly relaxed I was.

Then, each weekend we would drive into the mountains. It was like walking into one of those famous landscape paintings: suddenly we were surrounded by the Arcadian scene of children playing in lakes or waterfalls, behind them the warm pink stone of a distant city in the sunset. We would always eat lunch surrounded by the rhythmic drone of cicadas and protected from the heat by a canopy of wisteria. As always, the food would be a combination of simplicity and extreme sophistication. If anyone was still hungry, or even awake, at the end of the meal they could just wander into the orchard to collect another course.

They were blissful days, but they were, I knew, essentially escapist. Nothing I was writing was remotely connected to Italian reality: it was all cuisine and culture and nothing else. By contrast, the front-page scoops of Italian newspapers, and hours of chat shows, were dedicated to something very different. They seemed obsessed with a strange kind of news story, which wasn't properly news at all. Everything seemed to be about iconic crimes from decades ago. Unfamiliar with the *misteri d'Italia*, I often found the headline splashes incomprehensible: 'Sisde Silted Up The Monster Of Florence', for example. There's nothing the dictionary can do to help explain that sentence. And if you ask a friend what it means, they will pause for a long time before slowly sitting down and explaining, with slight embarrassment, the implications of the story. That particular headline referred to the discovery that the Monster of Florence, who decades ago had murdered copulating couples in Tuscany, enjoyed protection from the secret services because he was, allegedly, working on behalf of a clique of aristocratic perverts. Another example of a front-page scoop might be about the kidnap and murder of Aldo Moro, or else something called Gladio.

It was as if a large number of Italian journalists, academics and judges were still trying to solve whodunits from many years ago. The list of the mysteries was endless, as were the theories they spawned. The weekly revelations surrounding such crimes – like that one about the Monster of Florence – often appeared incredible. Invariably, the secret services were involved. Accusations normally ricocheted towards parliament, where someone was suspected of being the *Grande Vecchio*, the 'grand old man' who had pulled the hidden strings of Italy's post-war history.

It all sounds like an acute case of paranoia, especially when people try and link up the mysteries and end up with theories that look like something cobbled together from the *X-Files*. Yet, when you start reading newspaper cuttings and books on the mysteries you realise that there really is something very unusual going on. It's not just that there's so much murderous intrigue, or that there's such an appetite for it; it's that nothing is ever resolved. That's why the front pages of newspapers are still dominated by facts about those iconic crimes, because there has never – despite the yearning to know the truth about Italy's many 'illustrious corpses' – been an adequate explanation for what really happened.

In the mystery industry, the word *strage* is a particularly emotive one. It means 'slaughter' and is used to refer to those bombings, from the 1960s to the 1980s, in Milan, Brescia, Bologna and else-where, in which all evidence suggested the participation of Fascist terrorists, but which have rarely, if ever, seen the convictions of those responsible. At random intervals, the slaughters killed ordinary members of the public, in banks, on trains, at railway stations. If their effects were horrific, the consequences were per-haps even worse, showing that the physiology of Italy's democracy was assaulted by the 'cancer of secrecy', by a 'bacillus' which 'fed upon itself, degenerating and corrupting the texture of the state.'[1] The sheer inscrutability of Italy's slaughters, and the desire to understand, finally, the mysteries of those 'Fascist' bombings, led to the creation in 1988 of a bizarre parliamentary commission. It's called the *Commissione Stragi*, the 'Slaughter Commission'. Its full title is 'The Parliamentary Commission of Inquiry into Italian Terrorism and into The Reasons for the Failed Individuation of Those Responsible for the Slaughters'. The more I read about the Slaughter Commission, the more intriguing I found it. I was fasci-nated not so much by the historical task the Commission had been set, but by something rather different. Why is it that there are so many mysteries in Italy? Why is it that no journalist or historian or judge can ever say what's been going on? I was interested not in finding out the truth about the slaughters (an undertaking which I suspected would be doomed from the outset), but in explaining to myself why, in Italy, truth never seems to emerge. How does that Italian 'veil' – beautiful and concealing and intriguing – really work?

My first brush with the Slaughter Commission came in the

summer of 2000, when I received an invitation to one of their press conferences in Rome. I spent the four-hour train journey reading newspaper cuttings from the 1960s and 1970s. Accompanying each article would be a photograph of another slaughter: a pavement peppered with blood, corpses lying with limbs at odd angles; torsos slumped over steering wheels or broken bodies found at the bottom of stairwells. Rather strangely, the venue given for the Slaughter Commission's event was *Botteghe Oscure* – 'Dark Stores' – the street in Rome formerly synonymous with the Communist party and now home to its reincarnated self, the Democrats of the Left. I walked up to the first floor where the Commission's most recent report was being presented. The room was full of those politicians and judges famous for their investigations into the slaughters from 1969 to 1984. A report, coming in at a modest 326 pages, was being handed round. It was entitled 'Slaughters and Terrorism in Italy from 1945 to 1976'.

Of course, all was not quite as it seemed. I quickly flicked through the doorstep of paper on my lap and realised something was amiss. The work wasn't that of all twenty parliamentary *deputati* and twenty *senatori* supposed to make up the Commission, but simply the work of a breakaway eight members of it, all 'Democrats of the Left'. Hence, I realised with sinking heart, the location. The report, which was presented as a bringing together of all the recent trials and research, certainly didn't pull its punches: the slaughters 'were organised, promoted and supported by men within Italian institutions and by people linked to American intelligence . . .' The central plank of the report was that America's arrival in Sicily in 1943 represented the beginning of the 'American war against Italy, which was to impede with every means the autonomous decision of who to have govern us . . .' Nor was the Vatican spared a swipe: the saintly seat, 'having maintained an attitude ambiguous, to say the least, to Fascism, declared itself in favour of whatever intervention necessary on the part of the USA . . .'

The Slaughter Commission was supposed to be part of an Italian peace process, something like the South African Truth

Commission. But that day in Rome was rather like watching an arguing couple who, each time they approach each other, seemingly about to make up, suddenly realise they can't do it, can't resist the opportunity for one last verbal volley. Those who wrote the report even made explicit their disdain for the 'culture of pacification' because the price of a 'sort of general amnesty, cultural, political and legal' is too high: it would require assigning 'equal dignity to the warring sides . . . with reciprocal recognition and legitimation'. 'We don't want to re-raise The Wall,' says one of the politicians from the Democrats of the Left at the press conference, 'just throw some light on some pages which have been kept buried . . .' 'We don't want to use history as a cudgel' assures the Commission's President, Giovanni Pellegrino.

The climax of the document is the allegation that Senator Maceratini, the current parliamentary head of the National Alliance (the reincarnated *Movimento Sociale Italiano*, the postwar Fascist party, then in the opposition coalition with Silvio Berlusconi's *Forza Italia*), had 'never done his accounts with the past'. Maceratini, the report said, was the filter between the far-right and the neo-Fascists. 'It's documented,' the report went on, 'that even in the years following those of the so-called "strategy of tension", Senator Maceratini continued to have political links with personalities from the subversive right who have already been investigated and each time convicted with definitive sentences for terrorist episodes or for reconstituting the Fascist party . . .'

Within minutes there was a swift response from the right. Gustavo Selva, one of Maceratini's colleagues in the National Alliance, said that the Slaughter Commission's research 'seems like a document from the Red Brigades [the left-wing terrorist organisation] . . .' Another spokesman called it 'Stalinist', another said: 'Incredible, worthy of a little Maoist group from the 1970s'. For his part, Senator Maceratini affirmed that he's 'proud' of having 'operated' in *Ordine Nuovo* (a splinter group to the right of the MSI). Asked if it was true that as recently as 1997 he had meetings with members of the extreme right, he replied, 'It's possible that

they happened,' before slipping into the classic defence of a convenient mnemonic gap: '. . . but I don't have a dazzling memory.'
The entire day felt like something from the Cold War: knee-jerk
accusations and denials, visceral loathing. Low blows were aimed
from moral high-grounds. There was even a sense of excitement,
of glee, at the opportunity to return to the fray. The Slaughter
Commission, I quickly realised, was as much a part of the problem as the solution, raising ghosts as much as laying them to rest.
It became very obvious that there's nothing in Italy, least of all
history, which isn't fiercely politicised.

'Think it's true?' I asked one of the Italian reporters next to me,
who duly put his chin in the air and shrugged his shoulders in
dramatic slow-motion. '*E che ne so io?*', 'What do I know?' He
looked at me and smiled, as if the question were rather risible.
Later I go for a drink with a friend. 'Of course it's true. It's not that
mud in Italy doesn't stick,' he says; 'it's that there's so much of it
that it doesn't even matter if it does . . .'

There was one particular piazza in Milan which kept being mentioned in newspapers' front-page scoops from the past. In the
centre of the piazza is the fountain that gives it its name: Piazza
Fontana. It has the feel of a swollen side-street, leading somewhere else. Barely a few hundred metres away, in Piazza del
Duomo, people gawp at the flying buttresses of the cathedral.
Backpackers plait coloured threads into their hair and share
benches with older, more earnest sightseers with their guidebooks
open on their laps. But nearby, Piazza Fontana remains
untouched by tourism.

Historians, though, have seen in its dreadful bombing a pivot
in Italian post-war history. The epic enigma of that bomb on 12
December 1969 has become emblematic of the entire country's
subterfuge, and the slaughter is endlessly revisited in the hope of
finding, as Corrado Stajano wrote, 'the key to understanding the
history of the last twenty [now over thirty] years'. Understand
Piazza Fontana, the theory goes, and you can uncover the sinister
truth of modern Italy. It has become a sort of historical Holy Grail

which, if located, could prove a source of beatific, and horrific, revelations. The bomb has hung over the country like a fatal contagion. Many who might have come close to explaining what happened on that day, and in the days and years immediately after, have become themselves additions to Italy's long list of 'illustrious corpses'. Suspects, witnesses, *carabinieri* and magistrates, all became additional, indirect casualties of the Piazza Fontana bomb ('the mother of all slaughters'), victims of an escalating cycle of recrimination. With each subsequent death, the imperative for an explanation for Piazza Fontana became both more pressing and more improbable.

If you approach Milan in the spring, the air in the suburbs will be full of white *piumini* – pollen from the poplar trees – which waft in the air like overgrown, ethereal snowflakes in the sun. In the city, squeezed between chic boutiques at regular intervals, are narrow bars, full of mirrors and curling chrome. Men and women are drinking thimbles of coffee. If you walk along the city's wide boulevards or alongside its narrow canals, the place feels more Teutonic than Latin: bustling, business-like. Sparks fall like rain from scaffolding overhead, and trams clatter past. The city is industrious and wealthy. It's home to two of the country's most famous industries, fashion and football. It's also home to the *borsa*, the country's stock-exchange, and you can often see small-crowds gather on the pavements outside banks, from where big screens project to the outside world the latest stock market quotations. Milan, many proud Lombards will tell you, is the real capital of Italy.

I'm standing in the square reading the imposing marble tribute to the victims of the bomb on the wall of the bank. It was erected on the tenth anniversary of the bomb, and condemns the 'subversive attack' (no mention of an ideological motivation) in the name of 'liberty and justice'. It lists the sixteen names of those killed in the bombing. Another, much smaller and now rusting plaque was put on the lawn opposite the bank two years previously, in 1977: 'To Giuseppe Pinelli, Anarchist railwayman. An innocent killed in the grounds of the police headquarters, 16.12.1969. The Students and

Democrats of Milan'. Despite the attempts of the socialist mayor to have the second plaque removed in the 1980s, it still stands, testimony to a country's unhealed wound.

Now, more than three decades after the original explosion, a new trial (the eighth) has started. Cynics within the press have denounced it as at best a chasing of shadows which left the scene a long, long time ago, or – at worst – an irresponsible rearguard action by the left, still bearing unfounded grudges against former Fascists and their friends in Berlusconi's (then) opposition coalition. The trial, say the cynics, has come too late to be of either relevance or consolation. By now the events of 1969 are so distant that they appear like fossilised ancestors, to be regarded with nostalgia or ridicule, or else ignored. For others, though, Piazza Fontana contains a Shoah-like symbolism, such an obscene departure from normality that they are compelled to bear witness, repeatedly retelling the events and the accusations. Some of the weary campaigners on the left even suggest that there is an active, historical denial of the truth, and that Piazza Fontana has deliberately been turned into a distant event – Piazza Lontana, or Piazza 'Far Away'.

The Piazza Fontana trial was, like the Slaughter Commission, an opportunity to watch history being written and rewritten, squabbled over by those politicians who were under accusation, or else defending the accused. The extraordinary thing was that nowhere was there anything resembling a consensus about the most simple facts. Everyone is agreed that the Piazza Fontana bomb changed forever the direction of Italian history, but thereafter the country's left and right diverge irreconcilably. Even in debating an event from 1969, any compromise is impossible. The very mention of Piazza Fontana only serves to antagonise the country's right and left and to set off snarling from both sides of parliament. I couldn't understand why, so long after the event happened, it still meant so much to so many people. After all, the number of victims, in a crude mathematical count, looked small compared to other atrocities all over the globe.

There was only one phrase from the Slaughter Commission

that hinted at why Piazza Fontana was so important. During the entire post-war period (in the words of the President of the Commission) neither of Italy's warring halves ever quite 'took their fingers off the trigger'. It was a melodramatic sentence, but it was exactly what I had been told by endless Italians. Ever since 8 September 1943, they said, there had been (if only between the most extreme halves of the country) a civil war.

On 10 July 1943 the Allied powers landed in Sicily, from there to begin the bombardment of Rome (on the 19th). Within a week, Benito Mussolini's twenty-one year rule was over: a meeting of the Gran Consiglio del Fascismo *in Rome had passed a motion critical of the Duce by nineteen votes to seven, and the next day, 25 July, King Vittorio Emanuele III forced Mussolini's resignation. After the so-called 'Forty-Five Days' of limbo between opposing powers, and as Eisenhower was disembarking his troops south of Rome in Salerno, Italy signed an armistice of unconditional surrender to the Allies. On the same day, 8 September, Marshal Badoglio announced the armistice to the Italian people, urging them no longer to fight the Allies. The* voltafaccia *was completed on 30 October, the date on which the King declared war on Italy's former ally, Germany.*

For the next eighteen months, until the liberation day proper of 25 April 1945, the country experienced the full throes of civil war. Benito Mussolini had been arrested and imprisoned on the Gran Sasso mountain in the Abruzzi. In a glider and parachute operation headed by the SS commander Otto Skorzeny, he had been rescued and established at the head of the Repubblica Sociale Italiana, *or 'Republic of Salò', based near Italy's northern border on the shores of Lake Garda. Its dominion, protected by what became known as the Gothic Line, reached as far south as Rome (which had fallen to the Germans) and Naples. Further to the south were the Allies, beginning their tortuous advance up the peninsula.*

Italians were caught between the Allies in the south, and Germany in the north: given the side-swapping of Vittorio Emanuele and Marshal Badoglio, it was difficult for the Italian populace – both civilian and military – to be sure quite which was now the legitimate regime. It was in that almost existentialist vacuum that the civil war was born: a sense of uncertainty as to what or who actually represented the real Italy. The poignancy of the conflict was guaranteed by the fact that both sides, those faithful to the German regime and the partisans aligned against them, could present the other as the party guilty of betrayal. For the former, the partisans were classic turncoats (voltagabbana), *simply opportunists who betrayed both Mussolini and Italy; for those partisans, however, the supporters of the* Repubblica di Salò *had betrayed king and country, preferring to side with Hitler's Nazi-Fascists.*

As many as 82,000 people took a direct part in the partisan war in the north. The Comitati di Liberazione Nazionale *established a few independent republics in the north of the country. The pockets of resistance were recognised by the Allies in the Protocols of Rome in December 1944, granting the Resistance a subsidy of 160 million lire a month; the CLNAI, for its part, became subject to the orders of the Supreme Allied Command. The ferocity of the Fascist reprisals in Italy is well documented, and succinctly epitomised in the German commander Reder's 'March of Death'. Beginning on 12 August 1944 at Sant'Anna di Stazzema, where 560 men, women and children were massacred, it continued until its conclusion on 1 October at Marzabotto, which lost 1,830 of its population. Nor were the atrocities simply committed by the one side: on 6 July 1945 (almost three months after the Italian liberation) a group of former Resistance fighters executed 51 Fascist prisoners in Schio. Long after the armistice, partisans across Italy were still executing Fascists who had been regional commanders during the war, or even the 'philosophers' of the regime.*

Those two years of civil war are central to any understanding of Piazza Fontana, and of the subsequent era of 'civil war' (the terrorism of the anni di piombo). *In both periods it was northern Italy that was the battleground for the political soul of the country. The periods even shared some of the same protagonists, because many of the Fascists agitating for an alternative politics in the post-war years (Prince Junio Valerio Borghese or Pino Rauti) had been 'blooded' during Mussolini's Republic of Salò. Moreover, the knee-jerk resort to violence*

between 1943 and 1945 left 'the country with a residue of political terrorism, inspired by Anarchist, Fascist and Communist doctrines, as
well as some scores to be settled by the adherents of those doctrines'.[2]
Also, and vitally, the civil war offered a precedent of civilians taking up
arms against a rotten body politic, beginning a debate about the
morality of resistance. It was a debate invoked decades later, as people
began to ask 'how and why violence is legitimate when it has to be
practised without an obvious institutional cover . . .'[3]

For many on the left, Italy's post-war politics was the perfect
example that there was unfinished business from the civil war. So
quickly was Italian and German Fascism replaced by Russian
Communism as the international bête noire, so keen were the Allies
to check Italy's partisan 'wind of the north', that immediately after
the war 'the social groups which had supported the Fascist regime . . .
managed to climb back into their former positions of influence'.[4] The
vast cracks in Italian society were swiftly papered over. An amnesty
for 40,000 Fascists who had committed horrors during the civil war
was announced in 1946; only those guilty of 'especially heinous
crimes' were excluded from the amnesty. In one, infamous example,
the gang rape by 'Black Brigadeers' of a partisan woman wasn't considered sufficiently heinous; in the words of the judge 'such a beastly
act is not torture, but only the worst offence that can be made against
a woman's honour and modesty, even if she was somewhat "free"
having been a partisan messenger.'[5]

The theory was to colpire in alto, indulgere in basso, to indict
Fascist leaders but indulge the foot-soldiers. Rarely, however, were even
those in the highest military and political ranks indicted. Studies of the
post-war period revealed a continuity of personnel between Mussolini's
ventennio (twenty years) and Italy's First Republic: in 1960, for example, of the 64 first-class provincial prefects, all but two had served under
Fascism, as had all 241 deputy prefects, and 135 questori (provincial
chiefs of the state police). As late as 1973, 95% of senior civil servants
had been appointed to the service before the fall of Mussolini.[6] In
another example, a former officer of OVRA, Mussolini's secret police,
was given a post at the Ministry of the Interior.

The stumbling block of Italy's post-war democracy was thus a *widespread sense that there had been a* tradimento, *that Italy had betrayed the partisan members of her population. There was a belief, as one historian has it, that 'the ideals of the Resistance were excluded from the so-called democratic and parliamentary compromise, which had even reached a pact with the neo-Fascist right, represented by the* Movimento Sociale Italiano.'[7] *The MSI was for more than fifty years the symbol of the Italian state still flirting with Fascism. To many, its very existence was an obvious example of the inability of Italy to remember her dark past. In July 1960, for example, the party organised a conference in Genoa, and announced that it was to be chaired by Carlo Emanuele Basile, who had been the Fascist prefect of the city during the Republic of Salò and who was responsible for the executions of partisans and anti-Fascists.*

Since the country still hadn't been purged of its Fascist contingent, the myths and symbolism of the resistance were endlessly invoked by those who later took part in the lotta armata, *the armed struggle. Renato Curcio, founder of the Red Brigades, lost an uncle who had fought against the Fascists. Years later, in November 1974, he wrote to his mother from prison at Casale Monteferrato, recalling the uncle*

who carried me astride his shoulders. His limpid and ever-smiling eyes that peered far into the distance towards a society of free and equal men. And I loved him like a father. And I have picked up the rifle that only death, arriving through the murderous hand of the Nazi-Fascists, had wrested from him . . .[8]

Remembered and romanticised, Italian partisans became role models for the next generation. The ranks of the left (be they armed or artistic) were swelled in the 1960s and 1970s by those from northern Italy (such as Pier Paolo Pasolini and Giangiacomo Feltrinelli) who had either fought themselves or lost relatives in the resistance. It became a proud point of reference; when in the early 1970s a new, left-wing guerilla force (the Partisan Action Group) was formed, it published a magazine appropriately called New Resistance. Another member of the Red Brigades, Alberto Franceschini (whose grandfather had fought as a partisan), spoke of the 'red thread that tied us to the partisans'.[9]

The years after the Second World War, though, were initially ones of bonaccia *– what Italo Calvino called the years of calm before another storm. The referendum on the monarchy in 1946 had narrowly decided in favour of a republic, and when the new Italian constitution was ratified two years later, the male members of the royal family of Savoia were barred from re-entering the country. The following decades saw a lightning transition of Italian society from one founded predominantly on agriculture to one based on industry: between 1950 and 1970, agriculture's share of the workforce fell from 42% to 17%. In 1961 the abrogation of a Fascist law against internal immigration meant that within years millions of Italians had migrated either from the countryside to the cities or from the 'Mezzogiorno' (the agricultural south) to the industrialised north. The Christian Democrats engineered an economic miracle, relying, largely, on steel, cars and concrete.*

Traditionalists were, however, 'clinking the sabres'. It was an apt description of the threatening noises and rumours with which the far right reminded the country of its presence. There had, as early as 1964, been a confused gambit to take power, a sort of crawling coup by the secret services and their leader. Since Italy's most obvious Mediterranean paragons – Greece, Portugal and Spain – were in the late 1960s and early 1970s under military Fascist regimes, there was an almost permanent hysteria on the Italian left regarding the possibility of a right-wing coup. (The film, Vogliamo i Colonnelli, *literally 'We Want the Colonels', was its most obvious expression.) That noise of 'clinking sabres' and the hysteria it produced were the permanent backdrop to the* anni di piombo, *a perception from both sides that the country was on the brink of a violent turnaround and had to be defended.*

As early as December 1969, Britain's Observer's *Italian correspondent coined a phrase which was to become standard usage in reference to the far right: 'the strategy of tension', implying a sustained campaign of destabilisation by Fascists to promote a coup, the so-called 'Greek' – or later 'Chilean' – solution. 'Elements from the far right and from officialdom,' the* Observer *journalist wrote, 'are plotting a military coup d'état in Italy, with the encouragement and support of the Greek government'. Twenty-four hours before the Piazza Fontana bomb had exploded, one magazine had emblazoned its cover with the Italian tricolour, accompanied inside by the reassurance that 'the armed forces could be called upon to restabilise immediately the Republic's legality. This wouldn't be a coup d'état, but an act of political will . . . isn't the confusion we are now witnessing,' posed the rhetorical journalist, 'due to the fact that the institutions are by now insufficient and outmoded?' The head of* Confindustria, *an alliance of industrialists, had already exclaimed that 'the parliamentary system isn't made for Italians', and went on to invoke instead 'a mythical faith in order'.*

The months preceding the bomb had been dubbed the autunno caldo, *the hot autumn, because of endless industrial disputes. During 1969, the number of workers involved in strike action rose to over seven and a half million, the hours duly lost increasing to over 300 million. At the same time, the country had witnessed, between 3 January and 12 December of 1969, some 145 explosions. Stand-offs between the forces of order and protesters of various guises had already claimed lives. Just one month before the Piazza Fontana bomb, a policeman had been killed in Milan during a union meeting. On 15th of that month, one colonel announced 'given the present situation of disorder in the factories and in the schools, the army has the job of defending the internal frontiers of the country: by now the army is the only bulwark against disorder and anarchy.' Italy seemed to have reached an impasse, a confrontation between irreconcilables: a liberal country modernising at an exponential rate, and those traditionalists and 'forces of order' who – after two decades – were still struggling to come to terms with democracy. The climate, suggested both left-wingers and foreign journalists, was self-evidently ripe for a coup and – so the theory went – Piazza Fontana was to have been its tragic starting gun.*

Much is known about what happened that Friday afternoon in 1969. The bomb had been placed in a black bag under a round table on the ground floor of the bank. At the time it was crowded with merchants from the rural suburbs. Seven kilograms of trinitrotoluene, or TNT, exploded, leaving in their aftermath what someone later described as a scent of bitter almonds. One eyewitness, a client of the bank, described hearing a frightening explosion: 'I saw that everything was collapsing around and in front of me. The wooden counters of the bankers had literally jumped into the air while the room was filled with shards of glass. Many around me had fallen. Some were certainly dead, others were wailing.'[10] One newspaper the following day wrote of 'a hell of screams, of shouts, of desperation, of panic, of lamentation'.[11] Shoes were found with severed feet still inside. In all, sixteen people died, fourteen on the actual day; 88 were injured. On the same day, a bomb was placed at Milan's Banca Commerciale Italiana. *In Rome, bombs planted in the underground walk-way of the* Banca Nazionale del Lavoro, *and at the* Altare della Patria *(the 'Altar of the Fatherland', the spiritual centrepiece of Italy) caused further injury.*

Butterfly-net techniques of arrest were carried out, bringing in a haul of Anarchists in Milan. Improbably, when one of their number, Pino Pinelli, was asked in for questioning, he rode behind the police escort on his scooter. At around midnight on the Monday night after the bomb, a journalist in the courtyard of the police headquarters heard a thud. The body of Pinelli had fallen from the fourth floor of the building, hitting the corner of a wall, bouncing off another, before coming to rest on the ground. He had been held in custody for 72 inconclusive hours. Marcello Guida, the questore *coordinating the Piazza Fontana bomb investigation, claimed that Pinelli's alibi had collapsed, and that his suicide jump had been 'a desperate gesture, a sort of self-accusation'.*

February 2000. The first day of the trial for the Piazza Fontana bombing, and there's a big presence outside the courtroom. Not just camera crews and journalists, but also a few hundred students in grunge uniform who are playing loud drum and bass, mixing their tracks with interludes of cod-history over the PA. Most are smoking grass, ignored by the insouciant *Carabinieri*.

Given the ferocity and indignation of the prosecution, and given the age and evasiveness of the defendants, the atmosphere of the court is like a Nazi war-crimes trial conducted decades after the war. When I first started attending the trial, it seemed as if amazing revelations from the past were about to come out into the open, as if some long-absent truth had finally been found. That's certainly how it was presented in the left-wing press, which spoke of decades of *omissis* (omissions) and *depistaggi* (the deliberate derailing of investigations) coming to an end. The famous *muro di gomma* (the 'wall of rubber' against which all previous investigations inevitably, impotently bounced) had been scaled, the *omertà* was at an end. The epic *segreto di stato* of Piazza Fontana was about to be revealed in all its grotesquerie.

Inside, the courtroom is an oval bunker. Lining the walls to the left and right are eight enormous and barred prison pens, a reminder of the maxi-trials that used to take place here against entire terrorist organisations in the 1970s. Two judges sit below an imposing crucifix. To their left and right on the dais are the so-called 'popular judges' or jurists, wearing tricolour sashes. They in turn are flanked by other jurists without the gaudy sash (each juror has to have a possible replacement, because the trial is expected to be so long). Accordingly, and this being Italy, the start of the trial is delayed by a lawyers' strike. It begins a week later.

The first decision of the court is whether to move the trial to Catanzaro, over a thousand miles to the south in Calabria. It was on the basis of a law about public order dating from the era of *Il Duce* that various Piazza Fontana trials were removed to Catanzaro during the 1970s. There accusations were blurred and confused, witnesses whisked abroad. 'You see,' explains one journalist next to me in the press gallery, 'there's nothing south of Rome which is left to chance.' In a portent of things to come, the judge speaks for hours on the subject – a judgement described the next day by even the most sober newspapers as 'very tedious'. The request for a transfer to Calabria is turned down.

The apparent trouble with the trial is that nobody (neither Amnesty International, nor the European Court of Human Rights nor the Italian populace in general) maintains much faith in 'the togas', the judiciary. For its snail's pace and contrary decisions, the Italian judiciary has recently been blacklisted by

Amnesty International, and in 1999 the country topped the list of condemnations from the European Court of Human Rights. By the end of that year, the European Court still had almost 7,000 cases to deal with from Italy, making up over 20% of its impending workload. Moreover, since the judiciary is politicised to a degree unthinkable in most modern democracies, Italian justice often looks more like 'revolutionary justice', like Robespierre and his sans-culottes dispatching a whimsical terror in all directions. Political enemies can be laid low not by ideological debate, but by a timely accusation, thereby subjecting them to the near-stagnant waters of the legal system (there's no habeas corpus, very rarely a jury). That habit of sordid smear and political finger-pointing is called *giustizialismo*, and is one of the reasons why there's such a breezy attitude to the lengthy criminal records many politicians have: if you point out that the Italian parliament (of 650 senators or deputies) currently has fifty politicians *inquisiti* (under investigation), people simply shrug: 'the magistrates must be out to get them, that's all'. Most people I spoke to, especially with regard to the Piazza Fontana trial, said that it was probably a case of a grudge, and that magistrates didn't know the difference between *perseguire* and *perseguitare* (between 'to pursue' and 'to persecute').

Moreover it became obvious that the courts, like the Slaughter Commission, are acutely politicised. No one pretends to believe that the judiciary is separate from the legislature, so if someone receives a conviction it's often treated not as a moral indictment but rather, say, like an electoral defeat: it's a temporary set-back. They haven't committed a crime, just had a decision go against them. People will forget about it. Increasingly, the Piazza Fontana trial seemed less a historical reconstruction, less a righting of historical wrongs, and more simply a continuation of politics by legal means. It wasn't coincidental that the case arrived in court at a time when Italy had its first left-wing government since the war. The right, too, had obvious interests in the outcome of the trial. Despite the acute political sensitivity of the trial, two of Berlusconi's *Forza Italia* parliamentarians were acting as defence lawyers in the case. One proudly donned his *Forza Italia* lapel-pin each day. There was no sense of a conflict of interest, no need to separate judiciary and legislature. Pino Rauti, the Fascist politician whose organisation is accused of planting the bomb, was also recently in alliance with Berlusconi's party for the European elections in 1999.

The other reason anything emerging from the togas is taken with a spoonful of salt is the culture of *pentitismo*. Originally intended to weaken the Red Brigades and then used to break the silence of *mafiosi*, (by allowing criminals the opportunity to 'repent' and to point the finger), *pentitismo* has by now become a simple mechanism to stitch up enemies. There are, at the time of writing, 1,171 *pentiti*, suddenly turned from poachers into the judiciary's most revered gamekeepers, and many have produced convictions which are little short of staggering. In the south, the smear normally used is involvement with Cosa Nostra; in the north it's the suggestion that the accused participated in the *lotta armata*, the armed struggle of the 1970s. In one infamous case in the 1980s, a *pentito* pointed the finger at a famous television presenter, Enzo Tortora, who he accused of being involved in dealing cocaine along with the *Camorra*, the Napolitan mafia. The case became another absurd show-trial, and Tortora was sentenced to ten years' imprisonment. He was later absolved, but died soon afterwards. On his urn were written the words of Leonardo Sciascia: *che non sia un' illusione*, 'Don't let it be an illusion'.

In between hearings I watch a documentary from the late 1980s. The journalist is asking an Anarchist, the 'monster' first accused of planting the bomb and who was absolved in 1975, where or when the truth got lost. Pietro Valpreda, with a shock of grey hair from each temple, looks stern and says: 'Immediately after the slaughter, as soon as the judges arrived from the powers in Rome . . . I believe that since then, the truth has totally disappeared . . . even though something continues to emerge, not in an active form, but in a negative form . . . not "I did" but "I don't remember", "I couldn't have done . . ."'

The prosecution in the new trial alleges that the slaughter at the bank in Piazza Fontana was part of the programmatic terrorism of Italian Fascists. 'It's probable,' wrote Guido Salvini in his *Istruttoria*, the lengthy prosecution document which precedes any trial, 'that the bombs of 12 December 1969 had the end of promoting a coup which was already planned for the end of 1969 on a wave of fear and disorientation which, as with the bombs on trains and in banks, affected ordinary citizens.' Salvini identified *Ordine Nuovo*, the Fascist party then led by Pino Rauti, as 'the prevalent structure responsible in terms of material execution for the attacks of 12 December 1969, and for those which preceded them and continued to operate . . . causing . . . the slaughter outside Milan's questura on 17.5.1973, very probably the slaughter of Piazza della Loggia in Brescia, and the chain of major and minor attempts, including some near-slaughters on trains from the beginning of the 1980s'. A more catch-all accusation could hardly have been hoped for: over a decade of bombings laid at the door of the avowedly Fascist organisation, *Ordine Nuovo* and, indirectly, its leader, Pino Rauti.

Two of the accused (Delfo Zorzi and Carlo Maria Maggi) come from the ranks of *Ordine Nuovo* in the Veneto, the north-east of the country. Zorzi, having avoided extradition by virtue of being a Japanese citizen, is absent throughout the trial. Zorzi – or Roi Hagen as he is now called, in deference to his assumed nationality – is now a wealthy businessman in Tokyo, having spent the 1980s and 1990s importing and selling Italian designer labels to the Japanese. In 1969, he was twenty-two. One of his schoolfriends described him to Salvini as 'a person of very strong character, often hard, very brutal and without those reactions which arose in many of us at the sight of blood during beatings . . . he had a closed character, introverted and very reserved, carried almost to a type of mysticism.'[12] He had studied oriental languages in Naples, and afterwards opened the first Karate salon in the Veneto. During one police raid on his house, a significant arsenal had been unearthed: a P38, a Beretta and a Smith & Wesson, as well as other explosives. His was a perfect emulation of the writings of Julius Evola, Italy's post-war Fascist philosopher par excellence: a heady blend of neo-nazism and oriental spiritualism. He once plastered across walls in the Veneto, 'six million Jews aren't enough'.

Although Zorzi is absent from the trial, another of the accused – Carlo Maria Maggi – is ever-present, sitting impassively in the front row of the court in a cream suit and dark glasses. By 1969 he was thirty-five, already qualified as a doctor and working in one of Venice's hospitals. Outside his working life, however, Maggi was the leader of the Veneto division of *Ordine Nuovo*. He was a regular presence on the firing range in the Lido, and was a member of the so-called 'children of the sun', an organisation which at the solstices used to burn wooden swastikas on hill-tops. In November 1991, Maggi was sentenced to six years' imprisonment for 'reconstituting the Fascist Party' between 1969 and 1982.

The accusation rests, of course, on the testimonies of two *pentiti*. Carlo Digilio, nicknamed *Zio Otto* ('Uncle Eight' because of his love of the Lebel 8 handgun), was for years an informer for the CIA in the Veneto. His contact – one 'David Carret' – is constantly invoked throughout the trial, though he has never been identified or located. As an explosives expert used by *Ordine Nuovo* in the Veneto, Digilio claims to have brokered a deal for gelignite from a deep-sea recovery expert in Venice. Having taken possession of the consignment, Zorzi apparently showed Digilio three military cases stashed in the back of Maggi's car days before the Piazza Fontana bomb: inside each were wired explosives, 'at least a kilo in the small ones, a bit more in the larger one'. Later on, Zorzi is said to have boasted to Digilio: 'I participated directly in the placing of the bomb in the *Banca Nazionale dell'Agricoltura*'. The other *pentito* in the case is Martino Siciliano, one of Zorzi's school peers. 'It was us who did that stuff, us as an organisation,' Zorzi apparently boasted to Siciliano days after the Milan bombing.

The accusations go much further however. The prosecution and various historians suggest that the Piazza Fontana bombing was actually organised from within the Ministry of the Interior. 'The Piazza Fontana bomb,' one army general has written, 'was in some way organised by the "Office for Reserved Affairs" of the Minister of the Interior. SID [the secret services] took over to cover everything up.' The allegations centre on Elvio Catenacci, a man from that same Office for Reserved Affairs. Catenacci had, according to the accusations, recruited Delfo Zorzi; he had immediately dispatched one of his men to Milan after the bombing, and had systematically interfered with evidence. The allegation that the secret services were somehow involved recurred throughout the 1970s: two of the Fascists originally accused of the bombing, Franco Freda and Giovanni Ventura, were close friends of Guido Giannettini, an officer in SID. All three were sentenced to life imprisonment in 1981; all three were later absolved.

Put simply, the new accusations suggest not only that Fascists from *Ordine Nuovo* planted the bomb (subsequently blamed on Anarchists), but also that they were nudged by men from the Ministry of the Interior, the secret services and by a mysterious CIA agent in the Veneto. With no sense of *sub judice*, the Slaughter Commission has echoed the findings of the initial investigation, describing with its usually robust rhetoric the bombing as a *strage atlantica di Stato*, more or less a 'slaughter by the Atlantic [i.e. American] state'. In the words of the President of the Slaughter Commission, Piazza Fontana's bomb wasn't an obscure incident of extremist terrorism but rather a shrewd prompt for a political turnaround:

What happened in 1969 was a phenomenon . . . which for many years was assumed to be extremist neo-Fascism. But . . . there appeared if not one director, at least a centre of fomentation, instigation, finance and partial co-ordination. The mutation of radicalism of the right was a phenomenon induced by sectors of the security services . . . belonging to a strategic dimension of international inspiration.[13]

George Bush senior was even on the wish-list of witnesses presented by the prosecution. It was a great story, but I – like everyone else – had no idea if it really represented *La Storia*.

The 'suicide' of Pino Pinelli, the Anarchist in police custody, became 'an awkward death', his name 'like a collective remorse'. That was how Camilla Cederna, author of A Window on the Slaughter, *described his death in 1970. As the police account of events became increasingly inconsistent throughout that year, a handful of journalists began interrogating the official line of the Anarchist bomb, and its allegedly repentant perpetrator who had fallen from the fourth floor of the police station. The 'controinformazione' began to portray Pinelli's as the suicide that never was, to hint heavily that he had, rather, been 'suicidato' – 'suicided' – and quickly made the scapegoat for much darker political forces. The previously anonymous railway worker was immortalised as the anarchist who had suffered an awful, 'accidental death' (the phrase, famously borrowed by Dario Fo, came from the coroner's report of July 1970). Walls began to be daubed with 'Calabresi è assassino' (Calabresi was the police commissioner in charge of Pinelli's interrogation), or 'Valpreda è innocente, la strage è di stato, unico giudice il proletariato' ('Valpreda is innocent, the slaughter is by the state, the only judge is the proletariat').*

Whilst investigations into the actual Piazza Fontana bombing were continuing, two overlapping court cases began in an attempt to resolve the riddle of what exactly had happened to the Anarchist suspect. In the first, starting in October 1970, Luigi Calabresi sued Pio Baldelli, editor of the left-wing magazine Lotta Continua *('Continuing Struggle'). The magazine had repeatedly insinuated that the police had suicided their suspect. In the second case, the mother and widow of Pinelli presented an accusation of murder against the police officials who had been in charge of the interrogation. What emerged from those trials was a disconcerting tangle of confusion and contradiction. When Pinelli's body was re-exhumed, evidence suggested that his had been a 'passive' rather than an 'active' suicide leap: there were no injuries to his arms, despite the fact that even suicides instinctively protect their head in a fall. Nobody had heard a scream as he fell. There was evidence of a blow to the back of the neck (a possible cause for the police request for an ambulance two minutes before the 'suicide' jump). No one could explain quite why the window was open in winter, or why four policemen were unable to impede Pinelli's alleged action. One of the policemen claimed to have grabbed one of Pinelli's shoes when he was at the window, although the victim had shoes on both feet when he was found. The cases brought by or against Calabresi were abruptly halted, however, when, in May 1972, he was murdered with five shots on the pavement outside his house.*

I begin to get used to the commute to the courtroom in Milan. The same trains, thoroughly spray-painted and looking like the rainbow-colour of spilt petrol. Inside, columns of cigarette smoke pirouetting upwards before being sucked out of the windows. Percussive confusion: everyone staring into their mobiles, laboriously writing and receiving messages, experimenting with their ring-tones, so that the whole carriage becomes an atonal, electronic chorus. As the train rattles across the *Pianura Padana*, the basin of the Po, single rows of poplar trees loom into view, looking like the upturned teeth of a comb on an empty table. Facing Milan, the Apennines lie to the left, the Alps to the right, but for most of the year they're hidden by the gypsum-sky, by the blanket fog of the plain.

The courtroom has the same sense of bathos as a modern church, unable to capture the import or solemnity of its subject matter. Journalists tap their short bulletins into laptops; lawyers nip out for cigarette breaks. There are TV cameras from Japan permanently rolling, since Delfo Zorzi is still a fugitive from justice. Today is the first day of the deposition of the *pentito*, Carlo Digilio. He has recently suffered a stroke and so his deposition is relayed by video from a clinic in Lake Garda. It's hard to know whether the resulting fiasco is a result of technical incompetence or a deliberate attempt to undermine any credibility in the witness. The courtroom becomes an echo chamber of *pronto, pronto*, as the video stalls. The picture frozen on the screens shows a balding man, slumped in a wheel-chair in a cramped room.

When the connection is fixed, the relay of question-and-answer is punctuated with long pauses. The prosecuting lawyer reads out long, fluent phrases apparently given by Digilio years ago, and asks him to confirm them. Digilio breathes heavily into his microphone, before finally slurring his assent. He confuses dates and names, and by mid-afternoon he complains about 'the humid, sweltering heat', and the court is adjourned until the next day. Everyone retires to the nearby bar, and lawyers leave their indiscretions. 'As a first run, it was frankly embarrassing, for the prosecution obviously,' says Gaetano Pecorella, the *Forza Italia* deputy defending Zorzi. The left-wing press concede the next day that it was a 'difficult hearing'.

During the ensuing days and weeks, Digilio's version of events, tortuously told, begins to emerge: 'Mine was neither an ideological nor a political adhesion,' says Digilio. 'I entered *Ordine Nuovo* at the suggestion of David Carret on behalf of the Americans. I am a nationalist, nothing more than a man of the centre right . . . A few days before the 12 December 1969, the day of the *Immacolata*, Zorzi . . . asked me to examine the explosives closed in three metal boxes with English writing. They were those [used to contain] the belt-feeds for machine-guns used by the Italian army, inherited from the United States. The explosives were placed in the boot of Doctor Maggi's [Fiat] 1100. I asked Zorzi: "but where are you going with all this load?" The reply was: "to Milan."'

'It was the right thing to do,' are the words Digilio claims Zorzi used in the aftermath of the bombing. 'He spoke of the Piazza Fontana slaughter,' continued Digilio, 'as a war report. He spoke of it as if he had been the head of the command. He said that he had had the courage to do it, the others were weak.'

A few weeks later, in the witness chair in front of the horseshoe of judges, Pino Rauti is rubbing his hands in a scholastic manner. He's a short man, wearing a cheap blue suit. He's got slicked-back white hair, and eyes that seem to fall away at the edges. One of the Italian journalists tells me Rauti is playing the 'Andreotti gambit': the important, cultured man dragged through the courts by spiteful, lesser beings. Rauti was, in the 1960s, the leader of *Ordine Nuovo*: 'the motto of *Ordine Nuovo* is the same as that of the SS: "our honour is called faith,"' he wrote back in the 1960s. His is a cantankerous performance. He frequently calls the prosecution lawyer by a lesser title, and is each time corrected. During his deposition one journalist from the 'Communist daily' (*Il Manifesto*) guffaws melodramatically, rocking her hands – pressed together in praying position – backwards and forwards (the gesture usually used by imploring footballers). The judge suddenly interrupts Rauti and asks for the journalist to be ejected from the court.

In 1956, Rauti and his followers left the Fascist party, the *Movimento Sociale Italiano*, and formed their own study centre, *Ordine Nuovo*. The move had been precipitated by a perceived softening of the MSI, and Rauti remained outside the party until 1969. During that time, the new movement made its position explicit: 'the Aryan blood of the SS is still warm and so is that of the Kamikaze and of the Black Legionnaires and those of the Iron Guard who fell in the name of and for the eternal *Ordine Nuovo*.' Rauti presented a paper at a conference in 1965, where Communists were described as 'some sort of an alien presence, like the extra-terrestrial races of science fiction . . .'

Although Rauti denies chairing a meeting of *Ordine Nuovo* in Padova in April 1969, shortly before the spring bombing campaign, it's certain that he went on an 'educational' tour of Papadopoulos's Greece in the summer of that year. When an electrician came forward as a witness, claiming that he had unknowingly supplied the timers for *Ordine Nuovo*'s bombs, Rauti (identified by the electrician's wife) apparently visited the shop to counsel silence. (Asked about this in court, Rauti indignantly replies that it's inconceivable that a respected politician would do such a thing.) The strange thing – if it's true – emerging from the trial is that Rauti and his Fascists weren't isolated extremists, but rather pawns of a very clear, strategic plan. In his *Istruttoria*, the prosecutor, Guido Salvini, wrote of *Ordine Nuovo* that it was 'one of the organisations of the right characterised by the most extensive collusion with the apparatuses of the state . . .' Rauti's cantankerous performance in the witness stand isn't because he denies his Fascism (which he proudly admits), it's because after years of appearing the most threatening extremist in Italian politics, he now seems little more than a man manipulated by much greater forces. During his deposition, newspapers report that in the early 1970s, Rauti was receiving cheques from the US embassy.

It gets even stranger, though. As I emerge into the hazy Milan sun of the June evening, I watch Rauti chatting amiably with journalists, talking about his bridge-building towards Berlusconi's right-wing coalition. It's partly wishful thinking on his part, but they have been in alliance in the past (Rauti claims to have swung the European elections the way of Berlusconi's 'Pole of Liberties' when they shared the electoral ticket in Abruzzo, Caserta and Calabria). I'm amazed, not because Rauti might be on the fringes of a rather dark, right-wing coalition – it's simply that he's still there. A man whose organisation has been accused of almost every Italian slaughter is still in politics: smiling, suited, flirting with the female journalists. I join the huddle around him, and ask for an interview. He courteously invites me to Rome.

Italy's capital is normally sneered at by those in the north. Many friends in Parma or Milan have never even been there. It's a city sated with august classicism. The man-hole covers are still initialled with SPQR, *Senatus Populusque Romanus*. There are palm trees outside embassies and governmental palaces. Here the graffiti is very different to Parma: swastikas and celtic crosses, obscene phrases against 'the blacks' and *gli ebrei*, 'the Hebrews'. It's a strange, beautiful place, almost knowingly theatrical. It has the perfect balance of modernity and antiquity.

The political definition of Rauti and the MSI in the 1970s was *doppiopetto*: a word that means double-breasted, and sums up that ambiguous combination of respectability, duplicity and aggression. (*Dare il petto*, 'to give the breast', means to be up-front or aggressive.) The seat of the 'Tricolour Flame', Rauti's political party, is a short walk from the Vatican. Rauti, the secretary of the party, sits mock-presidential between threadbare flags and ageing posters.

In 1943, at the age of seventeen, he volunteered to serve under Mussolini during what he calls the 'civil war'. He was captured by the British in Algeria in 1945, while trying to reach Spain to 'continue the fight'. Ironically, he graduated in law from inside a prison in Reggio Calabria. 'I've been in prison a dozen times,' he says proudly. 'I consider myself something of an anomaly as a politician. One Russian publication once said that Rauti, with his glasses, seems like an ordinary accountant, but he's actually a dangerous revolutionary.' He prides himself that he is, to Communists, 'a black beast'. He revels in using the words 'Communists' and 'Russia', just as much as the left in general jeers 'Fascist' each time his name is mentioned.

'The *anni di piombo*,' he says, 'were ugly, dramatic, numbing, bloody years in the history of this country. But I have no regrets. We had so many youngsters killed by the Communists. There was never any tranquillity. Hundreds of our young people from the right were put in prison. They were terribly dramatic years, in which our youngsters responded to violence with violence.' The only thing dangerous about Rauti now is his charm, his steely politeness, his ability to brush off any question with amiable, sometimes barbed, banter. What, I wonder, does he make of the wave of trials trying to resolve the many riddles of those years? 'There will be no legal truth,' he says confidently. 'There have been court-cases and counter-cases, absolutions, inquiries, new pros-ecutions. The current thinking seems to be suggesting that what happened to, and because of, the right was in some way connected to the CIA. There was a sort of goading of opposing extremes at the centre of which was the power system of the Christian Democratic party. One day there would be something from the left, then something from the other side, and all the while the Christian Democrats appeared as the saviour of governmental stability. It was precisely in that period that that party received its maximum franchise . . .'

'So Fascists were inadvertently the puppets of the Christian Democrats?'

He becomes impenetrable, simply staring at me, waiting for the next question. 'Listen,' he says eventually, 'about some things there have been partial conclusions, but about the darkest incidents there are only question marks.'

'And your own, personal involvement?'

'It's true that I was involved in some things thirty years ago, but I have always been absolved. We should turn the page. All these cases are just attempts by the Communists to demonise me and the right. Times change,' he goes on, 'no one wears the clothes they did thirty or fifty years ago. I might admire the Roman empire, but I don't go around riding a chariot, right? But I'll tell you this, we haven't as a political party renounced our history, we haven't renounced the ideals that are generally called 'Fascism'. Italians are at risk of physical extinction. We have the lowest birth rate in the world, bar none. I'm not racist, but there's a limit to tolerance. There has been such a rapid influx of immigrants, from Morocco, from Algeria, from China. These people have different colours, smells, flavours, climates. Why should they be on the peripheries of our society instead of back home amongst their own?'

That evening, sitting in a bare hotel room in Via Verona, I finally find the perfect description of Italian politics. It comes from a columnist for *Espresso* magazine: 'In Italy, as in chemistry, everything is created, nothing is destroyed, everything is transformed . . .' In other words, given the catalyst of time, appearances might change but the elements involved remain exactly the same. On either side of the equation, past and present, the same personalities exist, only configured slightly differently, arranged in new, confusing coalitions. It's that which causes the surrealism and sensitivity when writing, decades later, about the slaughters or the *anni di piombo*: most of those names which recur throughout the history books or in the court cases are still highly active in contemporary politics. It seems there's no crime or conviction sufficient to end an Italian politician's career, no historical event that can't be *smemorizzato*, conveniently forgotten.

It would be understandable if Italy had undergone its own peace process. But, unlike Northern Ireland or South Africa, the past isn't faced before being forgotten; it is simply never faced. Nothing is ever, ever admitted. 'The one constant of Italian schools,' writes Giorgio Bocca, 'is that of removing the history of the previous half century . . . the fear of history seems congenital, ordinary people have somehow understood that to talk about history, to interrogate history, isn't prudent, that there's something inconvenient in history . . .'[14] The result is that nowhere in the world is as good at reinvention or rehabilitation as Italy. It's called *gattopardismo*, the 'leopardism' of Lampedusa in which everything pretends to change, but remains exactly as it was.

It's similar to the notion of *trasformismo*, which is usually used to describe the 'revolving-door' image of Italian governments (hinting that the actual doorman, and those going in and out of the lobby, remain for decades the same people simply in rotation). Another slightly bewildered British journalist once called it the Italian version of musical chairs, in which no chair is ever removed. The political music might change, and people will shuffle into other 'armchairs', but basically the same players always remain in the game.

By the time investigators, in the early 1970s, had identified Rauti and members of Ordine Nuovo *as the probable perpetrators of the Piazza Fontana bomb, the bombing of 12 December 1969 was already beginning to seem not simply an isolated, tragic act of terrorism, but rather a reflection of the entire 'strategy of tension'. Suspicions regarding such a strategy were increased by the long list of 'illustrious corpses' which began to be added to the original victims of the bombing; adequate evidence, it seemed, that Piazza Fontana wasn't the inspiration of a few fanatic delinquents, but rather the product of a well-drilled organisation. (Illustrious Corpses –* the title of Francesco Rosi's 1975 film based on a work by Leonardo Sciascia – was fictional, but the atmosphere was similar: mysterious murders which seemed anything but coincidental.) As the* Presidente della Corte d'Assise di Roma *wrote in 1971: 'it's necessary immediately to fix a date for the trial. I have received a list of the witnesses who have died mysteriously and public opinion is worried . . .'*

Pasquale Juliano, a Paduan policeman investigating Franco Freda, another Fascist suspect, was accused of irregular conduct and suspended; the only witness in his defence, himself a former policeman, was found by his wife at the bottom of a stairwell. (He had predicted his own violent death, saying to a friend: 'You'll find me in the basement with a blow to my head, or in the lift-shaft'.) Other strange deaths followed. Armando Calzolari, a treasurer for the Fronte Nazionale of the 'Black Prince', Junio Valerio Borghese, went missing in December 1969. His body was found over a month later, on 28 January 1970, at the bottom of a well on the outskirts of Rome. Left-wing journalists suggested at the time that he had been killed because he was about to make revelations regarding the Milan slaughter. Another victim, Vittorio Ambrosini, a 68-year-old lawyer and brother of the President of the Corte Costituzionale, had hinted that he knew the names of those involved in the bombing. In October 1971 he fell from the seventh storey window of a hospital. (It was intended 'to be passed off as suicide' claimed one former Fascist to Guido Salvini in April 1995.)

The problem with the Piazza Fontana trial is the way in which it seems entirely divorced from reality. There are so many words. Words everywhere, and not a shred of common sense. Documents multiply amongst themselves, which sire new pieces of paper, loosed from all logic. The longer I spent following the trial, the more it seemed like something out of Kafka. Legalese that promises clarity only ushers in confusion. One English academic often sitting beside me in the press gallery sighs: 'You know that the bill simply to photocopy the documents of this case would be about 16 million lire? That's five thousand pounds of photocopying!' The transcripts of another recent trial (in which the seven-times Prime Minister Giulio Andreotti was accused and absolved of involvement in the murder of the journalist Mino Pecorelli) came to 650,000 pages. The number of documents gathered by the Slaughter Commission is now well over one million. Inevitably, after the first, spectacular accusations, media interest in the Piazza Fontana trial is ebbing away because it's all so mind-boggling, increasingly impossible to see the wood for the trees.

I'm beginning, finally, to understand why so much scandal, even murderous, is simply ignored in Italy. It's too confusing to find the truth. It takes so much time. There is so much legalese and mystification that it's impossible to say explicitly, concisely, what happened. The way in which that mystification and confusion occur is very simple. Italy has more laws than any other European country. The oldest university in the world, in Bologna, was founded for precisely that reason: to decipher and recipher the Justinian codes, the *Corpus Iuris Civilis*, the *Digesto* and the rest of the Roman laws. What's important is not the principle, but the points of law. Codify, recodify, encrypt. *Quod non est in actis non est in mundo*: anything not written down, documented, simply doesn't exist. The standard compliment for a history book here isn't that the argument seems convincing, it's simply that the book is *documentato*, that it's based on documentary evidence. The Codice Rocco from 1931 even demanded a *certificato di esistenza in vita*: it wasn't sufficient to be alive, you had to prove it with a document.

Italy's great novel of the nineteenth century, Alessandro Manzoni's *I Promessi Sposi*, has a lawyer who is appropriately called *Azzeccagarbugli*, 'pettifogger' or 'bamboozler'. Debate relies not upon common sense or precedence, but upon producing alternative documents which trump the others in their intricate absurdity. To be convincing you have to deploy impenetrable pomp. That is how Italian power works, by bamboozling the listener: 'Using erudite law, which is by its very nature inaccessible to the many,' one Italian academic has written:

Italian power became something naturally distant from the population, as the language of command was distant and diverse from ordinary language. Law detached itself from life. It became something for specialists, intellectually refined . . . abstract. The use of something as coarse and democratic as an Anglo-Saxon jury would be unthinkable . . . the law will remain always a thing of bamboozlers, of cryptic language, which is of liars, a power used only to take in and deprive the weak.[15]

The irony is that Italy, so painfully legalistic, is as a result almost lawless. If you've got so many laws, they can do anything for you. You can twist them, rearrange them, rewrite them. Here, laws or facts are like playing cards: you simply have to shuffle them and fan them out to suit yourself.

***

28 September 2000. A *colpo di scena* in the courtroom – a show-stopper. Martino Siciliano, the other *pentito* on whom the Piazza Fontana trial pivots, is due to start his deposition. Siciliano was at the same school as Zorzi in the 1960s, and is described in one paper as a 'controversial character, psychologically flawed, divided between collaboration with justice, the need for money [and] fear of his ex-boss, Delfo Zorzi . . .' In recent years, Siciliano has more or less auctioned himself to the highest bidder, accepting employment and money from Zorzi, before taking a wage and a modest, protective escort from the Italian state. Zorzi calls his former friend a 'Falstaff', 'an alcoholised megalomaniac' serving 'Communist justice'.

Then the *colpo di scena*. Siciliano goes missing. Since his arrival from Colombia, he had been staying in a hotel on the outskirts of Milan. All that's left in his hotel room is a book entitled *Little Money, Much Honour*. His brother claims that Siciliano, who had previously provided hundreds of pages of interviews, had lost faith in the state, having been 'treated like a tramp'. It's unlikely that those interviews, conducted by Salvini, will now be admissible as evidence. None of which goes reported in the press. During the weekend following his disappearance, journalists are on strike. By the following Monday, the press are more preoccupied with Italian gold medals in the Sydney Olympics and the weekend exploits of Ferrari, the so-called *cavallino rampante* (the 'rampaging little horse') than with the disappearance of another witness.

A little later *Panorama*, a weekly magazine owned by Silvio Berlusconi, finds a bizarre scoop. Martino Siciliano, the AWOL *pentito*, hadn't actually been receiving millions of lire from the official slush fund for that purpose. He had been receiving money directly from Guido Salvini, the investigating magistrate to whom he had made his confessions; a financial collaboration which seems at best unwise, and certain to cast doubt on the veracity of the *pentito*'s confessions. Another scoop for the defence is that Carlo Digilio, the infirm *pentito* in a Lake Garda clinic, has identified a photograph of the man he claims was his CIA contact. Defence lawyers, though, track down the man, and claim the CIA agent is actually an old American in a small town in Kansas, and reveal that he wasn't even in Italy when the alleged meetings with Digilio, in Venice's Piazza San Marco, took place.

The case against the Fascists seemed to be collapsing. I wasn't even particularly disappointed. By then, my flat was strewn with thousands of documents, each one promising amazing revelations, but in reality only referring me to another document. I had begun to understand why the mysteries sire endless court cases and scoops, but never reach convincing conclusions. I had begun to understand why 'understanding' in Italy is often impossible: everything is too politicised, there's no objectivity anywhere and there's no difference, in terms of personnel, between the past and the present. I decided to give up on my commuting to Milan. Piazza Fontana, which had fascinated me for months, was becoming just too exasperating.

There were other reasons, though, to leave the court case behind. Writing about Italy's long list of 'illustrious corpses' gives a sense of the country as nothing more than an arena of murderous intrigue, whereas in reality I had never felt, since moving to Parma, either happier or safer. If the country does occasionally appear incredibly violent, it's more often blissfully peaceful.

A few days after deciding to give up on the Piazza Fontana trial, I was in a *trattoria* with Filippo. For months he had been a kind of cerebral tour guide, pointing me towards interesting places or people. We were sitting at a bare wooden table with a chipped jug of wine between us. He was squeezing lemon juice onto his mince of raw horse meat and capers. I had a plate of steaming polenta topped with wild boar.

'So now you understand why we say Italy is a brothel?' he asked at the end of our conversation about Piazza Fontana.

'I think so,' I said. 'Or at least, I'm beginning to get the idea. But . . .' I was trying to explain why I wasn't convinced by the metaphor anymore. 'But it seems all too pejorative. I'm blissfully happy here, I don't feel like I'm in a brothel. I want to write about something simpler. I want to write about . . .' I was looking over his shoulder, looking for inspiration. I saw the row of garish yellow-and-blue Parma shirts hanging up behind the bar. 'That's it. I'll write about football.'

Filippo began laughing. He put down his fork and guffawed for about a minute. When he had finished, he leant towards the next-door table and shared the joke. 'He says,' he was pointing at me, 'he says he wants to write about something simpler, something more complimentary about our country . . .' He paused for dramatic effect. 'So he's going to write about football!' They, too, started laughing. For another minute there were yelps of amusement all round.

'Zio Tobia,' he said eventually, slapping me on the back, 'if you write about football you really will understand that you're living in a brothel!'

3

Penalties and Impunity

> Ours wasn't only the victory of a football team, but also a victory for those values in which we strongly believed: dedication to a communal cause, altruism and perseverance, the capacity for sacrifice, loyalty towards opponents, agonising attention to every detail. We had to win but also to convince with a great style, respecting the opponents and enthusing our fans . . .
>
> Silvio Berlusconi on the glory years at AC Milan

Comparing Italian and British football (not necessarily at the top level, but down the divisions) is like comparing snooker with darts. One is cerebral, stylish, slipping the ball across the smooth green felt; the other a bit overweight, slightly raucous, throwing the occasional arrow in the right direction. The more you watch Italian football, the more you realise why Italy, having been introduced to the sport by the British in 1893, has won three World Cups: Italians are simply very good at the game. They play the most beautiful, cultured and skilful football imaginable.

Talk to any Italian about the strengths of the Italian game, and they will always mention the two vital ingredients lacking in Britain: *fantasia* and *furbizia* – fantasy and cunning. Fantasy is the ability to do something entirely unpredictable with the ball. The British, I'm endlessly told, will always try to pass through a defence, or run past it, but they never actually outwit it. That's what Italian fantasists do: they produce a nanosecond of surprise that springs open a defence. It can be a back-heel, a dummy, a pretence of being off-balance. It's the one side of football that can't be taught. It has to be instinctive, suddenly inspired, which is why the *fantasisti* are so admired: they are touched by an indefinable genius. The fantasy on the pitch is clearly infectious. Watching a game on television, or even with friends, is like listening in on some serious literary criticism: *un passaggio sopraffino, filigrana* ('an extrafine, filigree pass') or else *un passaggio sincopato, che splendore ritmico* ('a syncopated passage of play, what rhythmic splendour').

The other side of the fantasy is the *furbizia*. It's the ability to tilt the game in your favour through slightly sly, but perfectly legitimate, tactics. When a player falls over, he instinctively grabs the ball with his hands, as if to bounce the referee into giving him a free-kick. Players will beg the referee to book opponents. A goal is never, ever scored without a handful of defenders raising their arms in hopeful protest to the linesman or referee. Watch young, amateur Italians and they will already have learnt all the guile from their favourite players. I sometimes go and watch a teenage student of mine, who plays in a semi-professional league. He's a tall central defender called Francesco. Towards the end of one game, when his team was hanging on to a one-goal lead, he doubled up and raised his hand just as an attack was on its way. The game stopped for five minutes as Francesco wobbled around, staring at the grass. He was pointing at his eyes. The parents around me started muttering: 'Good old Francesco, always so professional.'

As the seconds ticked away, it slowly dawned on me that he was looking for his contact lenses. The game eventually restarted but only for a couple of seconds before the final whistle. At the end, I congratulated him on the win. 'I didn't know you wore lenses,' I said.

'Of course I don't,' he laughed.

The players are, though, strangely dignified. Many opposing players will kiss on both cheeks before kick-off. If one scores against his old team (cause for exultation in Britain), in Italy he refuses to celebrate. To do so would be an affront to his former employers and fans. Sometimes, they not only don't celebrate a goal against their former team, they actually break down and have a little weep. (Gabriel Batistuta is a long-haired Argentine who played for Fiorentina for almost a decade. When, having signed for Roma, he scored a vital goal against his old friends, he scrunched up his face in a grimace of pain.) All of which is described by gushing commentators as *un gesto bellissimo*, 'a very beautiful gesture', which it often is. Another beautiful gesture is the way the players, whenever an important match is won, strip off to their underpants and throw their dirty shorts to excited fans.

I once met the Parma and Italian national captain, Fabio Cannavaro, after a game. He was an example of pure class and politeness. He stood up when I came to the table and pulled out a chair for me. He wanted to know what the game looked like from the stands. He asked whether I thought they should have played 3-5-1-1 instead of 4-4-2. The whole game was dissected as if it were a game of chess: the opening gambits, exposed flanks, the endgame and so on. You quickly realise that the national stereotypes of Britain and Italy (the one reserved, the other impetuous) are actually reversed when it comes to football. Italians play such a calculated game that they are usually astonished by the unregulated passion of British football. And the reason they can be so tactical is the other key word of Italian football: *tecnica*. No one ever needs to hoof a ball into the stands, because the players actually have the skill to put it exactly where they want: they can juggle it, dribble it, spin it. They can trap a speedy ball dead on the spot, or play it off with a perfectly weighted pass using their collarbone or their studs. And like the white ball in snooker, in Italy the ball only leaves the green when absolutely necessary, when a defence needs to be prised apart.

The nobility of the players is often reflected by the fans. When someone who is a genuine footballing legend plays against your team, he's as likely to be applauded as whistled. When, after two years of injuries, Ronaldo finally returned to the Inter Milan line-up, and moreover scored a goal, the Lazio supporters (seeing his goal announced on the big-screen of their stadium hundreds of miles to the south, in Rome) instinctively applauded for a minute. Thus the theatricality of the pitch is matched by the grand gestures of the fans: fantasists are occasionally given a minute's standing ovation and the stadium suddenly feels, rather than thuggish, like a large theatre at the end of an emotional scene. (Enrico Chiesa or Francesco Totti are the usual candidates for such adulation.) When the players do head off to pastures and pitches new, they're greeted not with hatred and sneers by their former fans (as in England) but given standing ovations, again, for what they've achieved.

Compared to their British equivalents, the intelligence of Italian fans is often extraordinary. I've spent hours on the terraces listening to fans arguing heatedly about the adjectives which could best capture the beauty of particular players: 'He's so rococo!' someone will say about a long-haired midfielder with muddy knees. 'Rubbish, he's more pugnacious than that. He's rustic, a noble savage.' 'No, I repeat, he's rococo. So deft, slightly one-sided.' Even the best English players from years ago are still lovingly recalled: David Platt, Ray Wilkins, above all Graeme Souness. Talk football with any fan of Juventus (the team from Turin, called the 'Old Lady' of Italian football) and they will recall the best goals scored by John Charles, the Welshman the Italians nicknamed 'The Good Giant'.

And if Italian journalism usually looks like a press release from the President, Italy's sports journalism is – like the football – just about the best in the world. It's as withering and straight-talking as political writing is sycophantic. No one is pardoned anything. There's even something called *La Pagella*, where each player is given a mark out of ten for their performance. (The only 10 I've ever seen awarded was for a player who gave mouth-to-mouth to a collapsed colleague; an 8 is normally considered the top conceivable mark even for a fantasist.) Football journalists are almost as famous as the players; one of the country's longest-running TV programmes is called *Biscardi's Trial*, where three or four men shout simultaneously at each other in an atmosphere of epic indignation. It sounds ridiculous, but is actually riveting. There are also the high-brow programmes hosted by the country's 'philosophers of football'. Hours of television are dedicated each week not just to the matches, but to long documentaries about the history and culture of *calcio* (football). If you didn't know they were talking about football, you would think it were a war documentary: weeping men pouring over sepia photographs, unfolding letters from fifty years ago. Football, it's very obvious, is more than just a sport: it's an inheritance, the nation's sacred heirloom.

Only slowly, and only after that conversation with Filippo, did it dawn on me that there's a very large cloud hanging over the game: the lack of transparency. As with rumours about people with terrorist pasts or Mafia associations, there is always a merry-go-round of accusations, of conspiracy theorists and their deny-all adversaries, arguing about whether it's all a stitch-up. I've often spent long evenings in old wine cellars as someone explains in intricate detail a vital goal from the 1950s which was scored from offside, or a referee who suddenly became very wealthy upon his retirement from the game. If you ever appear sceptical about such paranoia, you're told that you're naïve and that, even though (despite being British) you understand football, you don't understand Italy.

The extraordinary thing is how much the football-fixing debates mirror, almost word for word, discussions about Mafia or terrorist association: some brave observer puts their head above the parapet, suggesting that all is not quite as it seems, that there's something dodgy going on. To which the reply is first a dismissive ridiculing of the idea, followed by increasingly threatening noises if the accuser continues with his accusations. By far the most intriguing personality in Italian football is the man whose job is exactly that: to defend Juventus against weekly paranoid accusers. His name is Luciano Moggi, a man with drooping, reptilian eyelids and who seems like something straight out of a *Godfather* film. He's always sardonic, unruffled, but he's often (especially when he smiles) ferocious. He cut his very sharp teeth at Napoli during the glory days with Diego Maradona, since when – at Torino and Juventus, the two teams from Turin – he has become the *eminence grise* of Italian football. (The TV parody of Moggi is a man who, when he captures an opponent's chess piece, calmly crushes it with a hammer.)

***

It is, then, only a suspicion. There's nothing to go on in terms of evidence. But it's enough to look at the facts to know the score: it's 1-0 to Juventus and it's quite obviously going to stay that way. Nothing's going to change that scoreline, not even a goal. In the dying minutes of the crucial, penultimate game of the 1999–2000 championship, Parma's Fabio Cannavaro jumps, almost folds his body in half at the waist as he heads the ball. It bounces against the inside of the bottom of the post, and into the net. In the caged pen for away supporters, Parma fans go beserk, waving blue-and-yellow flags and letting off smoke-flares.

But strangely the score remains 1-0. The goal is disallowed. All around me indignant *Parmigiani* start screaming abuse at the referee: 'You've earned it today alright', 'You've been bought by Agnelli', 'You're a cuckold'. Not allowing the goal seems particularly perverse since the action began with a corner, and there could have been no off-side. Cannavaro had a free header, and clearly hadn't elbowed any defender. The referee, examined after the game, can't remember or recall quite why he didn't allow the goal. There's no explanation. Fans of Lazio, chasing Juventus for the title, duly riot in Rome. A mock street funeral is held for Italian football and the cover of the *Corriere dello Sport* announces on its front page: 'Sorry, but this is a scandal'.

It's not the first time something of the sort happens. At the end of the 1997–1998 season, Inter Milan were denied a blatant penalty against Juventus which could have given them the title. A few minutes later the referee Piero Ceccarini awarded Juventus a penalty. They duly won their 25th *Scudetto*, the league title. Talk to statisticians about that season and they'll tell you, with eyebrows raised, that Juventus had been the most 'fouling' team all year (814 fouls) but with the fewest yellow (65) and red (3) cards. The referees are obviously, the rhetoric goes, on the side of Juventus.

In most places such criticisms could be dismissed as the whinings of bad losers. Here, though, there is serious suspicion that referees aren't always as independent as they should be. After all, if all the magistrates, newsreaders, newspaper editors and industrialists are obviously politically aligned, why shouldn't referees throw in their lot with one side or the other? Even the normally sober *La Stampa* (owned by the same man who owns Juventus, Gianni Agnelli) remarked that the 1997–1998 title would be a bitter trophy given the lack of credibility the club now had: 'One can't remain indifferent when confronted with certain coincidences which are so singular and, let's say it, so "nutritious" . . . there's the suspicion that the rules aren't the same for everyone . . .' The editor of the *Gazzetta dello Sport* even wrote that it was 'an open disgrace', and that the refereeing had been 'one-way'.

It may be true. During another Juventus–Parma encounter (at the Tardini stadium during that 1999–2000 season) there was another extraordinary refereeing display. I am standing on the terraces next to Ciccio who, like most Juventus supporters, is from the south, about a thousand miles from Turin. He's very short, coming up to chest height, but makes up for it with his aggressive defence of anyone in a Juventus shirt. We are drinking slugs of the coffee liqueur sold underneath the stands, enjoying the partisan banter of the terraces. All around us fans are lighting up large spliffs, doubtless another reason for the rampant paranoia surrounding Italian football. It's an incredible scene: smoke mixing with coloured flares, flags flapping between banners, the weak winter sunshine of a Parma January. A lot of southerners from Sicily and Puglia are in bomber jackets supporting the team from Turin. Most of them, students from Parma university, have bought tickets for the terrace for home fans and so mingle with the sedate, muted Parma crowd who are dressed as if they were going to the opera.

'Listen, it's all a fix,' I say to Ciccio before kick-off, repeating what I've heard for months on television debates about football-fixing; 'everyone knows that the referee will have been given a script by Juventus . . .'

'Why do you have to show your lack of intelligence speaking like that?' says Ciccio, smiling. He will never admit it, but he knows that the Old Lady of Italian football simply has a greater chance of winning than Parma, and not simply because of who's on the pitch. Juventus seems quite literally to have all the luck, which is related to the immense power it has off the pitch. 'Being cynical' in British football means being able to decide a game with a well-taken goal against the odds. In Italy, being 'cynical' in football implies having a 'society' (a club structure) that brings pressure to bear on everyone involved in the sport. The more one watches football in Italy, the more one suspects that the real game is not on the grass, but in the boardrooms, corridors and presidential suites. The more powerful the president (Berlusconi, Agnelli etc), the more chance you have of winning.

Juventus are duly gifted a penalty (the Parma defender is sent off). Ciccio wants no talk of a stitch-up. Alessandro Del Piero steps up and slots home the penalty. 'You see, Zio Tobia, you seem like a sore and stupid loser when you talk like that!' He's laughing, jumping up and down celebrating the goal as he slaps me on the back.

'Better a sore loser than a crooked winner.'

'You really are so naïve. You're simply up against a better team.'

'Right, starting with Agnelli,' says an old *Parmigiano* in front of us, turning round to scrutinise the southerner. He's banging his blue and yellow cushion on his knees in despair.

The strange thing, and it might just be an impression, is that the longer the game goes on, the more desperate the referee appears to seal the result. Having already awarded a penalty, the referee then sent off another Parma player, reducing the yellow-blues to nine men. The second player to be sent off, Dino Baggio, makes his feelings perfectly clear as a red card is raised above his head: he rubs his fingers and thumbs together, an obvious enough sign that he thinks the referee had been bought (a gesture for which he would subsequently serve a lengthy suspension). The accumulation of injustices (not just sendings-off but bizarre off-sides, non-existent corners) is so relentless that it's hard not to detect a conspiracy, especially where Juventus is concerned. On this occasion, though, Parma somehow pull a result out of the bag. The last minute of the game: a through ball to Hernan Crespo, who feints and then fires with his famous left foot. The stadium goes berserk, the Parma coach, in his cashmere overcoat, rushes onto the pitch and throws himself on top of the now prostrate Crespo. Delirium: nine men against eleven, and Parma manage to pull off a draw. 'Bet that wasn't in the script,' I whisper to Ciccio, who by now is on the verge of tears.

It is, as I say, only a suspicion, but there's something about Italian football which is not – as they say – entirely 'limpid'. Part of the paranoia comes from the fact that the referee is a much more important figure in Italy than in Britain because players, as well as displaying an imperious grace on the ball, are also full of guile. By a rough, personal estimate, there are about three times the number of penalty appeals in Italy. Not because the Italian game has more fouls (it actually has a lot fewer) but because players know instinctively when and how to fall over: 'Pippo' Inzaghi (formerly of Juventus and now at Milan) has made a career out of being both a brilliant goal-hanger and a credible *tuffatore*, a diver. The result, of course, is that refereeing becomes acutely sensitive, and suspicions about the referees' interpretations, and about the motivations for those interpretations, become evermore exaggerated.

Presidents of the football teams almost behave as if they wanted to increase those suspicions. In 1999, the President of Roma sent Italy's most important referees pristine Rolexes for Christmas, an unfortunate scandal which became known as the 'Night of the Rolexes'. Other investigations have revealed that referees have enjoyed holidays paid for, very indirectly, by Juventus; referees have also enjoyed the company of what's called in Italian a *sexy-hostess* courtesy of various clubs. And quite apart from the dubious gifts they receive, the psychological pressure exerted on referees is greater in Italy than anywhere else. During the week between the Sunday matches, television programmes spend hours on the crucial refereeing decisions: vital incidents are shown again and again in snail-pace slow-motion, played forwards and then backwards, as the entire studio debates whether a shirt has been tugged, or a supporting leg clipped inside the area. The importance of having a referee 'on your side' is shown by the fact that the leading clubs vehemently oppose what's called the *sorteggio integrale*, the practise of pulling the names of match referees randomly from a hat. That, of course, would be too random. Instead, only 'reliable' refs are allowed to be responsible for the big games of the big clubs.

There's so much smoke that it's hard to know if there really is any fire, whether there's any truth to the rumours about Italian football being played on an unlevel playing field. Then, during the fateful 2000–2001 season, the sordid workings of Italian football finally did come out into the open. On the pitch it was going rather badly: no Italian team managed to reach the quarter finals of the Champions' League or the Uefa Cup. There was much hand-wringing as fans and commentators realised that the traditionally shrewd Italian game had been surpassed by quick, cavalier sides from Spain, England and Turkey – teams in which many of the superstars were home-grown rather than imported from Rio. Nervous presidents began sacking their managers: eight of Serie A's eighteen teams changed manager, one team (Parma) had three different ones during the season.

Off the pitch, things were even worse. It was revealed that a match between Atalanta and Pistoiese had been subject to strange betting patterns: large amounts, placed by relatives of the respective players, had been bet on an Atalanta advantage at half-time, but an eventual draw at full-time (which was, of course, exactly what happened). Six players were suspended: not for having bet themselves, but for having failed to denounce exactly what was going on. That was just the tip of the iceberg: the Perugia coach, Serse Cosmi, was then caught on camera describing what had happened in Serie C (the third division). The year before, he said, Juve Stabia was happily mid-table: it had failed to make the play-offs and yet was mathematically safe from relegation. So 'it began gifting games'. One striker from another team, Cosmi continued, was expected to win the league's top scorer award: his previous seasonal highest tally was eight goals, but that year he scored 28. 'They came to an agreement,' said Cosmi, 'they lost 4-3, it was enough that he scored three goals. Things from another world. Penalties were showered around, games finished 5-4. The south is like that, if they want someone to win the top-scorer award . . .'

Cosmi had been caught by surprise, thinking that the cameras weren't rolling, but he had only revealed what everyone had long suspected.

More serious revelations were to come. Juan Sebastian Veron was probably the best player in Serie A. He had won the Uefa and Italian cups with Parma, and the *Scudetto* with Lazio. A shaven-headed Argentinian with a goatee, he plays in the hole between midfield and strikers, and often scores from very long range. If defenders then close him down, he invariably, casually, slips the ball to an attacker. Then it was suggested that Veron had been playing under a false passport (which was true, though Veron was entirely absolved of any involvement). As the season went on, more and more names came out, mostly South Americans, accused of the same thing: of having found fictitious Italian grandparents to adopt them and ease their passage into Serie A. There is a ceiling to the number of 'extra-community' players a team is allowed to field, so once a player is Italianised they're automatically more attractive and their market value rises by some 30%. The crime itself wasn't particularly serious, but in footballing terms the scandal was seismic. Not for the first time, it appeared that Italian football was slightly crooked. Whilst some teams had been adhering to the rules, others had been wilfully importing and fielding players who had no right to play. Clubs, it emerged, had either forged passports, or not even bothered to look at them. Accusations and libel writs flew in all directions. Fabio Capello, coach of Roma and therefore sworn rival of the other Roman team, Lazio, suggested that Lazio's historic *Scudetto* of 1999–2000 was therefore a con. More subtly, the fact that some thirty players were caught up in the scandal added to the already fragile sense of the superiority of football *all'italiana*: Serie A, it was obvious, was reliant not on native play-makers but on imported stars.

Since so many teams had fielded illegitimate players, applying the law and its sporting penalties (deducting points from offending teams, banning players or imposing hefty fines) would have meant invalidating many results from Serie A. The problem was so widespread that no one quite knew what to do: whether to go to the civil, rather than sporting, magistrates; whether to penalise teams or rather blame and ban the players themselves. Veron himself, at the centre of the row, began to get increasingly petulant, and the engine of the Lazio team suddenly found himself unable to get out of second gear on the pitch. The irritating law, it was obvious, was making life difficult for everyone, so a solution was found. It was a solution I was to see used frequently in Italy. The reasoning goes something like this: 'If so many people are guilty, let's change the law and play people "onside". To prosecute the ocean of offenders would lead to utter collapse, because there are simply so many of them. So let's not prosecute.' The solution, as always, was to fudge right and wrong, to change the rules suddenly to suit the rulers. Thus, mid-season, the law limiting the number of foreign players allowed to play was wiped out, allowing teams to field whoever they wanted. Those who had been honest were penalised for not having been more *furbi*; anyone who had played by the book, buying Italian players and checking foreigners' passports, was suddenly at a disadvantage. It would have been fairer literally to have moved the goalposts.

Of course, days after the ruling was changed, a foreigner scored a vital goal. Roma were visiting Juventus and being thoroughly outplayed by the Old Lady. Capello, knowing about the rule-change about extra-community players, sent on Hidetoshi Nakata, his Japanese star, who promptly scored one goal and set up another. Roma had clawed its way back into the game, and scraped a 2-2 draw.

Then another type of dependency emerged. Italian football, it became clear, was being fuelled by banned substances. During the 2000–2001 season, players began testing *non-negativo*, then confirmed as *positivo*, for the anabolic steroid Nandrolone. They weren't simply the journeymen players, but the stars: Fernando Couto at Lazio, Edgar Davids, the Juventus midfielder. A few years previously, the chain-smoking Czech coach, Zdenek Zeman, had alleged that many of the Juventus players had quickly become suspiciously muscular. He was ridiculed, then threatened and sued, and his career in Italy was effectively at an end. As the new crisis deepened, journalists queued up to talk to the unemployed coach (still living in Rome), who confidently repeated his accusations: 'At the time they made me seem like a madman, but they knew very well that what I was saying wasn't madness. The fact is they didn't listen to me or anyone else. I'm very sad, because it's a very sad time for football . . .'

On the day the non-negativity of Edgar Davids was leaked (fifty days after the actual test), I was back on the terraces watching Parma–Juventus with Ciccio. When the name of Davids was read out over the PA, the stadium erupted into a chorus of *drogato*, 'drugged'. Even the most partisan Parma supporter, though, would admit that Davids was the best on the pitch, increasingly powerful as the game went on: strong and subtle, able to boss the midfield with sudden changes of direction and speed. The game finished nil-nil. That evening, and for the weeks which followed, there were endless debates about Italy's crisis of *frode sportiva*, 'sporting fraud'. There were partial confessions, veiled accusations. It never quite came out explicitly, but there was a very clear tension emerging between players and their respective clubs. Players claimed to be totally innocent ('My body is the house of my soul' said Davids), and hinted that they had been slipped substances unawares. The club doctors were mentioned as possible sources of the contamination. One medical expert claimed that since Nandrolone and other integrators are available commercially from England and America, it might be difficult always to understand what was contained in the imported substances. (Nandrolone, though, in Italian is spelt *nandrolone*). Moggi, the Juventus troubleshooter, distanced himself from the affair, underlining that Davids had been playing with the Dutch national team on the week of the positive test (as had Frank De Boer and Japp Stam, both of whom were later to test positive for Nandrolone). As ever, the accused cast themselves as victims, citing the usual, extraordinary slowness of the justice system: one player had waited 88 days between his test and the 'non-negative' result. Another player, a midfielder from Milan, almost admitted that everyone was taking performance enhancing drugs, and publicly pleaded that players be given more guidelines not about which substances were legal, but about what were the accepted levels of illegal drugs. (The clubs duly attempted to increase the legal level of Nandrolone permitted, though the action was overturned by the Italian FA.)

But the best response to the crisis was, of course, not moral but aesthetic. Italian football, more than any other, prides itself on its beauty. To put that in jeopardy is infinitely more serious than allegations of match-fixing or drug-use. The real complaint, then, against the steroid use was not that it was wrong, it was that it promoted ugly football. One newscaster (a Juventus supporter) said in a debate that the game had become too 'physical, antagonistic', rather too much like the English version. Tackles flew in, players were too aggressive, there was no longer any room on the pitch for the golden boys of Italian football, the *fantasisti*. Strength and speed, the argument went, had become more important than silky skills. Steroids were wrong not per se, but because they threatened the *bellezza* of Italian football, and made it more like its vulgar, Anglo-Saxon incarnation.

In Italy, political power has always been intimately linked to football, and there's nothing new about one determining the other. If you're an important politician, chances are that you also own a football team; if you're a football president, you're probably also in parliament, or else very close to it. The conflation of football and politics is the reason that Italians, as is well known, 'lose wars as if they were games of football, and lose games of football as if they were wars'.

Mussolini was probably the first politician who fully understood the political implications of the sport. Physical perfection and sporting finesse became metaphors for the virility of Fascism, as athletic organisations drilled millions of Italians in gymnasia. Local governments were forced to build 'lictorian' (Fascist) sports grounds; by 1930 there were over 3,000 across the country. Bologna's was inaugurated in 1926, followed by the Berta stadium in Florence, the Mussolini stadium in Turin and the Vittoria stadium in Bari. Footballing triumphs came to be exploited as examples of the strength or superiority of Fascism (Italy won the World Cup twice during the 1930s).

The suspicion about Italian footballing stitch-ups dates from that period: Bologna, il Duce's home team and almost home town, won a succession of championships towards the end of the regime (1936, 1937, 1939 and 1941). Given Mussolini's connections to Bologna, and given the fact that both the football and gymnastics federations were under the leadership of the Bolognese Fascist Leandro Arpinati, those victories are still seen by conspiracy theorists as examples of the dubious continuum between football and politics: when it's politically convenient, teams can be helped to win titles. Indeed, when during the war it was necessary to reinvent Rome as the all-important imperial capital, the city duly won its own Scudetto in 1942. Football had become, say the suspicious, the most watchable, political propaganda.

The result is that, when teams now win titles, it's almost obligatory for the losers to claim that the powers that be had penalised them. Massimo D'Alema, when he was the country's Prime Minister in the late 1990s, bemoaned the prejudice against his team AC Roma, blaming the cartel of northern powers for the fact that, throughout the 1990s, only Juventus and AC Milan (belonging to Gianni Agnelli and Silvio Berlusconi respectively) won the Scudetto. A Scudetto for Rome, he said, would be worth three championships, such was the prejudice against any team from the capital. He openly referred to what, for any romanista, is the open wound of 1981: it was another crucial match for the championship, three days before its conclusion. As usual it involved Juventus, this time against Roma. Once again, it was being played in Turin, and the visitors had a legitimate goal by Ramon Turone disallowed for a phantom offside. Had they won that match, Roma would have almost certainly won the championship. But the goal was disallowed, and Juventus took the title. Another example, for many, of the Old Lady's uncanny ability to benefit from glaring refereeing errors.

Much of the suspicion surrounding football comes from the fact that the owners of Italy's football teams are the country's most powerful men, rather like medieval barons who countenance no dissent. Silvio Berlusconi at Milan, Gianni Agnelli at Juventus, Cecchi Gori at Fiorentina: all three are or have been parliamentarians with extensive media control (Cecchi Gori was until recently the owner of Tele Monte Carlo, the third pole of Italian television after RAI and Berlusconi's Mediaset). A football president probably doubles as a newspaper owner, owner of a television channel, head of his own financial empire and patriarch of a famous family. Matches probably aren't fixed, but (it's hard to explain this to someone outside Italy) the psychological pressure on a referee not to give a penalty against the Prime Minister's team is surely felt. Thus, the little teams with lesser presidents – Lecce, Reggina, Perugia, Verona – frequently and rightly complain that they've been penalised because they're not important, or else because their presidents aren't part of a political entourage. (The big clubs are called the Seven Sisters, of which Parma is the obvious Cinderella. But even in the Duchy of Parma, the football team is owned and sponsored, filmed and broadcast, by different organs of the Parmalat empire, which is owned by the Tanzi family.)

The most obvious conclusion from watching Italian football is that the country is based upon a few, very powerful, oligarchies. It's not dissimilar to the Renaissance, with a dozen important families who have carved up the spoils of the country. Because it is, invariably, a family thing. The same surnames recur again and again, regardless of whether you're talking about politics, television or football, regardless of whether you're reading a contemporary newspaper or one from the 1960s. The sons and brothers (occasionally a sister or a mother) become part of the footballing entourage, which is often an apprenticeship before they enter parliament or start editing the family's newspaper. Many of the sons of famous club bosses are agents, which means that they take a percentage on every deal done by their fathers. There's no notion of a conflict of interests, due to the desperation, the absolute determination, for 'strapotere', all-encompassing power.

To understand Italian football, and therefore its politics and media, it's useless to use British terms of reference. In Italy the equivalent of British monopolist, or American anti-trust, laws don't exist. There's no notion that there are areas of objectivity that must be observed, be it in refereeing or in news reporting. There's no central state that acts *as a check on the various Citizen Kane characters. The most obvious example of that 'strapotere' outside football is media ownership. In Italy there's no fourth estate: newspapers, with a few exceptions, are divided amongst the oligarchies. It's called 'lottizzazione', 'sharing the spoils'. Besides owning Juventus, the Agnelli group owns one quarter of all Italian national or provincial newspapers (and, more importantly, controls 13% of all advertising revenue in the country). Berlusconi, besides AC Milan, owns the Mondadori publishing house and therefore the copyright on a quarter of all Italian books. Il Giornale, a national newspaper, is his (or, technically, his brother's, which keeps it at least in the family), as are three out of the seven national television channels. He, too, has the financial lever of Publitalia, an advertising company without whose revenue many programmes and publications would abruptly collapse (Berlusconi controls roughly 60% of all television advertising sales).*

Almost all the media is, and always has been, 'schierato', which is to say 'marshalled' or 'lined up'. In the old days the three state channels, RAI 1, 2 and 3, were divided up between, respectively, the Christian Democrats, the Socialists and the Communists (even now, on RAI 3, the daughter of Enrico Berlinguer – one of the historic leaders of the post-war Communist party – reads the news; her uncle just failed in his bid to become leader of the Democrats of the Left). The RAI channels are the only national, televisual opposition to Berlusconi's three Mediaset channels. That is why it's often impossible, watching the news or reading newspapers, to have the least clue about what's been going on: each channel or publication, intimately linked to political power, has its own, very obvious angle. The same people who are making the news are also paying people to report it and broadcast it. It's called 'appartenenza', the 'belonging' to a particular political formation. To form anything resembling an objective idea of events, you would have permanently to zap between channels, and buy at least a dozen newspapers.

Many on the left are fairly hysterical about such oligarchies, and about the concentration of so many things in the hands of so few. It certainly makes journalism either craven or, if you're daring, dangerous. When one American journalist, writing a biography of Gianni

Agnelli, decided to try and penetrate that power system with an objective, financial analysis his house was broken into, and the American embassy warned him to leave the country before finishing his book. Italian oligarchies, he not surprisingly concluded, are 'antipathetic to democratic pluralism'.[1]

Berlusconi, of course, is the oligarch par excellence. He became owner of AC Milan in 1986, saving the club from the threat of bankruptcy. In the official hagiography of Il Cavaliere, it was the fulfilment of a childhood dream: 'The San Siro [Milan and Inter's shared stadium] is my dearest memory, hand in hand with my father . . .' Even that official version describes the baby Silvio learning to bend the rules: at the turnstiles 'I made myself tiny to be able to let the two of us use just the one ticket . . .' During the first year of his ownership, two of his television channels, Canale 5 and Italia 1, ran long montages of Milan glory, with a persuasive voice-over: 'Make yourself a present of a new Sunday with the azure sky, the green of the lawn, and the red and black of the new Milan . . .' A record number of fans, almost 60,000, quickly snapped up season tickets.

The achievements of Berlusconi's Milan are amazing. In fifteen years under his leadership, Milan have won a total of eighteen trophies: Scudetti, European cups, Supercups, Intercontinental cups. He brought together three of the greatest Dutch stars – Marco Van Basten, Ruud Gullit and Frank Rijkaard – and blended them with stylish Italian defenders like Franco Baresi and Paolo Maldini. Arrigo Sacchi, a little-known coach who was then manager of Parma, was picked as the new coach of Milan. Sacchi introduced what was then a revolutionary new style of 'total football' in which players paid little attention to traditional positions in an all-out siege on the opponents' goal. Gone were the days in which Italian teams played 'catenaccio', 'lock-out', defensive football. (Before then, the mantra of Italian football had come from Annibale Frossi, who claimed that the perfect game of football was the artistic and philosophical equivalent of a blank canvas: a no-score draw.) Later, Fabio Capello became coach, and the Liberian George Weah inherited the mantle of prolific goal-scorer.

As ever, though, the success story is mixed with scandal and Milan's trophy cupboard contains skeletons as well as trophies. The club, indeed, is the reason for one of Berlusconi's many legal prosecutions. In the summer of 1992, Milan paid Torino the then extraordinary sum of 18.5 billion lire for a young footballer called Gianluigi Lentini. It was later claimed in legal proceedings that the Lentini transfer had been the subject of shady financial deals. The President of Torino football club (who doubled, of course, as a member of parliament) alleged that six and a half billion lire of the transfer fee was paid 'sottobanco' – without receipts or contract – to a Swiss bank account, an obvious way to avoid taxes; it was claimed the actual player, Lentini, had his proposed salary slashed from four billion lire a year to little more than a billion and a half (with the obvious suspicion, according to the Torino President, that he was 'topped up' in cash from Berlusconi's slush funds in Switzerland); most damning of all, it was claimed that when the Milan directors had paid a seven billion deposit on the player, they didn't ask for the usual 'receipt' of payment, but instead wanted shares in Torino. It was that, more than the financial scams, which incensed neutral observers, because it meant that Milan had played much of the end of 1992 season owning controlling shares in another club. All the allegations were denied by Berlusconi. The magistrates who investigated financial irregularities in the early 1990s were called 'Clean Hands'; the Lentini scandal duly became known as 'Clean' or 'Dirty Feet'. Berlusconi's response to the scandal was to become, during the next ten years, a familiar refrain. He was, he said, the victim: 'I have the sensation of living in a police state . . . I feel the object of a witch-hunt.'

When Berlusconi burst into politics in the aftermath of Clean Hands, voters thus had his record at Milan at the front of their minds. There were, as usual, two sides to the coin: the epic success of Berlusconi's football presidency, countered by the strange financial deals that he was accused of conducting in the dark. Berlusconi gambled that because so many people would be dazzled by the success, few would worry about the scandal and thus, not for the first time in Italian history, he openly aspired to conflate politics and football: his political party was baptised Forza Italia *—a chant from the terraces, as in 'Go Italy!' His parliamentarians were originally referred to as his 'azzurri', the generic term for players in the Italian national side. When he announced the formation of his new political party, and his own candidature for the post of Prime Minister, Berlusconi even spoke of the move in overtly footballing tones: 'descending onto the pitch'. Forza Italia's regional offices were often little more than the former fan-clubs of the Milan football team which were dotted up and down the peninsula. Berlusconi, it was clear, intended to run the country as he ran his club (which could – depending on whether good football is more important than correct accounting – cut both ways).*

The intimate link between football and politics is, with Berlusconi, ubiquitous. When, in May 1994, his first government faced a crucial no-confidence vote in parliament, his team AC Milan were simultaneously competing for the Champions' Cup with Barcelona in Athens. That evening, once Berlusconi's team were 2-0 up (they would eventually win 4-0), parliament voted in his favour. Some people have followed the analogy between football and politics even further. Romano Prodi (Berlusconi's rival in the 1996 elections and who won the contest) presented himself as a keen cyclist, an image which, politically, recalled the old days of proportional representation: a mass of competitors, the result announced after months of competition and difficult calculation. Berlusconi's footballing mentality meant that he was ideal for the new, first-past-the-post system that was to revolutionise Italian politics. Italian politics was suddenly more like football: a show-down between two sides; abuse could be hurled at the opposing fans and their players, be they sporting or political.

Spring 2001. The crisis of Italian football was coming to a head. It centred, appropriately enough, on the reigning Italian champions, Lazio. Someone had allegedly forged a passport on behalf of Juan Sebastian Veron. Their coach, Sven-Goran Eriksson had been wooed away by the English FA. Their Portuguese defender had tested non-negative. Worse, though, for the image of Lazio and

Serie A, was the racism and violence, reflections of a more general, sociological malaise.

It started when Arsenal visited Lazio in the Champions' League. As the Lazio fans, traditionally from the far-right, barracked Arsenal's Patrick Viera with choruses of 'boo-boo', the Lazio defender Sinisa Mihajlovic repeatedly called him 'nigger'. At the following match the Serb was forced to apologise and denounce his own racism over the stadium's PA system. And yet the racist fans clearly enjoyed the collusion of the club and the *Carabinieri* lined up outside the stadia. Anyone who has ever been to a football stadium in Italy will know that it's impossible to get into the place with a cigarette lighter, with coins and sometimes even keys. They will almost certainly be confiscated when you're dusted down by the hoards of *Carabinieri* on the gates. And yet, despite such stringent checks, the following banners (both about fifty metres long) had both recently appeared in Lazio's stadium: 'Jews: Auschwitz is your town, the ovens your houses' or, a tribute to Mihajlovic and his fellow Serbs, 'Honour to the Arkan Tiger'. In another instance of incompetent policing, a motorbike was ridden up the spiral walk-way which takes fans to the upper tiers of the San Siro and thrown onto the opposing fans on the tier below. Quite how a motorbike was able to get there, when no one's ever managed to take even a hip-flask into a stadium, baffled the embarrassed commentators.

Watching football matches became like watching newsreels of matches in Britain from the 1970s: fans goading the police or other fans into close-quarter fights, train stations vandalised, cars repeatedly set on fire. Every Sunday evening there seemed to be new pictures of looted shops seen through the haze of police tear gas. In one post-match incident, a player from Como, Massimo Ferrigno, punched his former team-mate Francesco Bertolotti into a coma which lasted over a week. A month later, a bomb was thrown into the home of the co-owner of Napoli, Corrado Ferlaino, because the club was performing badly. (The same reason was given for the calf's head sent in the post to the President of Reggina.) Worse was the volley of smoke-flares which, at almost every match, went to and fro between fans like a gently lobbed tennis ball. It looked quite picturesque unless you saw it up close: one policeman had to have a finger amputated. In an even more tragic incident, a fan was killed as a paper-bomb was thrown from opposing fans during a play-off in Sicily.

Towards the close of the 2000–2001 season, Parma were placed just behind the chasing pack for the title; with Inter Milan and AC Milan struggling, a Champions' League place looked certain. 'Huh,' said Filippo, my taciturn and supremely cynical friend with whom I often watch the games from the *Curva Nord*, 'you just watch in the next few weeks. The teams from Milan will do anything they can to get into the Champions' League . . .'

'Such as?'

'You just watch the penalties they're awarded,' he said, laughing bitterly.

Parma, though, was itself to become the centre of suspicion. When one of the Parma players scored a goal against Lecce, he looked embarrassed, as if he had messed up the script. There was no celebration, only a banging of his fists against the post. Then Parma were playing Verona. Suspicions were raised before the game by the fact that the Verona and Parma presidents are good friends and business partners. Giambattista Pastorello borrowed money from the Tanzi family – the Parma benefactors – to buy Verona, so the relationship is, to say the least, intimate. They often loan players one way or the other to help each other out. The teams even wear the same yellow-blue strip. During the penultimate game of the season, with Parma already guaranteed a Champions' League place and Verona desperate to avoid the drop, Parma lost 2-1 at home. There was, of course, more conspiracy theorising for days on end.

It may be, of course, that Juventus and Italian football are actually clean and free of corruption. It may be that people from Parma are just bad losers. 'But,' as Filippo says, 'I wouldn't bet on it. I wouldn't bet on anything here unless I knew the score. Literally.'

Most neutrals, for various reasons, wanted Roma to win the

title, mainly for the worthy reason that Roma had played the best football. Also, the Argentine Batistuta, having delighted Italian aesthetes for a decade without winning much, was reaching the twilight of his career, and most people wished him well. The other, well-publicised reason for neutrals supporting Roma was a promise made by an actress. Sabrina Ferilli is a *romanista* and the owner of Italy's most famous pair of breasts – in various B-movies they're shown off like *caciocavallo*, those huge tear-drops of smooth creamy cheese. She had promised to perform a striptease should Roma manage to win the title. In the run-up to the end of the championship, news programmes could talk about little else other than the prospect of 'la Ferilli' baring her bosom. It was, literally, 'big news'. Roma did, of course, win the title, and 'la Ferilli' did her teasing striptease (down to a skin-coloured bikini).

The season, though, didn't end there: as ever, there were legal cases that promised to drag on for years. The President of Napoli, a man whose face is like an over-inflated football, half of it covered by a hedge-like moustache, began legal action: he insisted that Parma and Verona must have come to an agreement, and that Napoli had been the victims, dropping down to Serie B. More seriously, and probably more based on fact, at the beginning of July it was announced that two of the leading lights of Juventus, the *amministratore delegato* Antonio Giraudo and the doctor Riccardo Agricola, were to be tried for 'sporting fraud' for administering illegal pills and illicit syringes to Juventus players. The man who had conducted the investigations was even, the press noted gleefully, a Juventus supporter.

At the beginning of the following season, Edgar Davids' ban from football was reduced. Nobody really noticed. In short paragraphs at the back of the sports pages, it was reported that the magistrature had decided to reduce the Juventus midfielder's ban to just four months. Since a large part of the ban had been served during the summer months, he would be allowed to return to football almost immediately (17 September). All the other sentences were reduced or annulled, be they for forging passports, match-fixing or use of Nandrolone.

All of which made me think that the real problem wasn't about penalties, about whether the referees lean slightly towards the Old Lady of Italian football or the Prime Minister's team when they blow their whistles and point to the spot. The debate is really about another type of penalty, or the lack of it. It's the fact that, as Italy's moral minority always complains, *non paga nessuno*, which basically means that no one in Italy is ever, ever punished for anything: 'nobody pays'. Ever since I had arrived I had heard one half of the country, that law-abiding half, complain bitterly and incessantly about the *furbi* who appear to bend and break the law at will, without ever facing the consequences. In Italy there are no penalties other than on the football pitch. Crime is never followed by punishment because, at least for the powers-that-be, there's guaranteed impunity. You can get away with anything. As long as you play the game, you'll be played onside. Take Nandrolone, field illegal players, fiddle the accounts, put up Fascist banners: *non paga nessuno*.

Perhaps none of which really matters. Italian football remains the most stylish and cultured and clever incarnation of the sport. The *Azzurri* will always be the hot favourites to win any international tournament because, whatever goes on in the boardrooms, the actual foot-soldiers are still the best in the world. Also, I would rather play football in Italy – in the parks or on the beaches – than anywhere else. When you roll up with a friend, looking for a game, everyone will instinctively welcome you. Then, once they realise you're English, they will pretend to be having second thoughts: '*Mamma mia*, not an English footballer!' The seriousness with which they play, whispering advice to each other as they sprint across the sand, or signalling where you should put the ball just by moving their eyes, is incredible. They hardly ever foul; if, by accident they do, they will pick you up, bow and apologise. That's the nobility of Italian football. Afterwards, once you're in a bar with them all, it's normally impossible – thanks to their hospitality and generosity – to buy even one drink.

And anyway, long before the end of that football season, the plight of one individual had become the complete negation of my theory of Italian impunity. Almost as if to compensate for the absence of justice, one man had been sentenced to an exemplary prison term for a murder committed decades earlier, in 1972. Here, finally, was an example of that rare thing, a genuine Italian punishment (with the irony that it had been meted out to the one man millions of Italians were convinced was actually innocent). Adriano Sofri had become the country's most famous 'murderer', and – since his case overlapped so intimately with that of Piazza Fontana – I travelled to Pisa prison to meet him.

4

'The Sofri Case'

He thought about those other informers, buried under a light layer of earth and dry leaves, high in the folds of the Apennines; miserable men, a mud of fear and vice. They had played their game of death, on a thread of lies between Partisans and Fascists, they had played with their lives . . .
Leonardo Sciascia

Heading out of Parma to the south-west you quickly reach the Cisa pass which takes you over the Apennines towards the Ligurian and Tuscan coasts. It's a spectacular road that lifts you above the fog of the plain: supported on concrete stilts it struts over valleys, and its long tunnels puncture the mountains. A few hundred metres below the asphalt, picturesque mountain villages huddle around their bell-towers, appearing from above like random piles of matchboxes. Now, in October, the mountain colours are crisp and autumnal: white wood-smoke gusting between dark green pines.

I'm driving towards Pisa prison. A few days before, the first penal section of the *Cassazione* court had, on 6 October 2000 in Rome, pronounced the final judgement on a murder committed almost thirty years before, in May 1972. It had taken eleven hours for the court to reach their decision, which was then curtly announced to the gathered journalists at ten p.m.: 'this court rejects the appeal for a retrial . . .'

It was the definitive, closing chapter of a case that has obsessed the country, one which had, throughout the 1990s, become every bit as politicised and emblematic as the Dreyfus affair almost a century before. The appeal to the *Cassazione* was the last resort: a final opportunity to reopen the case. That opportunity denied, the conviction (announced six months previously) for the 'Calabresi crime' stands, and Adriano Sofri will remain in prison until 2017, almost fifty years from the date of the crime.

'The Sofri Case' is, in many ways, the complementary inverse of the on-going Piazza Fontana trial: a tardy and dubious attempt to apportion blame (this time on the extra-parliamentary left) for one of the iconic moments from the *anni di piombo*; to indict not only an individual but also the wider movement of which he was representative. If evidence which is belated and confused in the Piazza Fontana trial has allowed the left to point an hysterical finger against various historical nemeses, the Sofri case has offered the same opportunity for the right. The Piazza Fontana crimes were the very reason for the Calabresi crime: Calabresi was the police commissioner in charge of interrogating Pino Pinelli, the Anarchist suspected of the bombing who subsequently fell to his death from a window of the police station. As with so much of the *anni di piombo*, Piazza Fontana appears the original sin from which all other crimes descend. 'The *anni di piombo* started with Piazza Fontana,' wrote Giorgio Galli in Genoa's newspaper *Secolo XIX*, 'and until the truth about that beginning has been ascertained, that about Calabresi will remain partial.'

Responses to the Sofri case tend to be knee-jerk assertions of either his guilt or innocence, and all commentators inevitably become *colpevolisti* or *innocentisti*, part of the guilty or innocent camps. For the left, Sofri is a *cause-célèbre* without compare, the sacrificial lamb of the right bent on judicial revenge for left-wing terrorism in the 1970s. 'They've buried him alive,' say his friends on the evening of the latest decision. Some hint darkly that Sofri, as a man of granite integrity (and one who knows his own symbolic value), might now resort to suicide, but he denies it in a press conference from Pisa prison the following morning: 'There are two things I'll never do: ask for a pardon [which would imply guilt], or commit suicide'. His brother, an academic in Bologna, declares: 'This is an ugly country; if I weren't an old *signore* nearing the end of my days, I would go away . . .' An editorial in *La Repubblica* calls the decision 'a monstrosity . . . the inhuman and uncivil vendetta of the State'. Sofri, runs the editorial, has to suffer the 'infamy of being an assassin – still worse the sender of an assassin . . . he will consider this a death sentence, and will testify until martyrdom his innocence.' Within days, a campaign for granting Sofri a Presidential pardon is begun.

Those on the right, however, were gleeful. 'Justice has been done,' declared one member of the National Alliance; 'let's hope that the *Lotta Continua* lobby [the movement of which Sofri was the leader] now shuts up, and remembers their history as killers, as definitively sanctified today by the Italian judiciary'. Another National Alliance spokesman says he hopes for an end to 'the obsessive, apologist song which has transformed Sofri into an icon which even he doesn't seem to recognise'.

The road comes out at the *Golfo dei Poeti*. I turn left, and stop in another small town, Bocca di Magra, and approach a man selling pancakes out of the back of a van. He's got thick waves of greying hair. This is Leonardo Marino, the *pentito* whose confessions are responsible for the Sofri case. I explain that I'm a journalist, and ask him a couple of questions. He repeats the phrases I've read elsewhere: religious language about repenting, about the need, after all these years, to tell the truth. Marino, once in the rank-and-file of *Lotta Continua* in the 1970s, has become a figure of ridicule for the left. He is the *pentito* who has pointed a finger at Sofri, and his two 'accomplices'. In 1988 he confessed first to his priest, then to the police, about his involvement in the murder of Luigi Calabresi. Almost every detail he recalled was wrong: the colour of the car, the place where the murder was planned, the weather conditions. There was little evidence, other than his, on which the accused could have been convicted. There was an eerie absence of the normally all-important *documenti*.

It's strange, now, to see him: whilst Sofri is in prison, Marino is selling pancakes on the Ligurian coast as if nothing had happened. During Sofri's first trial it was revealed that Marino had been in contact with the police long before his 'official' confession in the summer of 1988, leading many (not least Dario Fo in another invective comedy, *Marino Libero, Marino è Innocente*) to suggest that the whole confession was simply a put-up job by police.

An hour later I arrive in Pisa. The city is dominated by scholars and students and the atmosphere is very left-wing. Pisa's ancient university (where Galileo Galilei once taught), and especially its *Scuola Normale* (founded by Napoleon in imitation of Paris's *Ecole Normale*), have long been the educational cradles for future Presidents and Prime Ministers, for philosophers and scientists. During the 1930s, the city was a refuge of intellectual resistance to Mussolini: in 1937 Aldo Capitini published his *Elementi di un'esperienza religiosa*, an impassioned plea for non-cooperation with the regime, and two years later one of his colleagues published *La scuola dell'uomo*, a sort of paean to liberty. Walking around the city, back and forth across the bridges which criss-cross the river Arno, the political affiliation of the city is obvious: sprayed on walls at regular intervals, with what I'm told is typically Tuscan humour, is one recurrent sentence: *Cacciamo i Fascisti della faccia della terra . . . e non solo!* – 'Let's hunt fascists from the face of the earth . . . and not only from there!' Another piece of urban graffiti is appended to the south wall of a church: an enormous mural, a collage of colourful, floating bodies, painted in Pisa by Keith Haring shortly before his death. Like Parma, everywhere there are monuments, memorials and plaques, always appearing more provocative than reconciliatory. In the heart of the city there is a small park with the sculpted bust of a young man, Franco Serantini. Below the inscription explains: '20-year-old Anarchist mortally wounded by police at an anti-Fascist rally'. On the wall of the building opposite the bust someone has (evidently recently) sprayed: 'Franco, we will avenge you'.

The *Casa Circondariale di Don Bosco*, Pisa's prison, is a squat building, almost unnoticed from the road but for the perspex watch-tower inhabited by a bored, uniformed guard. Immediately inside the prison there's another plaque, this time commemorating the agents of custody killed in the line of duty: 'Repose with Christian piety' it says (dated 1977). The prison guards are good-humoured and disorganised, struggling to find the flurry of faxes and photocopied *documenti* that I have, for months, been sending to them and the ministry in Rome. Finally everything is miraculously in order, and I'm ushered across a courtyard and through a series of slow, hydraulic doors. The interview room is cold. In the corner, plastic chairs are stacked to the damp, brown ceiling. I sit down on one of the chairs and wait for the arrival of Italy's most notorious 'murderer,' Adriano Sofri.

Throughout the early 1970s, the anarchist Pino Pinelli and the police commissioner Luigi Calabresi became symbolic characters in Italy's unusual morality play, invariably hero and villain respectively. Despite the fact that he had been unknown and anonymous during his lifetime, in death Pinelli had become, like Che Guevara, the focal point for left-wing malaise. He was invoked in slogans daubed on walls across the country: 'Quando votate ricordatevi di Pino Pinelli' *('when you vote, remember Pino Pinelli'), and* Lotta Continua *issued a record of 'The Ballad of Pinelli'. Calabresi, on the other hand, became the scapegoat for all the alleged injustices of Italian society, and of Piazza Fontana in particular.*

As the libel trial continued between Calabresi and Lotta Continua, *however, the process of blurring fact and fiction was well underway. A series of films and plays began to add to the symbolic accretions of the Pinelli–Calabresi case. In October 1970 Dario Fo's* Accidental Death of an Anarchist *opened, with its unsubtle indictment of the police version of events:*

Do you know what people are going to think of you? That you're a bunch of bent bastards and liars . . . who do you think is ever going to believe you again? And do you know why people won't believe you . . . ? Because your version of the facts, as well as being total bollocks, lacks humanity.[1]

In the same year, Elio Petri's film, Investigation of a Citizen Above Suspicion *won an Oscar for best foreign film, portraying a policeman who had murdered a suspect but was persuaded not to confess. The parallels with the Calabresi case (even though the film had been shot prior to December 1969) were obvious. As were those drawn a year later with the release of* Sacco and Vanzetti, *a film version of innocent (Italian) Anarchists put to death in America, in which another Anarchist, Andrea Salsado, fell from the fourteenth floor of a New York police station. The momentum of indignation was such that, in June 1971, 800 intellectuals signed a motion in L'Espresso magazine describing the police as 'torturers'.*

That polarisation of politics was underlined on 16 April 1970, when the television news was interrupted shortly after 8.30 p.m. in various cities by the announcement of a new, revolutionary formation. As the images of the day's news rolled on, an inserted voice-over announced:

A new mass resistance has been born, the workers' rebellion against the landlord and the State of the landlords has been born, the rebellion against foreign imperialism has been born, the rebellion of the populations and of the working-classes of the south has been born. Born are the Red Brigades and the Brigate GAP [Gruppi di azione partigiana] have been reconstituted. The way of reforms, the way of revolutionary Communism, the way of the definitive liberation of the proletariat and of the Italian workers from the domination and exploitation of foreign and Italian capital brings a long and hard war. But on this route the partisan brigades, the workers, the cooperatives, the revolutionary students march compact and united until the final victory.

The wording reflected the character of the leader of the GAP movement, Giangiacomo Feltrinelli: melodramatic, apocalyptic, above all desperate to inherit the mantle of the partisan movement. Feltrinelli is one of the many 'fallen' from the anni di piombo whose memory has been both lionised and ridiculed, his name becoming a reflection of both the violence and the farce of those years. Feltrinelli's family was one of Italy's richest, thanks to their acres of forests in Carinzia, and his grandfather's road-building projects under Mussolini. Brought up 'like a prince of the royal blood in olden times,' Feltrinelli escaped from his family home in Turin during the civil war to fight with the partisans, later becoming a member and generous benefactor of the Communist party. Feltrinelli had, in 1950, founded a study centre and subsequently opened a publishing house and a chain of bookshops across the country. It was Feltrinelli who first published Giuseppe Tomasi di Lampedusa's The Leopard *and Boris Pasternak's* Doctor Zhivago *(a publication which soured his relationship with the Communist party in Italy and Russia). Increasingly, he travelled to Cuba and South America, duly publishing works on guerilla movements, on*

Che Guevara, and – as a close friend of Castro – commissioning the Cuban leader's autobiography.

The musical chairs of parliamentary politics were unable to offer any degree of stability or continuity which might have counteracted the descent into guerilla warfare. In the aftermath of the 'hot autumn' of 1969, a series of union leaders had been denounced for 'delinquent instigations'. A general strike was called for 6 February 1970, and the following day the Prime Minister, Mariano Rumor, resigned. After a governmental vacuum lasting fifty days, Rumor formed another coalition, before resigning again in July. At a time when the country cried out for a coherent leadership, the various competing factions of the Christian Democrats were engaged in futile feuding amongst themselves.

That summer, as the Italian Azzurri reached the final of another World Cup, there was a prolonged revolt in Reggio Calabria (towards the toe of the Italian boot). It had been announced that the seat of the new regional government, having been promised to Reggio Calabria, was to be the neighbouring Catanzaro instead. In an area of abject poverty and poor housing, where unemployment ran at over 10,000 and many still lived in sheds dating from the 1908 earthquake, the removal of long-awaited and vital public sector jobs was naturally resented. Reggio responded with a prolonged series of strikes, demonstrations and bombings which quickly became political in nature. Between July and September 1970, three people were killed, 200 wounded and 426 charged with public order offences. In that period there had been nineteen general strikes, twelve explosions, 32 barricades set up on roads and fourteen occupations of the local railway station. The area also witnessed the second slaughter of the 'strategy of tension': on 22 July, a bomb exploded on the Freccia del Sud – *the Southern Arrow train* – at Gioia Tauro, killing six passengers and wounding another 72.

Pasolini's documentary of the year following Piazza Fontana, called 12 Dicembre, *shows the pulsating chaos of Reggio in those months: wide, sun-drenched streets without cars or pedestrians, only mounted police aiming bullets or water-cannons at protesters. Blockades set up on street corners, black smoke from tyres and cars that had been set alight. Occasionally, an ambulance careering through the debris.*

The right began by denouncing the strikers and demonstrators as hooligans and scoundrels, but later began to exploit the unrest. The local secretary of one of the unions, Ciccio Franco, sided with the protesters, using the infamous slogan 'boia chi molla' *(execution for quitters).* 'It's our revolt,' *claimed* Ordine Nuovo, *'it's the first step in the national revolution in which this obscene democracy will be burnt.' It was, indeed, a propaganda coup for the far right, which was able to present itself as the champion of the impoverished, marginalised south. It later reaped the rewards at the ballot box (in 1971, in Catania, the neo-Fascist* Movimento Sociale Italiano *garnered 21.5% of the vote, and a year later the leader of the revolt, Ciccio Franco, became an MSI senator). In subsequent years, there was a concerted attempt to export the street* squadrismo *of Reggio to the largely left-wing, and more industrialised north, with Fascists marching under the slogan* 'L'Aquila, Reggio, Milano sarà peggio' *(the rhyme boasting that things would get worse in Milan). The rising toll of violence and the presence of two, increasingly extremist movements, which appeared diametrically opposed, was ominous.*

In December 1970 there was an attempt to impose on Italy the 'authoritarian solution'. It was a strange coup d'état, so subtle and secretive that when it failed many denied, as they still do, that it had even taken place. Prince Junio Valerio Borghese, the organiser of the coup, is one of the most controversial figures of Italian postwar history. During the Second World War, Borghese commanded the infamous Decima Mas, *a body of assault troops which was responsible for raids on the British fleet in Alexandria and which, after 1943, was savage in its treatment of Italian partisans. Borghese was later tried as a war criminal and sentenced to twelve years' imprisonment. On his (very early) release, he became President of the neo-Fascist party, the* Movimento Sociale Italiano, *before founding the* Fronte Nazionale, *a pseudo-military organisation to 'build a dam against red terror'.*

Coming in the aftermath of the Piazza Fontana bombing, and the subsequent polarisation of society, the coup itself was not entirely unexpected. 1970 had witnessed reforms which, insufficient to satisfy any but the most moderate on the left, were however adequate enough to unnerve the traditionalists on the right: regional government had been introduced in the spring, and in May, the Statuto dei Lavoratori, *a workers' charter, guaranteed various workplace rights. Most importantly, days before the Borghese coup, the bill legalising divorce (which had been passed in November 1969) became law. The coup took place on the night of 7 December 1970 (it was known as 'Tora-Tora,' in memory of the Japanese attack on Pearl Harbour on the same date in 1941). Borghese had prepared a proclamation to read to the Italian public:*

Italians, the hoped-for political change, the long-awaited coup d'état, has taken place. The political formula which has been used by governments for 25 years and has carried Italy to the brink of economic and moral ruin, has finally been abandoned . . . The armed forces, the forces of order, the most competent and representative men of the nation are with us and we can reassure you that the most dangerous adversaries – those who wanted to sell our homeland to the foreigner – have been rendered inoffensive . . . we raise the glorious tricolour, and invite you to shout with us our irrepressible hymn of love: Italia! Italia! Viva l'Italia!

Two hundred Forest Guards left their Cittaducale base in the north-east of Rome and made for the city centre in a convoy armed with sub-machine guns and handcuffs. Members and former members of a parachute regiment remained at their base, under the command of Sandro Saccucci (later to become a deputy for the MSI) awaiting orders. Across the country, other groups were ready for action. The Ministry of the Interior was occupied, and a stash of arms removed (counterfeit ones were later found in their place). Suddenly, however, just as the Guards were about to enter the state television studios, they were met by two unknown men, who ordered them to retreat. The operation was called off, with the bizarre explanation that it was raining too heavily.

The abortive coup was quickly dismissed as nothing more than the work of crackpot eccentrics, 'a jolly get-together among old comrades' according to General Vito Miceli, head of SID (the secret services) and another future MSI parliamentarian. The notion that there had been an attempted coup was ridiculed, indeed there was barely any evidence, bar those counterfeit weapons at the Ministry of the Interior, to suggest that it had even taken place. Gradually, however, the seriousness of the coup attempt became clear. General Miceli, it was revealed, had known about the coup well in advance, as had the army Chief of Staff, who was ready to provide weapons.

Indeed, within months another subversive organisation, Wind Rose, had been created by veterans of Borghese's abortive coup. It was an alliance of senior army and intelligence officers hoping, again, to take over the reins of government. 'The objective,' proclaimed one of their early manifestos, 'is to fight against the political, unionist and governmental braggarts, and against all those who cooperate and sustain the chameleons of this putrid democracy.' Borghese died in exile, in Spain, in 1974, the same year in which Miceli was arrested for his part in that other, related organisation, Wind Rose. Those who had taken part in the Borghese coup were accused of 'armed insurrection against the state,' but by 1984 all had been acquitted on appeal. As ever, there was not one conviction following the crime. Indeed, since then the coup has been portrayed as nothing more than a left-wing hallucination.

In any other country, the coup, if that's what it was, would be a sort of historical cul-de-sac, an example of a few politicians or militarists taking a wrong turning. But in Italy, because every intrigue is so secretive, the subject is never satisfactorily resolved. Confessions and revelations emerge from dubious pentiti, years and decades after the event, usually bringing confusion rather than clarity. Just as the Sofri case was reaching its conclusion, a pentito came forward claiming to have the missing link to explain one of the country's many illustrious corpses: the disappearance and assumed murder of a journalist in the autumn of 1970. The journalist, claimed the pentito, had been murdered because he had discovered plans for the coup. No one, of course, knew whether the confessions of a mafioso over three decades after the event were reliable, but they were certainly, in the then political climate, poignant: the brother of the murdered journalist was, at the time of the new revelations, Minister for Education; at the same time, on the opposition benches, were two members of the National Alliance who had been intimate colleagues of Borghese, posing for photographs with him before the coup.

In 1971 the iconography of Pino Pinelli, the anarchist who died during questioning in the Milan police station, was becoming evermore like that of Che Guevara: his name endlessly invoked on thousands of banners and city walls. Meanwhile, the destinies of the two men held in popular opinion responsible for their deaths (the policeman Luigi Calabresi and a former colonel of the Bolivian police, Roberto Quintanilla, respectively) became bizarrely intertwined. The latter had been killed on 1 April 1971 in Hamburg, at the residence of the Bolivian consul. The gun used by the killer, a Colt Cobra 38, had been purchased by the publisher, Giangiacomo Feltrinelli in Milan in 1968. Reports in the Italian press suggested that Feltrinelli had met the killer, a German called Monica Ertl, throughout the months preceding the murder. Others, of course, suggested it was another, sophisticated put-up job by the Italian police; more precisely, by that Office for Reserved Affairs at the Ministry of the Interior who were desperate to frame the rich revolutionary. In little over a year, both Calabresi and Feltrinelli would also be dead.

In May 1971, Pinelli's body was exhumed as evidence in the libel case between Lotta Continua's *editor and Calabresi. On 4 October, an arrest warrant was issued for Calabresi (though he was, posthumously, declared innocent of all charges in 1975). The spring of 1972 is the twisted, intricate knot of all the threads at the beginning of the* anni di piombo. *On 3 March, the Red Brigades conducted their first, highly publicised kidnapping. On the 16th of the same month, Enrico Berlinguer was elected leader of the Communist party (the funeral of his predecessor, Palmiro Togliatti, had been attended by over a million people). The publisher Giangiacomo Feltrinelli was killed as he allegedly attached explosives to a pylon outside Milan. In May, a young Anarchist, Franco Serantini, was killed in Pisa by police at an anti-Fascist rally. It was, crucially, at a meeting to commemorate the death of Serantini that Sofri allegedly ordered the killing of Calabresi (another policeman accused, of course, of killing another Anarchist).*

The first warning of what had happened to Luigi Calabresi was a call received at the central line of the Milan police station at 9.15 on 17 May 1972: 'There's a man shot in via Cherubini . . . it's commissioner Calabresi . . . he's bleeding from his head . . .' Calabresi was slumped on the pavement outside his house, next to his red cinquecento, with bullet-wounds to his head and left lung. One journalist who arrived at the scene recalled the 'leaden atmosphere . . . the police and carabinieri considered themselves at war against groups on the left.' Calabresi was transported to the San Carlo hospital, but pronounced dead within half an hour. He was thirty-five, and left a pregnant wife and two sons. Witnesses claimed to have seen a blue Fiat 125, number-plate Mi-16802, driven by a blonde woman. A man described as near six foot had fired the shots. The killing was, wrote Lotta Continua *the next day, 'a deed in which the exploited recognise their own yearning for justice'.*

In 1988, Leonardo Marino, the crêpe-seller on the Tuscan coast, came forward with his version of events. Marino claimed that Sofri had ordered the killing of Calabresi after the rally to commemorate Serantini, the murdered Anarchist. Sofri and his two 'accomplices' were sensationally arrested in 1988, starting twelve years of trials, retrials, arrests and releases until that final verdict in October 2000. Partly because of the paucity of evidence against the former members of Lotta Continua, *the imagery of the case became vital. Sofri was endlessly described as 'too intelligent,' as 'arrogant' and insufficiently contrite for the obscene rhetoric of the early 1970s. Just as the case was opening, Gemma Capri, the widow of Calabresi, published a book entitled* Calabresi, My Husband. *The timing was, to say the least, cynical. Elegant and blonde, she was present throughout each trial and retrial.*

From the outset, Sofri has shown an almost aesthetic disdain for the legal pontificating. Writing of his first trial, he says: 'The process has been diverted by gestures and tones closer to an autodafé *rather than a civil trial. Suddenly tears and sweat, imprecations and furores . . . have overpowered and replaced the confrontation of the facts.' Sofri accused the judicial circus of being in 'bad taste' ('demagogic and windbag-ish'). Relying on their intuition, people had, said Sofri, been taken in by the 'fat and crying'* pentito, *Leonardo Marino.*[2]

Sofri was, however, apologetic about the tone of his and others' writings from decades ago:

The articles which accompanied the Calabresi campaign were horrible ... The articles in Lotta Continua *are witness to a degenerative parabola which accompanied not only this case . . . The violence and the crudity and also the brutality of the things we were writing were precisely to do with the desire to obtain real justice . . . not to let what we thought had happened [to Pino Pinelli] in the Milan questura go unpunished . . . in the course of the campaign, that position became habitual, complacent: a sort of inert taste for insults, lynchings, for threats which took control of us, and not only us . . .*[3]

As another witness at the trial explained it: 'We were at war, it was the perverse logic of the era.'

As with the Piazza Fontana trial, there weren't simply individuals on trial, but an entire diaspora of former colleagues and 'extremists'. Lotta Continua *was a sort of cradle for an intellectual caste in Italy which has now, years later, graduated into the media and parliament. Former* Lotta Continua *members are regulars on cultural chat-shows, they work as TV anchormen, as senators and academics. The* Lotta Continua *lobby (many of whom were also accused by Marino in 1988, before charges were dropped) have thus fought to clear not only Sofri's name but also, by association, their own. And Sofri himself is second to none in terms of media manipulation and contribution: his by-line appears so regularly in newspapers and magazines that anyone who didn't know otherwise would think he was the country's most famous journalist, rather than its most famous 'murderer'.*

It would be too strong to say that Sofri has willed himself into this position, but in stubbornly and repeatedly requesting not liberty, but justice, he must have been conscious that he would become a secular martyr. *Sofri finds himself in prison,* wrote one journalist in October 2000, the day after the closure of his case, 'for not having doffed his cap to the bureaucratic cast of the judiciary'. By now, in the autumn of 2000, Sofri is the only one of the four accused of the crime still in prison. The pentito *Leonardo Marino was almost immediately released. Of the other accomplices, one (Giorgio Pietrostefani) escaped to exile in France after the Venice trial of 2000 (from where he has been interviewed by the press, but untroubled by extradition); and another (Ovidio Bompressi) also went into hiding, subsequently handed himself in, and was then confined to house arrest on medical grounds.*

Sofri, on the other hand, has cast himself as the niggling point of clarity and honesty, refusing the fudge of exile or illness. The case is now only Sofri's. It has become, in his words, a case not about 'my future life, but rather about the past, more dear and vulnerable . . . this affair risks hijacking not only my material existence . . . but that of my own soul.'

Sofri has an almost boyish face: he's very relaxed, very witty. He asks me to give him the 'tu', the informal address. He has a loud voice, and adds *capisci?*, 'understand?,' to the end of every sentence, projecting himself as the earnest professor he might, in other circumstances, have been. Deprived of any recording device, I have to transcribe his polysyllabic words at the speed of light.

'There's a very strong, virulent civil violence in Italy,' he says. 'It's abnormal, monstrous, grotesque. Italians wallow in the fact that they are *bravi ragazzi*, good people, measured and antique . . . But there's an endemic violence between neighbours which lurks like a kind of fever under the skin.' The Italian words he uses to describe this atmosphere are *una disponibilità alla riscossa*, which means more or less 'a disposition for revolt'. 'In the 1970s,' he says, 'there was an atavistic, militant tension, a belief that there was a moral need for thought and action. Many felt that the Italy that emerged from the Second World War was divided into two parts, Catholics versus Communists, all that Don Camillo stuff. And many saw the history of anti-Fascism as a kind of incomplete emancipation, another example that everything in this country remains either half-done or betrayed.

'But that notion of a "creeping civil war" is a beautification of the case. Both sides – the state and elements of the far right, and the blundering criminality of the left – just fed on themselves.

They fatally believed their own rhetoric, so what culminated was an *imagined* civil war, a *simulation* of a civil war. The *anni di piombo* were just the usual Italian struggle, the usual fratricidal/patricidal goings-on within city-states, a sort of multiplication of opposing views from the peripheries, from the bell-towers. My case, for example, is a storm in a teacup. I'm not saying it's not horrible, but it's not part of some epic encounter between two sides. My case shows simple personal hatred, denuded, revealed in its full horror: it's nothing more than the exultation of hate and grudge.'

Sofri is blunt and cynical. I ask him about the new trial for Piazza Fontana. 'The danger is that the trial might confirm an idea which I don't share, namely that there might be possible a degree of clarity about the Piazza Fontana bombing. This late recognition of what the "counter-information" of the left was saying at the time is strange. For the togas to talk about "a slaughter of the state", using exactly the same words as we did back then, sounds a little false. Those were our slogans of extremism. And the fact that it is based upon very dubious *pentiti* takes something away from the case . . . *pentitismo* is, as we all know, a very slippery mechanism . . .'

Sofri throws out grandiose concepts in every sentence, sometimes following them up later in the conversation, sometimes leaving them hanging dislocated in the air. His range of reference is bewildering, peppered with the leitmotif of Italian cerebrality, the suggestive subjunctive. He swaps languages without pause.

Why is it, I wonder, that no historian or court or journalist ever seems able to unearth the truth, or even a convincing interpretation, about Italian history? 'I think,' he replies, 'that things are actually much more simple than that. *Dietrologia* [conspiracy theorising] is an air that you breathe in Italy. It's the result of paranoia and jealousy, and it simply exalts an intricate intelligence. It's like Othello with Desdemona's handkerchief: one innocent object can spark off endless suspicions. It's a game which people play, almost to show off. I prefer not to see a conspiracy which exists than to see one where it doesn't.

'I don't say that there aren't many dark or dodgy things: people always say football matches are fixed because probably very often they are!' He guffaws. 'And there is a type of wretchedness about the Italian state, with its tricks and deceits and dirty businesses. But here a rationalist would cry. When one says things, with evidence and facts, you're not believed. When something's so obviously *verosimile* it can't be the *verità*, it would be too simple: it would be too obvious, too easy, so it can't be true . . .

'Look at my case. I've never said that it's inconceivable that the far left had something to do with the murder of Calabresi. I've simply asserted with frankness that I was never, never in any way responsible. It's the stuff of madmen. When we spoke of the "general encounter" for the autumn of 1972, we meant the possibility of renegotiating a whole host of communal contracts, not that some killing would be the spark for armed revolution.'

He leaves no doubt as to his contempt for the judiciary: 'full of ambition, symptomatic of the Italian delirium for omnipotence. Judges seem to think they are almost literary critics, re-evaluating novels. Or else they pretend to be the "good guardians". It's a monstrous deformity. We in *Lotta Continua* worked very much in the light of day, in fact sometimes with too much ostentation and pretension. Ours was an experimental adventure. Not an adventure in the sense of dangling yourself off a bridge with elastic tied to your ankle, not in that sense of extreme sports . . . ours was a communal interpretation of the world, a mixing of languages, an exciting crossbreeding of cultures. It all culminated in an extraordinary mimesis, a humane, though almost virtuoso, imitation of those around us. We were social, almost becoming others.'

He describes the typical trajectory of bourgeois children feeling the gravitational pull of the workers. 'We could use their language, learn their customs, appreciate and participate in their struggles. In the end, we realised it almost deprived us of our own identities. We realised we had to start taking things seriously. It all changed when women suddenly declared they were feminists . . . a few people did try to continue the mimesis, a kind of psychological transvesticism . . .' He laughs again.

'I now cull my political ideas from the same places as everyone else, from television and newspapers. That's one of the strange things, that people outside live as if they were in prison, stuck in front of the television. Most of my articles I have to write from memory, because it's not like there's a massive library here. But I get fucked off ['*incazzato nero*'] when people say I'm more free than them, because I can sit here with my thoughts. Prison is abominable – a torture, a physical torment, a sexual mutilation. We're like scavengers on society's rubbish . . .'

Leaving the prison, I go to a bar to read the day's papers. In one, it being the twenty-fifth anniversary of the death of Franco, one of the Spanish dictator's maxims is quoted: 'one is the master of what one doesn't say, and the slave of what one does.' The phrase, despite its provenance, seems apposite for Sofri. He is a talker, a man who loves words, especially – say many – his own. In fact, Sofri is frequently accused of pompousness, of arrogance, of a yearning to be the protagonist; he's an intellectual, according to a friend, who enjoyed the 1970s' engagé game of 'Cowboys and Indians'. And yet it's very rare to meet anyone who doesn't express 'reasonable doubt' about Sofri's conviction. At most some say he's guilty verbally, guilty of having been incautious with his words. He has been convicted simply for talking too much, for boasting and provoking. He is, I realise, a very literal prisoner of his own past, a slave of the words he had spoken.

A few months later: December 2000. With an election expected in spring, the political exchanges are getting worse. Two bombs, one allegedly Anarchist, quickly followed by the Fascist reply, have sent shivers down the spine of the body politic. 'Something strange is happening,' admits the Secretary of the Democrats of the Left: 'terrorists are shooting again . . . there's a return to a situation of tension . . .' Everyone describes a sense of déjà-vu, a sense of disbelief that, years after the *anni di piombo* were thought to have petered out, these bombs are still being prepared and planted. It seems absurd and surreal. As one dismayed journalist writes:

Here again are the ghosts which stink of dynamite . . . in most European countries governments of left and right alternate without any problems of public order or security. Not in Italy, where it seems [the bombs] will never finish. And the hands of the clock actually seem to have gone backwards . . .

The first device was found on 18 December, placed a few metres away from Piazza Fontana, amongst the steeples of Milan's gothic *duomo*. It was left in a black bag next to a public passageway, timed to go off at three a.m. The Anarchist trail is immediately under suspicion, particularly since the explosive used (called 'Vulcan 03' or 'quarry dust') was used in other, recent Anarchist bombs. The bomb is later claimed by a group called *Solidarietà Internazionale*. The response from the right is swift. On 22 December, a former 'black' terrorist decided to enter the offices of *Manifesto*, the 'Communist daily' as it calls itself, in Rome. On the fourth floor, shortly after midday, he asked for directions, explaining 'I've got to deliver a package to *Manifesto*'. His bomb, however, exploded before he reached his target, lacerating his legs and giving him multiple fractures. Doors were blown off hinges, and one photograph the next day showed a poignant image: one sole, dusty shoe, that of Andrea Insabato, the bomber, upon a mound of glass, papers and masonry. By chance Insabato was the only one hurt, but – as *Manifesto* wrote the following day – 'If the bomb hadn't exploded before expected, it could have been a slaughter'.

Piecing together Insabato's curriculum vitae as a terrorist was fairly simple. He was an adherent of NAR, the far-right *Nuclei Armati Rivoluzionari*, and of *Terza Posizione*, in the 1970s. He was arrested in 1976 when, at the age of seventeen, he fired a pistol against one of the offices of the Communist party in Rome. More recently, in 1992, during a football match between Lazio and Torino, he ostentatiously burnt the Israeli flag, shouting *ebrei ai forni*, 'Jews to the ovens'. Just days before the bomb against *Manifesto* he had attended, on the occasion of Jorg Haider's invitation to the Vatican, a rally in favour of the Austrian politician, carrying a Palestinian flag.

On its defiant front page (entitled *Siamo Qui* – 'We're Here') the day after the attack, *Manifesto* blamed the attack on the 'cultural humus which has allowed the neo-Fascists to be cleared through customs and which has offered them political legitimacy . . .' Inside, the editorial continued the attack, suggesting that Insabato was the product of 'the hypocritical right of Fini and Berlusconi which has never had the courage to deal with its bloody history, as has – with difficulty and pain – a part of the non-institutional left. This is the result. The sewer is still there, with its great unpunished and its little soldiers . . .' That robust response from the target of the attack was to be expected, but most other political commentators follow the same line: Insabato, after all, graduated from the same crucible of neo-Fascism – the *Movimento Sociale Italiano* – as did many of the political leaders of Berlusconi's right-wing alliance. Many have gone in different directions to Insabato, changing political livery and party names; but in the days and weeks after the bomb it emerged that there was barely a political party on the right which didn't have some link to Insabato, or which hadn't offered him a platform for his opinions. He emerged as an *integralista cattolico*, a member of the 'Christian Militia'. He had frequently attended rallies of another party of the far-right, *Forza Nuova*. Most significantly he had, in January 1995 in Rome's Hotel Ergife (where Pino Rauti was launching his new political party), taken the microphone and declared: 'We need to remember that the real enemy is Zionism, that Jewish sect which tries with every means to dominate the world.' Insabato, though, was swiftly branded a *cane sciolto*, an 'unleashed dog', by the far right.

More subtly, many suggested that politicians were responsible for the 'new terrorism' not directly, but indirectly: with all the finger-pointing, the hysterical 'Fascist!' and 'Communist!' jeers of the pre-election fever, politicians had unwittingly given rogue terrorists a sense of purpose and a rhetoric they understood. Such was the analysis, albeit more muted, offered by the *Procuratore della Repubblica* in Milan shortly after the bomb there: 'We had hoped,' said Gerardo D'Ambrosio, 'that the resort to bombs for political purposes was finished . . . unfortunately it's not so . . .

Every time the political exchanges get more bitter one can always expect that someone will try to exploit the situation . . .' Italian terrorism, lamented the then Prime Minister, Giuliano Amato, is 'a volcano which is never spent'. Another magistrate, investigating the new Red Brigades, called Italy's terrorism: 'an underground river . . . which suddenly re-emerges evermore violent.' Terrorism in Italy, he said, is 'almost physiological'.

For decades bemused historians and sociologists have analysed Italy's terrorist phenomenon. Many have echoed the line that 'terrorism does not invent, but rediscovers, recycles and readapts that which is already in the womb of the nation,'[4] suggesting that there's something uniquely Italian about the country's terrorism. Many of the early studies of the anni di piombo *thus suggested that the country had a 'psychosis of the bomb'. Ever since the* Risorgimento, *the argument went, the country had had a culture of violence that was 'living and important'. According to that theory, the historical roots of the* anni di piombo *were clear: in 1894 the French President had been killed by Italian Anarchists, as were, later, the Spanish Prime Minister and the Empress of the Austro-Hungarian empire. In 1900 Umberto I was assassinated; in 1921, in a theatre in Milan, another bomb claimed the lives of more than twenty people. In 1928, eighteen were killed during an attempt to assassinate another Italian monarch. Violence, from the* Risorgimento *to the* Resistenza, *had been the catalyst for every important turning point in Italian history. 'No other industrialised society,' wrote one academic in the* Rivista Storica Italiana *in 1980, 'has seen a terrorist phenomenon which, for duration . . . diffusion and rootedness can compare to that of Italy.' 'Violence has mesmerized us,' wrote another academic; the* anni di piombo *were simply the latest example of Italy's 'aestheticisation of violence . . . rendered photogenic, if not exactly accepted, conferred with that fascination which is at the root of its hypnotic power . . .'[5]*

Others discerned what was called 'Cattocomunismo', the quasi-religious, millenarian zeal of the terrorists. These evangelicals, having lost their orthodox faith, were still attempting to 'realise the other world in this world', to pass 'from an exigency of Christian totality to

Marxist totality'. One left-wing guru had, for example, spoken of Communists as a race born of a 'virgin mother', and of his political group as a 'combatant religious order'. 'The need,' wrote one journalist, 'for total and definitive answers, the rejection of doubt, are at the same time Catholic and Communist.'

The end of the Cold War, and the not-unrelated eclipse of the Christian Democratic party, have given studies a new dimension, contextualising the anni di piombo *within an international framework. Against the backdrop of the Warsaw Pact and the North Atlantic Treaty Organisation, Italy has been seen as a border territory, on a knife-edge between the two sides. The reasons for what has been called a 'tragic frontier experience' were both geographical (Italy being seen as literally on the front-line) and political (the country had the largest Communist party in the western world, winning 19% of the vote in 1946, and thereafter increasing its polling at every election until its peak in 1976 with 34.4%). The consequence was that Italy was subject to a McCarthyism that made the original, American version appear very mild by comparison.*

Thus, *historians have written of post-war Italy as being 'on the nerve-front between the West and Communism, for the entire Cold War under constant observation, and its democracy ever under surveillance'. If the terrorism of the 1960s and 1970s was chilling, it was because that violence was a reflection of the Cold War, isolated examples of a greater global conflict. As such, the acts of terrorism were 'signs of war, fragments of a planetary war fought underground which every now and again surfaced with its horror, its devastating potential . . . to destroy all that it touched: peace, the democratic confrontation, the truth . . . surfaced and moved on, leaving behind blood and darkness . . .'[6]*

In that respect, *Italy has been compared to Germany, another country torn in two by the 'spaccatura dell'Europa', by the rift of an entire continent. The difference being that Italy witnessed 'an invisible iron curtain, crossing populations, classes and consciences' which 'shattered' the unity of the country into 'two political, civil and moral realities . . . almost two countries'[7]. Whereas in Germany a wall had become a very literal, concrete example of a* divided nation, in Italy the cleavage was ever more subtle and sub-merged. The clandestine nature of the armed struggle was, in fact, revealed to the Italian parliament in 1990, when Giulio Andreotti announced that ever since 1945 there had been a military presence on the peninsula called Gladio (the so-called 'stay behind' of Allied troops); subsequent investigations revealed that weaponry and personnel from much of the anni di piombo overlapped with that of Gladio.

An equally serious problem was that Italy's post-war foreign policy zigzagged unpredictably, swerving from philo-Arabic policies (Colonel Gaddafi had even become one of Fiat's major shareholders) to support for Israel. The timing of Italian slaughters was often uncannily close to similar events on what the President of the Slaughter Commission called the chessboard of the Mediterranean, especially in the Middle East. Thus, according to some, Italy's anni di piombo weren't only a result of the Cold War, but also of the Arab-Israeli conflict.

The role of parliament during the period was also decisive. Parliament was described as a 'conventio ad excludendum', an imperfect two-party system in which one party was permanently in power, and the other permanently excluded. Either that, or the opposition was fatally accommodated, becoming part of the 'constitutional arch', the political 'marriage' of opposing parties: there was the 'opening to the left' (involving Socialists) or the 'historic compromise' (involving the Communists). The Christian Democrats were thus described by Leonardo Sciascia as 'invertebrate, available, conceding, and at the same time tenacious, patient, grasping; a type of octopus which knows how gently to embrace dissent to return it, minced, into consensus.' Opposition was, effectively, impossible. Thus, some commentators on the armed struggle used the birth of British parliamentarianism as an example of what exactly was wrong with Italy: quoting Thomas Hobbes, writers such as Giorgio Galli saw the birth of the British parliament as a means to contain a civil war. Verbal exchanges and the alternation of parties replaced cruder confrontations as representative democracy became 'the game which impeded a civil war'. That such exchanges were conspicuously absent in Italy meant that, in some

sense, the latent civil war never found itself absorbed, reflected or paci-
fied by parliament, and so raged on outside it.

Whilst I was packing a bag to go back to Britain for Christmas a
song came on the radio: it was the beautiful, lilting voice of Fabrizio
De André, the country's most famous and much-mourned
singer–songwriter. The song, from 1973, is called *Il Bombarolo* –
The Bomber – and is, like its subject-matter, an integral part of the
nation's fibre. 'Intellectuals of today,' go the lyrics, 'idiots of tomor-
row, give me back my brain, which I only need between my hands.
Acrobatic prophets of the revolution, today I'll do it by myself,
without lessons . . . I've chosen another school. I'm a bomber . . .'

And yet, whilst I was packing, the strange thing was that I did-
n't really want to go home. I wanted to see friends and family, but
it was somehow an incredible wrench to leave Italy, even only for
a few days. I had become as *campanilista* (as attached to my local
bell-tower) as everyone else. Even the thought of leaving Parma –
nicknamed the *isola felice*, the 'happy island' of Italy – was worrying. I looked out of the window and saw it snowing, the large
flakes jittering like molecules under a microscope. I could see the
rooftop tiles turning from pink to white. On the street below, people were putting skis on their roof-racks. Then, just as I was about
to leave for the airport, my next-door neighbour Lucia dropped
by to give me a sackful of her hand-made *cappelletti* (the little
pasta-wraps of Parmesan cheese which come served in a watery
broth at Christmas) as if to remind me of all the good food I
would be missing in northern Europe.

There was another thing I would inevitably miss over
Christmas. The sheer beauty of the country. The stunning style,
the visual panache, the obsession with *spettacolo*. That, I knew as
I sat on the plane, was what I would have to write about next: the
Italian aesthetic. Because there was one enigma which I had been
wondering about for months: how is it that the country which has
produced the greatest art in the Western world, which produced
some of the best films of the twentieth century, now has the
worst, most abysmal television on the planet?

5

The Means of Seduction

It was television which practically ended the era of piety and began the era of hedonism . . .
  Pier Paolo Pasolini

If I were a believer – not one of those who only goes to mass, but a believer who is perfectly convinced of his faith – I would say that Berlusconi is bad with a capital B . . . he has invested all that money in television in the worst way . . . he has lowered the cultural level of television and therefore of Italy . . . I blame him for that, because that cultural down-turn is the cause of so many things . . .
  Andrea Camilleri

I don't know whether it's because of the Reformation, which was iconoclastic and 'written'; or else because Britain has had, on the whole, the better writers and Italy much superior artists . . . but Italy is, unlike Britain, a visual, rather than a literary, country. Perhaps because there's such a forest of legal and bureaucratic language, very few people read newspapers, even fewer buy or borrow books. Every year or so there are official figures about book-consumption from ISTAT, the national statistical research unit, and the results are always the same: a massive percentage of Italian adults don't read one book a year. To survive, the *edicole* – the little pavilions on street corners which sell newspapers – have to double as fetish shops, selling gadgets and videos and soft-porn magazines alongside the newsprint. On public transport in Britain, half the passengers might be reading; in Italy, they will be eyeing each other, or else 'reading' the *Settimana Enigmistica*, a magazine of riddles and crosswords. There is, one quickly notices, no populist press, and there will be an Italian bestseller (Andrea Camilleri is the latest example) only once a decade.

Reading, when it's done at all, is done under duress. None of my students, I get the impression, has ever read a book for plea-sure. The more time you spend in the universities, the more you realise that they are part of what the Italian media calls the 'illiteracy problem'. A vast amount of teaching is done by dictation. When I ask students how they are taught in other classes, they describe professors who roll up and simply read their own books, chapter by chapter, to their students. If someone interrupts the dictation with a question about what has been read, the affronted professor will pause, then go back and read the sentence again, without explanation. Revision involves buying and rereading the professor's book, and learning it off by heart. Thus when those students then come to me for top-up lessons on language or literature, they have an acute fear of books and a sense of disorientation if asked to debate. They want to be told what to think, and they will then remember it and quote it back at you in exams.

Visually, though, the country is more cultured than any other. Each church feels like a museum: go into the *duomo* in Parma and, with a 500 lire coin, you can light up the entire cupola and admire the angels and apostles who usher the Madonna into heaven. This Assumption of the Virgin is the work of the city's most famous artist, Correggio (Antonio Allegri). Titian comment-ed on the work: 'Reverse the cupola and fill it with gold, and even that will not be its money's worth'. (Although Dickens, visiting centuries later when the frescos were crumbling, was more scathing: 'Such a labyrinth of arms and legs: such heaps of fore-shortened limbs, entangled and involved and jumbled together. No operative surgeon, gone mad, could imagine in his wildest delirium . . .') Every week, even in the smallest towns around Parma, a new art exhibition will open. A lot of my friends seem to be budding sculptors or photographers, or else are studying the popular degree course in *Beni Culturali* (the appreciation and restoration of 'cultural goods'). Many happily talk to me for hours, without a trace of pretension, about why one architect or artist is worthy of note.

Even on a more low-brow level, the visual finesse of the country is always obvious: everything is simply beautiful. When I look out of my window I can see exquisite, geometrical chaos. Ripples of pink tiles, each roof facing a different direction to the one next door. The city looks like something from a fairy-tale, or at least from another century. The whole place is immaculately lit up, with minimal white lights which, through the foggy air, look like candles. People ride bicycles that seem to have been in the family for generations. *Palazzi* are propped up by columns which look as delicate and thin as pencils. The house-fronts are all brightly coloured, normally the mellow, vaguely regal yellow which is called Parma yellow (a colour popularised by the Duchess Maria Luigia, Napoleon's widow, who reigned in Parma in the early nineteenth century.) The care put into buying shoes, tablecloths, handbags and clothes is extraordinary and, for a foreigner, unfathomable. When you buy a bouquet of flowers, it will take twenty minutes for the florist to prepare its presentation: leaves and sprays are added and discussed, paper and ribbons turned and twisted, and then removed if the colours are thought to clash. Shops are like stylised grottos: salami hanging like bats from the rafters, corridors of fresh basil and rosemary lining your path to the counter.

The consequences of a visual rather than literary culture are evident everywhere. It's often hard to find anything that is remotely ugly, be it a building or a painting or, especially, some-one's clothing. Italy, of course, produces the world's most esteemed fashion retailers, be they for the high-street or the cat-walk: Versace, Armani, Valentino, Max Mara, Benetton, Diesel, Dolce & Gabbana. The care about clothing means that you can go into a shop and describe the colour, cut, stitching style and buttons you want on a shirt, and the shopkeeper will invariably find it. Like in the restaurants, the more specific and picky you are, the more you're esteemed: 'I would like a black shirt of a silk-cotton mix, no pockets, horizontal button-holes, French cuffs but with a Venetian collar. Oh, and preferably minimally tapered towards the waist . . .' If you get that far, however bad your Italian, you will have the respect of everyone in earshot. (The sartorial vocabulary is, like that for food, enough to fill a separate dictionary.)

That preening might sound like vanity, but it's not. It's simply a precision about presentation. Even at two in the morning, groups of women gather outside shop windows and discuss the width of sandal straps in the same, amicably heated way that old men discuss Verdi. Fashion is followed slavishly. When the season changes, and it happens almost overnight, the cognoscenti all begin wearing the same colour: last year lilac, this year yellow. Personal grooming is taken very seriously, by both men and women. As you drive out of town, huge billboards advertise the transplant cure for baldness: 'Hair For Anyone Who Has A Head' says the slogan. Often if you casually say to someone that 'you're looking well' the reply is: 'Thanks. Yep, I've just done a [UV] lamp.' I, being British, would be embarrassed, but here there's no bashfulness about wanting to look good. Tanning techniques are minutely discussed and dissected. A mountain tan, I learnt, has a different depth and tone to a beach tan.

Linguistically, of course, beauty is ever-present. I sometimes play football in a team on the outskirts of Parma and whenever I arrive in the changing room – and it happens to everyone – I'm greeted with kisses: *Ciao bello* or else *ciao carissimo* ('Hello dearest').

'Listen,' I said to Luigi, our speedy winger, as we were lacing up our boots one Saturday, 'you've got a trial with an English team next week, right?'

'Yes, *carissimo*.'

'In England?'

'Yes, *carissimo*.'

'Well, Luigi,' I wanted to say it tactfully, 'just don't call the English players 'beautiful' or 'dearest,' and don't kiss them, OK?' The effect was as if I had told him that the English don't have friends. He couldn't understand how men could behave so coldly towards each other.

'But,' he was clearly bewildered, 'if I can't tell my new football friends they are beautiful and dear to me, what can I say?'

'I don't know. You have to remember, *carissimo*, that you Italians are just much more civilised than us.'

By now I'm so used to the sheer style that I can recognise a northern European at a hundred metres. They have grey hair, or none at all. They look awkward with their sunglasses. Young male backpackers don't have the complicated facial hair that is another Italian art form. Each time I look in the mirror I hear Italo Calvino's description of

... goofy and anti-aesthetical groups of Germans, English, Swiss, Dutch and Belgians ... men and women with variegated ugliness, with certain trousers at the knees, with socks in sandals or with bare feet in shoes, some clothes printed with flowers, underwear which sticks out, some white and red meat, deaf to good taste and harmony even in the changing of its colour ... [1]

Northern Europeans, Italians know, are simply less stylish. The British also, I'm often told, spend so much time reading they forget to wash. Either way, British personal presentation is like British football: inelegant.

That search for beauty and style has its logical extension: a simmering, but unmistakable sense of erotica. Every Italian town has one street that becomes, at that idyllic sunset hour when everything slows down, a free-for-all catwalk. Couples and widows and children and the card sharks from the square walk back and forth, greeting and gossiping with friends. In Parma people will almost always look you up and down to get an overall picture of your size and style. Women, often men, will hold your stare for a second longer than is subtle (which, I suppose, makes shades imperative). It often seems that flirting is the oil of all human interaction. Frustrated young men in Italy constantly complain that it's all *fumo e niente arrosto* ('smoke and no roast') that – crudely – all the flirtation is a road to nowhere. Whatever the destination, though, it's an amusing journey because there are so many siren voices, so many seductive distractions.

It was late spring when the sexual tension in my university class, latent throughout the long winter, came to the fore. Maria Immacolata ('Mary Immaculate'), my favourite student, began coming to class with little more than a chiffon sarong thrown over a minimalist bikini. She's the daughter of an ice-cream magnate from Bari, and was always the first to arrive, the last to leave. 'What I miss most from Bari,' she said coquettishly, aware that we were alone and that I was admiring her iodine skin, 'are the waves'. To illustrate, she rocked her pelvis backwards and forwards as if making love to the chair. Then, as casually as if she were asking the time, she said: 'Are you betrothed?' A few days later I found a fantastically explicit love letter rolled up and shoved inside the handlebars of my bicycle.

Eroticism is everywhere. Even going shopping, if you're of a mildly puritan bent, is unnerving. The underwear section of one national department store is called 'cuddles and seduction'. There are more *intimerie*, 'intimate' lingerie shops, in Parma than any other kind. The shop with the highest turnover per square metre of shop-floor in the whole of Italy is a lingerie shop on the out-skirts of the city. It is, you quickly realise, another art form, taken to giddy heights of detailed eroticism. I have even been asked by a sleek shop assistant, on one apparently simple mission to buy candles, what sort of girl I was entertaining: 'If it's a first date I would suggest either pine or opium as the appropriate scents.'

'But it's just for myself. Can't I go with something simple like vanilla?'

'Ah, you're English!' she said sympathetically, as if suddenly understanding my ignorance about the nuances of buying wax.

I used to ask my students to give ten-minute lectures in English on whatever subject they wanted. In the course of the year three girls chose, independently of each other, to lecture on lingerie. Never was the classroom so alive. There was a heated debate about when exactly a *perizoma* (a G-string) should be worn, about whether showing knicker straps outside your skirt is now out of fashion, about which *push-up* (wondabra) suits which form of breast. The male students, too, were suddenly awoken from their slumber, asking earnest questions about the implications of suspenders as presents and the strength of transparent straps.

That refreshing candidness about erotica means that never is there a sex scandal in Italy. Politicians, despite their Catholic avowals, proudly partner the most pendulous, beautiful celebrities, doing their credibility only good. In Britain sex-and-drugs is the dream tabloid story; in Italy it's just not news. One of Bettino Craxi's Socialist ministers in the 1980s enjoyed such a swinging lifestyle that he even wrote a book about Italian discos and their culture. Another book published on the golden years of Bettino Craxi was written by Sandra Milo, an 'actress' and acolyte of socialist circles. She described orgiastic parties, invariably placing herself and famous politicians centre stage. Being much more mature than the British about such things, most Italians, if told that their local politician is enjoying a sex-and-drugs lifestyle, would express envy rather than outrage. Thus Berlusconi's Undersecretary at the Culture ministry, a learned art critic called Vittorio Sgarbi, is admired for his fine taste in not only Renaissance art but also in women taken from the 'dubious actress' drawer. He has such an amorous reputation that he stars in advertisements for a coffee brand: he's married to an ugly woman until he takes a sip, and he's then surrounded once again by beautiful nymphs. Every week he's asked onto talk shows to give his opinions on the female form, and on the etiquette of sexual encounters. Berlusconi himself fell in love with his second wife, Veronica Lario, as she stripped off on-stage during a performance of Fernand Crommelynck's *The Magnificent Cuckold*.

Cuckoldry is, of course, the flip-side of the flirting. There is a knife-edge between flirting and infidelity, and given the ubiquity of the former, there's also a widespread paranoia about becoming a cuckold (which, as Italian referees know, is the worst insult you can level at a man). Long television chat-shows are dedicated either to how to cheat successfully on your partner, or how to avoid it happening to you. Another frequent billboard seen in Italy is the one with a giant magnifying glass, advertising the services of a private detective: 'Are you sure you can trust her?' goes the slogan. Graffiti on street walls often just publicises an enemy's shame: 'Rinaldi is a Cuckold!' There's a whole niche humour about cuckoldry, and understanding the various nuances about 'being horned' takes years. Listen to the endless conversations on the subject and it becomes obvious that, as well as that seething jealousy, there is a more mature attitude towards the improbability of monogamy: 'Horns are like teeth,' goes a Roman proverb, 'it hurts when they grow, but they give flavour to life.'

In a culture which is so visual, and which eschews anything written, television has become the crucial source of infotainment. The time spent in front of TVs in Italy is on average, according to ISTAT, around 240 minutes per day (the figure creeps up each year). Which naturally means that, as an instrument of political propaganda, it is unrivalled. It reminds me of something Sofri had said, about how Italians outside prison live the same life as him, as if they were actually locked up and stuck in front of the television. It is also omnipresent: in most bars and even restaurants the noise of a football match or a garish quiz show will accompany conversation. If you walk down any street you will hear the drone of a dozen television sets.

I had expected television to be another example of Italian visual brilliance, a continuation of the enjoyable beauty and erotica. Instead, switching on the television was like introducing an insistent shopkeeper into the living room. Almost all the time, the TV was trying to sell me something. Programmes are interrupted by promotional messages, which are also euphemistically called 'consumer advice' by presenters who walk to another part of the studio to chat about a new product. Then a few minutes later there will be an advertising break proper: the volume of the TV, at least on the three Mediaset channels, actually increases during the ad breaks. Football matches, if there's a pause for an injury or a free-kick, are interrupted and 'the line returns to Rome' for more consumer advice. Programmes, after a while, come to seem like sing-along fill-ins between the adverts, rather than vice-versa. (57% of all Italian advertising budgets are sunk into television; in Britain the figure is 33.5%, in Germany only 23%).

Watching the news is barely more engaging. Reports are accompanied by pop-music and proverbs. It's seemingly obligatory on each day's news to have a slot advertising a new Hollywood film, a slot on football, another on pop music and finally a fashion story. During the summer, each edition of the 'news' is accompanied by the 'deck-chair interview', a slot in which beach-bums can talk about the latest tanning techniques. Or else an investigative reporter is dispatched, microphone in hand, to interview holiday-makers about the latest trend in sand-sports: beach volleyball or frisbee-throwing techniques. And (almost without exception) during the 'news' the whole system goes into melt-down, and the newscaster reaches for the phone on his desk. 'Apologies, we're having technical difficulties.'

Breasts are ubiquitous, even boringly so. It's unthinkable to have a glitzy studio show without a troupe of dancing girls dressed up in bikinis, and often even less. During a recent election, one local television debate was hosted by a woman who, other than serving the men coffee, took off an item of clothing each time the political debate became tedious. A friend and I remained glued to the tedious discussion until she was stripped to the waist. A typical stunt from another show will have a woman in a bikini slipping into a glass bath tub filled with milk. To great yelps of delight from the studio, she will then strip off whilst hidden by the milk and pass the bikini to the excited presenter. Each channel has its own little starlet, who introduces the evening's entertainment, addressing the viewers as *cari amici*, 'dear friends', and smiling at the camera as it zooms in on her shapely form (perfectly displayed as, hands behind her back, she swings her shoulders backwards and forwards, her top perforated by a 'tear-drop' at the intersection of her bosom).

The best programme on Italian television is called 'Blob' (on RAI 3, the 'Communist' channel). It broadcasts out-takes from the cheapest TV of the previous 24 hours. It has a section called *protette*, a play on words which implies both 'protection' and 'pro-tits'. It works, of course, because it pretends to be taking an ironic view of 'scorching' TV, whilst re-running all the best bits: bosoms falling out of skimpy dresses, female presenters pole-dancing to pop music, or else a famous politician enjoying a coy lap-dance. Another lead news item, towards the end of the year, is who is doing which calendar, and with which 'artistic interpretation'. Actresses are interviewed in soft-focus, with their twelve semi-naked photographs superimposed. A few weeks later, when you go to the *edicola* there are row upon row of these mildly sexy calendars, hanging up next to the Communist daily and various soft-porn videos.

All of which is nothing compared to the hype surrounding 'Miss Italia'. Every year in Salsomaggiore, a small spa town near Parma, the most beautiful girls from throughout Italy gather to compete for the prize of becoming the country's 'Miss'. For an entire week the contest obsesses the nation: friends bet on likely winners, debate their various attributes. By the time of the gala final on Saturday, there's nothing else on the peep-show television. Sofia Loren was a competitor in the 1950s, winning the runner-up award of 'Miss Elegance'. Since the advent of the Northern League, there's also a competition called 'Miss Padania'.

It quickly becomes clear that Italy is the land that feminism forgot. It's not that there aren't many successful women in Italy, it's that they're never in the hungry public eye (unless they come with heaving cleavages). It's hard to think of any female role models in Italy other than those confined to the role of television confectionery. With a few notable exceptions, the Italian parliament is a famously male domain. In one survey taken recently, it was analysed how much television time was dedicated to male and female governmental ministers: for every four hours of masculine chat, seven minutes were spent interviewing women ministers. On Berlusconi's Mediaset channels, women were granted 57 seconds of air-time for the entire month of June (one half of one percent of the overall coverage). If they're not tinseled starlets on television, lay women are simply famous for being mothers or relatives: women are rarely famous in their own right, but instead by virtue of their (virtuous) relationship to their men. Berlusconi often quotes his mother ('as my mother once said about me – I'm a kind of wizard'); Cecchi Gori, president of Fiorentina football club, always used to sit next to his during Fiorentina football matches. To be close to a mother gives off an aura of goodness.

'How on earth can you put up with all this nonsense?' I once asked one of my female students, noted for her firm, feminist opinions.

'That,' she said smiling, 'is exactly what we ask of British food: how can you possibly swallow that rubbish?'

'Fine. But the difference is that we don't spend a third of our waking lives watching TV, consuming what's been put on our plate by the country's most powerful politician.'

'Fine. But I would rather have crap television than crap food,' she laughed.

Another instance of the importance of television in Italy is the fact that the country boasts a quarter of the world's terrestrial channels: 640 of a total of 2,500. Most local channels have a sexy, middle-aged lady talking on the phone to a viewer as she displays her tarot cards on the carpeted table and narrates how much money you can win if you put the following numbers down for this week's lottery. Others are dedicated solely to reading horoscopes or dispelling an amorous curse cast by a rival in love (there will be a mage, complete with aluminium foil mitre). Much the most common, though, are the channels selling dubious beauty products: for half an hour there might be a close-up of someone's buttocks as little pads send electric shocks into the flesh. On other channels there will be a man, pretending to be outraged that he's selling so much jewellery for so little money, placing plastic necklaces on busty girls.

As usual, I went to Filippo for an explanation. 'What you don't realise,' he said, 'what none of you British realise, is that Italy's a cultural desert. You come here to gawp at buildings and chipped statues from 500 years ago, and imagine that we're still at that level of cultural production. Which is, of course, absolute balls: Italy's now, culturally, completely arid. If I were you I would go back to the 50s and 60s. Switch off the television and watch some old films instead . . .'

'Italia, Oh Italia,' wrote Byron, 'thou who hast the fatal gift of beauty'. It's a line that could serve as the leitmotif for much of Italian cinema. During their golden era in the 1950s and 1960s, Italian auteurs *maintained a very ambiguous attitude towards the country's patho-logical need for beauty and eroticism. A series of self-reflective films appreciated both the magnificence and dangers (the 'fatality') of Italy's visual culture.*

Visconti's Bellissima *is the prime example because it cuts both ways: it is, as the title suggests, lush and stylish cinema, but the plot is about the threat to society posed by the cinematic need for shallow beauty. A film crew are holding auditions to find a child actress, and one mother bankrupts her family and almost her morals in the desire to see her child on the screen: 'You don't get if you don't give' says one of the film crew to her, seductively asking for either money or sex. She does eventually see her child on screen, but only by spying on the screen-tests where the film crew are ridiculing her daughter.*

It's the same with Michelangelo Antonioni. 'Beauty really is dis-comforting,' says one of his characters in La Notte, *as he pours himself a death-bed glass of champagne whilst admiring the nurse. 'Life would be so much easier if there weren't pleasure,' says another character, the writer, Giovanni Pontani, as he watches an erotic dancer whilst seated next to his wife. The settings of Antonioni's films could hardly be more luxurious: the Aeolian islands and Sicily in* L'Avventura *(a title which is also a euphemism for a fling), or the opulent party out-side Milan in* La Notte. *In both, the erotic temptations, the frisson of sexual infidelity, cause excitement and agony. In both, the shadow of disappearance and death falls across the frivolity, evoking the idea of 'Eros and Thanatos' where eroticism goes hand in hand with death, the dissolution of the self. The very thing which makes his films so beautiful to watch (languorous, moody women and their modern, worldly men) is the same thing which makes them tragic and emotionally depressing: human relationships don't last, all pleasures are ultimately hollow.*

Fellini's cinema shared the same themes and often the same actors. La Dolce Vita *was, like* Bellissima, *a self-referential film: both a celebration and a critique of the new, glamorous world of the cinema. And, like* La Notte, *it was a film about the thwarting of literary ambition (even about the way in which the visual had superseded the verbal). The film was denounced as 'obscene' by the*

Catholic hierarchy when it came out. The Vatican's mouthpiece publication, L'Osservatore Romano, *called it 'disgusting'. The intention of Fellini, though, was a moral one: 'There is,' he wrote, 'a vertical line of spirituality that goes from the beast to the angel, and on which we oscillate. Every day, every minute, carries the possibility of losing ground, of falling down again toward the beast.'*[2] La Dolce Vita *was an attempt to distinguish angelic humanity from the bestial, and it duly became more than merely a cheap take on loose-living. Thus the sexuality of the film is invariably derided: the diva Sylia is simply a 'kitten' (she even places a cat upon her head before the famous Trevi fountain scene). In that bestial atmosphere, Marcello Mastroianni's character concludes 'morals aren't right'. The result is a film that is both erotic and numbing at the same time. Its scenes are, like Antonioni's, a modernist mixture of titillation and ennui. Everything, especially the media circles Marcello moves in, seems exciting and yet soulless.*

Pier Paolo Pasolini's most famous film, certainly the most brutal, was an attempt to identify those fetishes of the flesh with Fascism. Salò, *a reworking of the Marquis de Sade's* 120 Days of Sodom, *was the story of young boys and girls selected for an orgiastic sojourn in the dying days of Fascist Italy. It's eroticism at its most obscene and animalistic. Characters don't have names, only rank (the masochistic Fascist is only ever referred to as Il Presidente). One boy is derided as a 'weak, chained creature'. The process of selecting the sexual slaves is presented like a cattle market, as officers from the regime compliment and criticise. 'Little tits to give life to a dying man' is the observation on one girl; the lips of another are pulled back to reveal imperfect teeth, and she's rejected. The film is a litany of vices, sexual and otherwise. Acts of religion are punishable by death; the eroticism is legalistic, so that the sex represents obedience rather than transgression. Against the soundtrack of lounge jazz, there's also pomposity. One Fascist reveller proclaims languidly: 'I'm provoked into making a certain number of interesting reflections . . .' The only possible conclusion from the film is that the path of pure hedonism leads to a new kind of Fascism.*

The connections between Fascism and erotica were also made by

Bernardo Bertolucci. The Conformist *(adapted from Alberto Moravia's novel) was, like all Italian cinema, a work of breathtaking style. It was a film that influenced a generation of American film-makers. Various scenes seem as immaculately posed as a painting: the long white benches of the mental asylum, the enormous, empty rooms of the Ministry where one of the regime's officials is seducing the woman sitting on his desk, hitching up her skirt and stroking her thighs. Against the backdrop of a murder plot there's the latent lesbianism in Paris, the brothel in Viareggio, such that Fascism, at least seen cinematically, appears highly aestheticised and eroticised. Like Pasolini (with whom Bertolucci had worked on* Accattone*) Bertolucci was deconstructing fetishism and Fascism, and tracing the links between the two. Fascism, in fact, was a subject-matter which produced probably his greatest film:* The Spider's Stratagem. *It's told in flashback: a young man has returned to his father's village to unveil a statue to his memory. He is set on unmasking the murderer of his father, a famous anti-Fascist, and returns to the village (in the flat Emilian plain) to visit his father's mistress and former friends. Only at the end does it become obvious that the whole narration has been a lie, and that the hero of the story isn't quite what everyone thinks.*

The irony is that the two humanists who have most often been the scourge of the Catholic church, Dario Fo and Pier Paolo Pasolini, have often used religious material – or at least moral criteria – to criticise the dehumanisation of modernity. They were endlessly accused of degrading Italy with their plays or films (even today there is usually a great sucking of teeth when the name Dario Fo, Nobel prize-winner, is whispered in Catholic circles), but they recognised what was happening long before anyone else: cinema and then television had unleashed the genies of eroticism and consumerism, and the country had somehow, according to the critique, lost its soul and its piety, even its politics, along the way. 'Consumerism,' wrote Pasolini, 'has cynically destroyed the real world, transforming it into total unreality where a choice between good and evil is no longer possible.'[3] He called it 'cultural genocide'. Dario Fo, in his play Big Pantomime with Flags and Puppets, *foresaw a world in which viewers are hypnotised by a televisual diet of football and advertisements.*

Witnessing an industrial revolution in the space of a few decades, various intellectuals argued that Italy's new-found obsession with possession (carnal or consumer) had eroded the moral fibre of the nation. Either that, or consumerism was a disguise, an attempt to pretend that poverty no longer existed. Italo Calvino wrote of 'the suspicion that all our ostentation of prosperity was nothing but a simple varnish on the Italy of mountain and suburban hovels, of emigrant trains and the swarming piazzas of black-clothed towns'[4]; with strikingly similar diction, Pasolini asked 'You know what Italy seems like to me? A hovel in which the owners have managed to buy a television.'[5]

And it's television that is now at the critical intersection of erotica and politics. The story of the 'new wave' of Italian broadcasting, coinciding with the end of the golden era of Italian cinema, began in July 1976. The Constitutional Court decreed that the state RAI channels would retain the monopoly on national broadcasting, whilst at the same time allowing unlicensed, private channels to broadcast as long as it was on a 'local' scale. In 1978 a new, local channel sprang up: Telemilano. It served the residents of a suburb of Milan called Milano 2, a residential complex of some 3,500 flats which had been built and sold during the previous decade by Berlusconi and his anonymous investors. By 1980 there were 1,300 private television channels; three years later, despite buy-outs and mergers, there were still more than 700. In 1980 Telemilano became known as Canale 5. In 1983 Berlusconi bought Italia Uno, and a year later he bought Rete 4. Those three channels eventually bought out almost all their rivals, such that the entire private sector broadcasting was unified under the Mediaset umbrella of Silvio Berlusconi.

The smaller the enterprise, of course, the more important the advertising revenue. Thus Berlusconi's nascent television channels were the early models for today's television. Programming was seamlessly integrated with advertising in the same way that now a programme is interrupted for a 'promotional message' and news items are there to plug a product. Rather than being 'alternative', the new private television channels and their low-budget programmes survived by becoming advertising vehicles. Often the advertising arm was barely distinguishable from the broadcasting business. The advertising revenue of the Mediaset channels was looked after by Publitalia, Berlusconi's advertising company which, by 1990, was responsible for 24.5% of the entire television advertising market (the figure is now nearer 60%). It was an arrangement that was to become a leitmotif for Berlusconian business: the buyer and the seller incarnate in the same person, the left hand closing a deal with the right.

The Mediaset studios are still based at Milano 2. If you go there, the whole place feels like something from The Truman Show: *it's a kind of unreal, bourgeois bubble. No one need ever leave the million square metres of the estate: there's a chemist, a school, a police station. There's a strange combination of concrete and greenery: all the blocks are a rusty red colour, and are linked by bridges and paths which weave over lakes and roads. It all feels slightly 1970s, not least the names of the blocks: Palazzo Aquarius and so on. The manhole covers have a simple M2 imprinted, along with Edilnord, the name of Berlusconi's construction company. At the centre of the complex you can see a tower of satellite dishes and the symbol of the Mediaset empire: the snake.*

Those three Mediaset channels, owned by Silvio Berlusconi, are even worse than the rest of the channels. Watching Mediaset is like watching out-takes from Sesame Street without the clever bits. There's a merry-go-round of about twenty personalities who seem to be on television rotation duties. The same VIPs (pronounced to rhyme with 'jeeps'), footballers and ageing compères appear on different shows on different channels, so that in the end each programme ends up looking like the last. Invariably the band strikes up half-way through the show, and everyone jumps to their feet to sing a syrupy song from the 1980s as the studio audience claps in unison and sings along. (Another of the favourite musical genres is 'cartoon theme music'.) Horoscopes are minutely discussed on the hour, and magicians and wizards and sexologists often sit alongside the panel of 'political experts'. The mawkishness of these programmes is amazing. *If you try and keep count of the number of times someone on Mediaset says* bellissimo *you'll be in triple figures after half an hour.*

Other than adverts and Europop singalongs, programming is reliant upon films. In one of his many masterstrokes, Berlusconi bought the Italian rights to hundreds of American films and mini-series, beginning the era in which Italy became a mass importer, rather than exporter, of 'culture'. The trend has continued, so that Mediaset broadcasting is now like one long cinema screening of snuff films and B-movies. They're broadcast, of course, under the title Bellissimi *and by now it's very rare to see a film on Italian television which hasn't been imported from America, occasionally Britain. It's rare to watch a film in which the lips move when the words are spoken. (Italy's most famous actors are now its dubbers.) And those who are fed up with incessant advertising breaks can, since the growth of video rentals, pop out to rent a video, probably from Blockbuster (also owned, in Italy, by Silvio Berlusconi).*

The law, however, maintaining RAI's national broadcasting monopoly was still in force in the early 1980s. Eventually, though, the law was changed because it had already been blatantly broken. Berlusconi wasn't broadcasting nationally, he was simply broadcasting the same programmes at the same times across the country, albeit on local channels. It was national broadcasting in all but name. Someone could watch the same imported film at the same time in Palermo or Parma, where different stations would coincidentally have a co-ordinated programme schedule. At one point, since such broadcasting was illegal, the programmes were taken off the airwaves; the ensuing outrage from viewers who needed the next episode of Dallas *or* Dynasty *enabled Berlusconi to present himself, as he would often do in later years, as the man representing 'freedom' against 'oppression'.*

The legislative sleight of hand by which Berlusconi's broadcasting scheduling became legal was known as Law 223 or 'the Mammí law' (named after the Minister for Telecommunications). It was proposed in 1984 and passed, eventually, in 1990. It sanctioned the de facto national broadcasting by Berlusconi, ending for all time the

monopoly of RAI and creating the RAI-Mediaset duopoly. Five gov-
ernment ministers resigned in protest at the legislation, already wary
of Berlusconi's omnipotence. The then Prime Minister was Bettino
Craxi, who had been best man at Berlusconi's second marriage and
was to become godfather to Berlusconi's daughter. Craxi's offshore
accounts later received a 23 billion lire injection from an obscure part
of Berlusconi's Fininvest empire (called All Iberian).[6] *Berlusconi was*
sentenced to two years and four months for the alleged bribe, though
on appeal he was acquitted because of the statute of limitations. The
crime, as so often, had passed its crime-by date. Berlusconi had
become 'His Emittenza,' an ironic play on words which evoked both
his 'eminence' and his broadcasting 'emittance'. Not only did 'the
Great Seducer' (another nickname) own the means of production, he
owned something much more important: 'the means of seduction'.

The tactic is blissfully simple. It requires a small box in the corner
of every room, plugged into the wall. It requires an aerial to
receive the right broadcasts. (Eventually, the notion of 'the right
broadcasts' might become irrelevant; if the owner of the 'right'
channels should also head the government, the rival state channels – rivals politically and economically – will also be his.) That
benevolent media tycoon pays himself for advertising space on
his own channels in order to promote his own products. As he
becomes inexorably richer, he also becomes the consumers' most
trusted entrepreneur. They recognise and agree with his
Orwellian mantra 'old is bad/new is good'. Eventually, the mores
of millions of viewers will be so familiar to him that they can be
turned into faithful voters, guaranteed to be receptive to any slick
promotion by a new political party.

By now the most convincing explanation, albeit the most mundane, for Berlusconi's political appeal is the simple fact that he
controls three television channels. Having a politician who owns
three television channels turns any election into the equivalent of
a football match in which one team kicks-off with a three-goal
advantage. Victory for the other side, even a draw, is extremely
unlikely. Certain programmes, like the parliamentary programme

on Sunday, *Parlamento-in*, are like long party political broadcasts. Some Mediaset channels are worse than others. Rete 4 has an anchorman – Emilio Fede – nicknamed 'Fido' because he's so sycophantic to his boss. He'll introduce a news story with a comment like: 'These stupid commies!' Rete 4 is the channel that anytime Berlusconi is making an important speech will beam it live, without comment or criticism, into millions of homes across Italy. The other two channels are only minimally more balanced. Even there journalists, like referees walking into the San Siro Stadium, appear overawed. Asking hard questions of Berlusconi is akin to criticising not only the politician, but everyone in the television studio who are employed by him, and so it's simply not done. The partiality, as with referees, might be accidental, subliminal, but it's very obvious.

Thus Berlusconi has been compared, not unfairly, to Mussolini: both had a balcony from which they could harangue, cajole and persuade adoring viewers. Berlusconi, being the head of Italy's 'videocracy', is only different because he owns an electronic balcony. The defence is that such partisan broadcasting is actually democratic: RAI is so riddled with left-wingers that Mediaset guarantees, not objectivity, but at least democratic pluralism. Without Berlusconi, the thinking goes, we would only be at the mercy of political henchmen.

But more than just painfully partial towards its boss, Mediaset television has achieved something even more disguised. It has seduced a society to the extent that politics and ideas don't seem to exist. Italy's noble visual culture has been reduced to endless erotica, and the small screen is now a cheaper, bittersweet version of *La Dolce Vita*: a world obsessed with celebrity and sexuality, to the exclusion of all moral values (Fellini, not surprisingly, for years objected to his films being shown on television). In many ways, the real problem with Mediaset isn't that it's political in the purest sense; it's that it's not political at all. The only thing on offer are bosoms, football and money. Even someone who enjoys all three eventually finds it all boring. '*Panem et circenses*,' says Filippo, 'that's what the ancient Romans called it: "bread and a bit of a show". Give that to the masses and they'll be happy'. An American friend, quoting Pynchon on paranoia, is even more dismissive: 'If they can get you asking the wrong questions, they don't have to worry about the answers!'

The new generation of voters, though, those who have lived with Mediaset's Benny Hill programming since infancy, know of no other form of television (and, as a consequence, the youth vote is an integral part of Berlusconi's success). When I tell some of my *Leghisti* students (those who sympathise with the Northern League), or the southern ones who sympathise with the National Alliance, that I really only watch RAI programmes, and then only after midnight, they are often appalled. 'But it's boring and Bolshevik,' they say. It's often only black and white documentaries at that hour, I'm reminded. That's the degree of hypnosis that Mediaset has achieved. It has turned viewers into *guardoni*, oglers. Its tinsel titillation is gripping: take the semi-pornographic Italian version of Big Brother, or else programmes like *Miracoli* (the weekly slot on the latest miracles) or *Proposta Indecente* ('indecent proposal'). The assault on anything measured or literary is such that the English word 'fiction' is now used in Italian to describe only saccharine TV drama. The best-selling magazines on the news-stands are those glossies with TV listings like *Sorrisi e Canzoni* ('Smiles and Songs', owned of course by Silvio Berlusconi).

In that ideological vacuum, Mediaset's greatest gift to its owner has been to promote the one thing for which he will always be admired: his wealth. Almost all the quiz shows are built around the opportunity to make money. Every evening, on every channel, millions, sometimes billions, of lire are lit up in bright lights, as the bikinis flirt with the excited member of the public, on the verge of pocketing a small fortune. Given the number of zeros on banknotes, another imported programme-format is called 'Who Wants To Be A Billionaire?' Lead items on the news are about which tobacconist sold the winning ticket for the lottery this week. Bingo, a game that is not exactly cutting edge in Britain, has recently become a highly fashionable Italian sport. All of which creates an environment in which someone's wealth, and all its apparel, become the hallmark of that person's worth. In marked difference to Britain, the yardstick by which people are judged isn't class but money. Boasting about money becomes like bragging about sexual conquests: it's important that everyone 'knows'. If someone enquires after your 'stock' in Italy they're inquiring after your wealth, not your breeding. In the end it's obvious that the nation's richest man will become, almost subliminally, the country's most seductive politician.

It's what has been called the 'sequin syndrome,' a disease which makes Mediaset seem caught in a 1980s, yuppie timewarp. Slowly it has begun to influence more than just the values of Mediaset. RAI, the state television network, has colluded in the cultural implosion: with a (largely ignored) licence fee which is only about £40, and with a subsequent turnover of 2,640 million euros compared to the BBC's more than 5,000 million, it has had to follow Mediaset's example and churn out glitzy variety shows to survive the ratings battle (called, in Italian, *lo share*). It, too, runs adverts every ten minutes. Its financial difficulties are then exacerbated because parochial sing-alongs have little international appeal, and thus never generate revenue from abroad.

The problem has become so acute that, in one of her very rare outbursts, *la signora Ciampi*, wife of the President of the Republic, recently said that Italian TV is by now *deficiente*, 'half-witted'. One magazine recently denounced 'the degree of servility shown by our television chatterers, ineffable adorers of men of power and above all of the landlord of all televisions,' adding that by now that attitude had become 'a booring, snarling servility', ferociously loyal to its leader.

Pasolini and piety are unlikely bedfellows, but by now one can see his point about television eroding the country's Catholic piety. The real tragedy, as nostalgic Italians often grumble, is that the country has witnessed a cultural collapse. Talk to anyone brought up in the 1950s or 1960s and they will say that all the hallmarks of the country – its intelligence, its beautiful language, the Catholicism, the style, even that simmering, cinematic erotica – have been eroded by television.

Meanwhile those who are blasé about a political leader owning so much of the mass media chuckle when they read about British scandals. 'What's all this about spinning?' I was once asked by someone who has a subscription to the *Times Literary Supplement*. 'What are spin-doctors?' I began to explain that certain people in Britain are rather worried about the slant the government can put on a story, the 'spin', thereby obscuring the reality. The result around the table was general hilarity: 'Is that all? You British are so prudish. Blair doesn't own three television channels, production companies, video outlets, dozens of magazines and a national broadsheet, does he?'

6

Clean Hands

The majority of Italians, although they had never extorted from, or corrupted, anybody, had always tried to interpret in the most limited way their obligations towards the state. They used 'recommendations' as a daily means of survival. The country plunged into the enthusiasm prompted by Clean Hands as if in a rite of collective liberation. With widespread indignation against the corrupt and the corrupters, largely fed by the press, an entire population deluded itself that it could in some way redeem itself of its own vices in the arena of civil ethics . . .

   Pietro Scoppola

A few years before I arrived in Italy, there had been a full-blown revolution. An entire political class had been removed. The way the country worked, economically and politically, was within the space of a few months completely turned around. Like any revolution, 'Clean Hands' meant different things to different people. For some it was the long-yearned for, blissful overthrow of the despotic regime that had ruled Italy for almost fifty years. For others, the hands of the revolutionaries were not 'clean' but very bloodied, having caused the deaths of dozens of innocent Italians who had dedicated their lives to the service of the Italian Republic. Clean Hands was (like the Slaughter Commission or the Sofri case) another of those historical case studies that was being fiercely debated in the run-up to the General Election. The way Clean Hands was seen by the electorate would almost certainly determine the outcome of the election, not least because one of those running for the highest office, Silvio Berlusconi, had first championed, and then been 'persecuted', by those revolutionaries. He had become an *indagato eccellente* (one of the 'illustrious accused'). Thus, he was the advocate of the 'restoration', desperately wanting to portray Clean Hands as nothing more than an interregnum of crazed Communists and bloody revolutionaries.

As usual, the debate was so confusing and contorted, that the only way to understand what was going on was to approach it in the first person. At least that way I felt that I was laying a thread of wool so that, when I had glimpsed the inside of Italy's economic maze, I could safely find my way out into the light once more.

The Italians invented capitalism. Or at least, in Pisa and Florence and various other city states, they invented the modern banking system based upon the extension of credit. It's still a country of bankers and instinctive, creative entrepreneurs. In Parma alone there are forty-two different banks, and that's before you start counting their various branches. Banks are like political parties and television channels: there's no end to the available choice (even if, in the end, they all look the same). In a large city, there will probably be a few hundred banks on offer. And, as with politics (like the 'white' Christian Democrats, 'black' Fascists, 'red' Communists), financial status is expressed in a prismatic language. 'At the green' means skint. 'In the red' is the same as English, but – the most commonly heard colour – 'in the black' means unofficial, untaxed and untraced.

If you believe the statistical rhetoric (and it all depends on how big you believe that 'black' to be), Italy effected the *sorpasso* – the overtake – of the British economy in 1987 (its GNP was 5,998 billion dollars, compared to Britain's 5,474). It's easy to understand how it happened: cars, clothes and food. Emilia-Romagna, the region which includes Parma and Bologna and which specialises in those products, has the highest per capita income in Italy. (The irony is that the richest province is the buckle on Italy's 'red belt'. Many of the brilliant entrepreneurs in the area are die-hard Communists who happily gather in the piazzas for the regular rallies and the waving of the hammer and sickle.) Driving between the two cities on the A1 motorway you will see, at one lay-by, a sculpture of a flying car. Cars drive the economy, hence the 'overtake' expression. At Bologna airport there's normally a new engine or piston-system displaying the native genius for engineering. Within a radius of a few kilometres are the factories of Ferrari, Lamborghini and Maserati.

If you stop off in Reggio-Emilia you'll find the home of Max-Mara, the famous clothing empire, whilst nearer Parma lining every road there will be a little outlet selling Parma ham or Parmesan cheese. In fact, it's apparently as profitable to break into a cheese factory as it is a bank: every few months I read in the *Gazzetta di Parma* about a cheese heist in which a band of robbers has broken into a Parma cheese production centre, and stolen the round ingots of cheese. (The generic word for the hard, gritty cheese is *grana*, which also doubles as the word for money.) On the outskirts of the town are the red and white chimneys of Barilla, the world's largest pasta factory. Nearby is Parmalat, the large dairy enterprise with outlets across the globe.

Seeing those businesses in action, the most obvious anomaly of the Italian economy is that, other than a handful of enormous companies like Fiat, enterprises are usually what's called SME (small-medium enterprises). The engine of the country's economy are often minute, local, family-run businesses which produce those textiles or foodstuffs or expert engineering. The percentage, for example, of the workforce employed in companies with less than ten employees is, in Britain, 7.2%, in America it's only 3.0. In Italy, the figure is 23.3%.[1] There's still – it's obvious when you walk around the narrow backstreets of any city – an artisan class that produces, in small outlets, the finest objects of the Italian economy: the furniture, the *prosciutto*, the suits and so on. Quite apart from their deserved economic success, these small enterprises give the country an other-worldly atmosphere because they're still involved in the old-fashioned art of manufacturing. Unlike Britain and its tertiary economy of financial services and management consultants, in Italy people still make things. Go into any of the tiny artisan grottos and before you even see the intricately blown glass or the marbled paper or decorative tiles, you're hit by the scent of oil, sawdust, the smell of a cooking kiln. In fact, supermarkets are a rarity: each shop is specialised, selling only tobacco or perfumes or newspapers.

There's another thing that you notice about the economy at the lowest level. There's a kind of generosity which means that people exchange presents in the way that the British shake hands. It's part of that *tessuto sociale*, the 'social fabric', which invariably seems better knit in Italy than anywhere else. Every time you meet a friend, they will offer you something, regardless of whether you're at their house or yours, or just passing each other on the pavement: a new CD, some piece of pottery they've found, a new crate of wine they want to share. Such is the extravagant generosity amongst friends that there's an old-fashioned exchange of merchandise in which the whole notion of money is almost an irrelevance.

When money does come into the equation (perhaps because of that preponderance of small enterprises) there's another thing about the Italian economy that you immediately notice. It's a cash society. Because of the confusing number of banks and documents, there's clearly a feeling that traceable transactions – receipts, Visa-slips or cheque-book stubs – are inconvenient. Cheques are hardly ever used. Paying with plastic is impossible in many places. If you are buying a table or an overcoat, even paying the bill in a restaurant, you'll often be asked whether you're paying in cash or not. If so, the prices are almost always *trattabili*, negotiable. That, of course, is the case in any country, but in Italy even adverts for houses worth hundreds of millions of lire announce through various euphemisms that they're ready to reduce the cost if payment is in *contanti*, in 'countables'. If you negotiate a job contract, a percentage of the sum will often be offered under the counter.

The dependence upon cash slowly alerted me to something else, which was the complete reverse of the generosity amongst friends and family. There is, unfortunately, nowhere else in the world where the words *imbroglio*, *truffa* and *inganno* (fraud, swindle and deception) are so often needed. I haven't seen him for years, but there used to be a man on stilts who I would see every day in Piazza Garibaldi. He would be shouting at the passers-by, many of whom stopped to listen to him, nodding in sympathy as his spittle fell on the pavement. There, by the base of his two-metre stilts, were long letters and documents that announced the injustice to which he had fallen victim. He was, apparently, quite famous, performing daring stunts across the country to publicise his plight. Listening to him was like those forays in the post office when I first arrived in Italy. Everyone seemed to have their own story of a scam or rip-off they had suffered. When one person started talking about their mishap, half a dozen others would chip in and start recounting their own swindle which was similar or possibly even worse.

I, too, sympathised because I had found myself, every few months, the victim of something similar, albeit much smaller. Incessant short-changing, clever financial scams, unorthodox payment methods and bizarre banking techniques all seemed to leave me out of pocket. Other peoples' *furberia* had reduced me 'to the green'. There had been the time when, to avoid the hour-long queues in the post office, I had set up a direct debit between Telecom Italia and my bank. The next phone bill was, inexplicably, overcooked by about two million lire: half of which was thanks to Telecom's inexplicable error, the other half because I had taken in a lodger who had been phoning what's called *hard chat* on my phone. My bank paid the bill, but then billed me itself because I was suddenly hugely overdrawn. To recoup the money from Telecom Italia then involved so many hours of queuing that I (again naively) decided just not to pay the future bills since the money they owed me was greater than what I owed them. I had, of course, to pay the bank a 'suspension of the direct debit agreement fee', but then I was at liberty to not pay Telecom Italia until they had settled their debts. They duly cut off my phone line, and it would cost another 300,000 lire to get reconnected. It took seven months of bureaucratic queuing for that to happen. The costs from the whole episode were somewhere near £1,000.

I usually tried not to grumble about it, because the amounts I had lost only ran into a few million lire. Everyone else around me seemed to have been conned out of much greater sums, having been abandoned by business partners or persuaded to invest in spoof businesses. As my blood reached boiling point, I would complain to various friends, who would then generously lend me their cars or their money, or else invite me to their country houses and sit me down to explain the way things work. 'First,' said Filippo, 'there's a reason that people you know in this country are amazingly generous. It's because anyone who you *don't* know will almost certainly try to be *furbo* with you. It's them against us, and' – he said as he poured us another glass of lemon liqueur – 'we're here to defend you, and vice versa.' He started laughing: 'But you, Zio Tobia, you've still got milk in your mouth', which – suggesting you're still at the suckling stage – is the Italian way of saying 'you're wet behind the ears'.

'Never, ever, set up a direct debit in this country. Not unless you've been introduced to both the bank and the billers. Don't ever put a cheque in the post, because you can't trust the post, let alone the postman. You have to "play the game". You have to join one side or the other, to have someone at your shoulders [which really means get some decent back-up]'. He said he would talk to 'his friends' to see if there were any jobs going.

That, I knew, would be a *raccomandazione*. Since the chances of applying at random for a job and getting it merely on merit are virtually nil, you have to accept the way things work and get parachuted into a cushy job having been heartily *raccomandato*. Thus, when you accept the kind advice and sit one of those competitions for a job, you will know that, despite a gymnasium full of thousands of hopefuls, the job is yours because it has already been piloted in your favour by friends. (Then, once you've got an almost normal job, you in turn will be expected, when organising a strict competition for future promotions, to cast a favourable eye on the 'recommended' candidates.) I duly got a job to teach at Parma university. Only at that point did my adventure within a parallel world begin. I discovered another bizarre world of bureaucratic absurdity. To teach at the university I had to be registered for VAT, which was only possible if I was registered as an Italian resident, which in turn was only possible if I had a *Permesso di Soggiorno*, a 'sojourn permit'.

Two weeks before the start of the academic year, then, I was outside Parma's *Questura per Stranieri*, the 'police office for foreigners'. Knowing the acute problem of queues in Italy, I arrived at seven-thirty, half an hour before the office opened. There were already about fifty people mingling on the pavement – Moroccan men holding hands, swapping cigarettes, a group of what I assumed were Eastern European women huddled together, lots of men from Africa wearing faded football shirts, their wives in lime green robes. Eight o'clock arrived and the antique door of the *Questura* was still shut.

Eventually the heavy door swung to, and a policeman – decked out in shades and epaulettes – ushered us in. When towards ten o'clock I arrived at the counter and shouted my request through bulletproof glass, I was given the application form for a sojourn permit. I went to the bar across the road and began filling in the form. More and more people came in, clutching their precious forms: Albanians, Ukrainians, Tunisians, Somalis. We passed around biros borrowed from the bar for the cost of a coffee. Jokes started flying around in pidgin Italian about how Albania, or Nigeria, was more efficient than this, and shouldn't we all just go back to where we came from. By the time I had explained the form to various people, and filled in my own, the *Questura* was already shut.

Seven-thirty the following day. The same crowd on the pavement, waiting for the office to open. We greeted each other like old friends. The man in the West Ham top was there. He shook my hand, delighted that the English were subjected to the same routine as Africans. After queuing for only 45 minutes, I proudly presented my application for sojourn in Italy. The application process, of course, would require months, but at least equipped with the carbon copy I could go to the *Anagrafe* – the provincial equivalent of Somerset House – to apply for residency. The *Anagrafe* is an infamous institution: any change of status – marriage, new house, identity card – has to be rubber stamped. Then to the tax office, to apply for VAT status: another morning gone. I was beginning to understand why people talk about doing an 'operation' in a bank, or an office: it really does require military precision to navigate your way through the documentation.

Worse was yet to come though. The university presented me three contracts for the three courses I was supposed to teach. Since they are formal pieces of paper, it's not enough to sign them: they have to be *bollati*, given an official postage stamp sold at tobacconists. Then, I was told, I had to be insured in case of personal injury incurred whilst lecturing on English literature: another 300,000 lire. A few days before the beginning of the course, I went to the faculty library to see what books were available. The stern *signora* from the secretarial office ran up to me: *Ma che fai?* 'What are you doing?'

'Trying to find a few books for next week.'

'These are for the exclusive use of permanent staff. You're hired as a freelance and must buy your own.' She produced the business card of a friend who could help me out.

'But I'm allowed to use the blackboard, right?'

'Haven't you read your contract?'

I hadn't of course. It slowly dawned on me, as months went by, that since I was working freelance at the university there was no date specified as to when payment arrived. Assuming things were done monthly, I had only looked excitedly at *quanto* – how much? – not at the much more important information: *quando*, when? Months went by: the deep blue sky of late summer gave way to the dense fog of autumn. The snow began to fall in December, and the local electricity monopoly, AMPS, wanted its heating bills paid promptly at the post office. Any tentative payment enquiry at the university accounts office was brushed off with brilliant ventriloquism: 'It is foreseen that the pre-agreed payment as stipulated in the contracts for freelance teachers will be honoured before the end of the academic year.' Months later, that line had turned into 'before the beginning of the next academic year'.

I went back to see Filippo, who began laughing. 'You've still got milk in your mouth! Of course she makes you get insurance and books from her friends. Of course she then pays you a year and a half later. What did you expect? You really are so naive.' He began, slowly, explaining the whole thing again. 'Cash,' he kept repeating. 'Cash. Documents and contracts and banks will always rip you off. You must insist on cash. And never tip. Tipping is for stupid foreigners. Italians never tip. Why would we? Tipping is like paying tax . . . a voluntary contribution towards someone you don't know and shouldn't care about.' The distrust was incredible. All the more so because 'credit' – that Italian invention – was originally based linguistically and financially upon belief, on trusting the other person.

I had even seen politicians urge tax evasion, though. Those in opposition would encourage viewers not to pay the TV licence because the RAI channels were in the hands of the 'wrong' party. Other political leaders regularly urge a *sciopero fiscale*, a tax strike in protest against unfair financial burdens from the government. The defence line for tax-evaders is always the same: either it's justified because the government is corrupt, and therefore our tax-evading corruption is actually 'fiscal resistance to corruption'. Or else it's justified because of the extraordinary tax levy on Italians, the theory of the so-called *oneri impropri* ('unfair burdens'). It's a defence line which Silvio Berlusconi has repeatedly used to explain his financial manoeuvres: tax-payers, he has said, feel 'morally at loggerheads with the state', observing that the state's laws go against 'our natural sense of justice . . .'[2]

Given that backdrop, in which everyone (from friends to parliamentarians) urges you to, sooner or later you will become '*furbo*'. However earnest the intentions, you're almost forced to collude with 'unofficial' money, with the 'black' side of the economy, simply because it's so widespread. To avoid doing so would be harder than avoiding the cracks between the cobbles. Renting property 'in the black' (with under-the-counter cash) is very common because it suits both sides: the landlord pays no tax, so the rent is lower. You're welcome to do it legally and above board, but then you'll end up in a bedsit somewhere under the ring-road. If you can compromise on your morals a bit, the opportunities are exponentially increased. If you want to buy a house, the scams are even more labyrinthine. Buying a property involves so many middle-men (not only estate agents, but 'notaries', the richest of all Italian professional orders) that it's not surprising that Italians are bemused with the ease and speed with which the British buy and sell houses. Here, the costs and complications are so high it's clearly best to keep it a once in a lifetime experience. The only way to save yourself 30 or 40 million lire is to take a few short-cuts. Many suggested to me that if I were to pay them in 'countables' they would accept a 1.5% instead of the 3% cut. With the notaries you can even pretend that you've bought the house for half the price, thus halving his cut (although there you will be left with a property which is worth, on the vital, stamped paper, only half of what you actually paid). Alternatively, there's something called a *scrittura privata*, a 'private document', a sort of 'for our eyes only' agreement. Thus you can buy a property for two different prices: the official one (cutting your costs, future taxes and so on) and the private one (which is the real price you agree to pay the seller). Not for the first time, it became difficult to distinguish quite what was going on. There seemed, at all levels, to be parallel paths – the official one written on paper, and the hidden one going on in verbal agreements between 'gentlemen'.

The other problem was that frequently I was offered a flat that, given the official/reality divide, wasn't actually in existence. The widespread practise of illegal building (*abusivismo*) means that you can find something that – given your modest budget – appears a bargain: a two bedroom attic flat on split levels in a part of the city that feels crumbling but lively. The estate agent notices your enthusiasm, and whispers in your ear about how negotiable they are when it comes to cash payments. The problem is that if the flat or a part of it, say the second level of the flat, is 'abusive', it simply doesn't exist in the annals of bureaucracy. To save money, the notary has been bypassed and in buying the property, you make the gamble that the 'unpardoned' building doesn't get discovered, because you would have inherited the abuse. You would, to officialise the abuse, have to pay for the pardon, or else keep it secret and risk the fine. It would be very unlikely that anyone would even discover your inherited abuse, but if you had snapped up the bargain you would already be on that well-trodden road to collusion with illegality. Anyone who had a grudge against you could simply do the ultimate in betrayal: denounce you.

Stay in the country long enough and you simply have to become 'cunning' in order to survive. With a shrug of honest admission, everyone in Italy will admit to having broken the law at some point (it's hard not to if being 'an accessory to tax evasion' involves leaving a shop without the till receipt). Catholics mention original sin and our fallen nature; politicians talk about being realistic rather than ideological about the law. Everyone has a bit of 'black' mixed in with the 'red' and 'green'. It's only a matter of degree. *Così fan tutti*: everyone's guilty of something, so if you go looking for dirt, you'll find it anywhere.

The whole debate about Clean Hands is about where to draw the dividing line (if it even exists) between what is 'cunning' and what is 'corruption'. And even corruption is a redundant term because here the word has so many layers. It is only a loose, generic word (like *prosciutto*) that needs to be divided into dozens of different cuts, each of a different quality and cost.

The other side of the economy is the complete opposite of those small enterprises: huge 'para-statal' companies employing hundreds of thousands of people. As with the politics, in economics there was a marked continuum between Mussolini's regime and the First Republic. The many acronyms from Fascism such as IRI, IMI and AGIP survived untouched. To those state enterprises, founded in 1933, 1931 and 1926 respectively, was added another in 1953, ENI. Thus the public sector workforce remained much as it was under Mussolini: IRI had in 1942 employed 210,000 people; by 1955 it was still employing 187,000 people and would, seven years later, become Europe's biggest industrial group after Royal-Dutch Shell.

The other catalyst for Italy's post-war reconstruction was Mediobanca, founded as an offshoot of the Banca Commerciale Italiana in 1946 and nestled just behind La Scala in Milan. It was, until his death in 2000, for over fifty years the private domain of a banker called Enrico Cuccia. Even there the continuities with the

Fascist period are marked: Cuccia had married the daughter of Alberto Beneduce, the man who had, under Mussolini, been president of both IMI and IRI. Mediobanca provided credit to the country's commercial ventures, receiving in exchange large shares itself or else positions on the board. (It now has a market capitalisation of almost £7 billion, and owns, amongst other assets, Assicurazioni Generali, Europe's third-largest insurer. Mediolanum, a bank in which Berlusconi has a 36% stake, is now part of the controlling shareholder group of Mediobanca.)

For all the subsequent criticisms aimed at the Christian Democrats, their rebuilding of the Italian economy was a brilliant piece of strategic management. Mediobanca, with its secretive system of overlapping interests, provided capital investment. Those semi-public corporations (often blamed for the later distortions of the Italian economy) for decades laid the foundations for Italy's industrial revolution. Thanks to their partnerships with private enterprises, those para-statal acronyms offered Italy the best of both worlds: the guiding hand of the public state combined with the acute, capitalist judgements of private enterprise. The result was that the raw materials and the physical infrastructure required for the country's economic miracle were quickly put in place. To give just one example, steel production, controlled by IRI through the Finsider company, reached three million tons by 1955; the obvious beneficiary was Fiat, which in turn increased production by some 400% during the 1950s.

Thanks to the low value of the Lira, and the low labour costs of the immediate post-war years, the 'miracle' was export-led. For much of the post-war years, the percentage growth of exports – cars, chemicals, clothes and so on – was in double-figures. The crisis only arrived in the 1970s. Since Italy was more dependent upon oil than many of the other industrialised countries, it was particularly susceptible to the hike in oil prices at the beginning of the 1970s. The end of the Bretton-Woods agreement on fixed exchange rates and the devaluation of the dollar (in both 1971 and 1973) meant that Italian exports (ever the success story of the economy) were hard hit. Industrial unrest was also causing a wage spiral. The hourly rates of workers between 1964 and 1968 increased by 22.8%; during the four years after that period, they rose by over 95%. In fact, inflation was perceived as a way out of the Italian crisis, not least because the continuing fall in the value of the Lira meant that the engine of the Italian economy – exports – could be kept competitive. (Meanwhile imports, of course, and especially oil, became as a consequence ever-more expensive, which itself fuelled the inflationary spiral.) It was in that period that the most surreal effect of Italy's economy took place: everyone became a millionaire, and calculators started to come equipped with that unique button of three zeros in order to save time when adding up.

The more serious problem was that the economy was being subordinated to the survival of various political parties. Since they depended so heavily on patronage, on the ability to place their supporters within the bureaucracy through 'recommendations', any attempt to cut down on the mushrooming public sector workforce would have been tantamount to political hari-kiri. Thus organisations like the 'Cassa per il Mezzogiorno' (the 'fund for the south') and the 'Ministry of State Participation' were just the most famous examples of the bureaucracy providing jobs rather than services. Despite its important role in post-war reconstruction, the huge public sector had 'become the centre of party power, paving the way to the so-called spoils system'.[3] It served politicians to do exactly what was worse for the Italian economy: exponentially expand the size of the bureaucracy, thereby increasing the size of their grateful clientele. By the beginning of the 1970s, just over 30% of all salaries and wages in the south of Italy were due to public administration jobs. The circumstances were exaggerated in the south, but even nationwide the percentage of employment in the public sector had doubled from just 9% in 1951 to over 18% in 1990.

There was nothing particularly new about the size and inefficiency of Italy's bureaucracy, which had, for centuries, been the brunt of bitter criticisms. 'In Italy,' wrote Stendhal, 'and especially in the neighbourhood of the Po, everyone's conversation turns on passports.' He describes in The Charterhouse of Parma *one clerk who 'waved his hand several times in the air, signed his name, and dipped his pen in the ink to make his flourish, which he executed slowly and with infinite pains . . . The clerk gazed at his flourish with satisfaction, added five or six dots to it, and finally handed the passport back . . .' Luigi Barzini was even more scathing. Bureaucrats, he said, 'are as a rule impatient, overbearing, hurried, ignorant, indifferent to other people's problems, insolent and sometimes corrupt . . . Italians of all classes (unless they are important people with powerful friends) spend a substantial part of their time standing in angry queues, in front of office windows, or waiting endlessly merely to have some simple right recognised. What their rights are, nobody knows for sure. Uncertainty is used, in Italy, as instrumentum regni.'*

There were other problems. Mediobanca was the epitome of the 'salotto buono', an exclusive club of few high-financiers whose interests overlapped wherever possible. In fact, there had been 'a massive rush towards the concentration of capital. Between 1966 and 1967, twenty-nine companies possessed over 34% of the entire equity capital.'[4] That trend would continue during the following decades, witness to both the financial muscle of a few, very large corporations and the small size of Italy's stock exchange. Given the size of the Milan Borsa, it had traditionally been simple artificially to inflate or deflate stock prices. Shareholder rights were minimal, consolidated accounts were until recently unheard of, public information was nearly impossible to obtain. Business empires were split into the usual 'Chinese boxes'; if you opened the lid on one company, you didn't see the contents but just another box. Meanwhile many of the largest and most influential companies remained unquoted and in private, family hands.

Even today, that habit of Chinese boxes is incredible. Take, for example, the takeover in 2001 of Olivetti (and therefore of Telecom Italia) by Pirelli. It was masterminded by Marco Tronchetti Provera (former husband of Cecilia Pirelli) and his Benetton allies ('Benetton Edizione Holding', responsible not just for the clothing empire, but also a Formula One team, and almost all of Italy's motorway service stations and the motorways themselves). In the deal, £4.3 billion was paid for a 23% stake in Olivetti (in a move which would have been illegal elsewhere, a premium was paid only *to certain shareholders). The resulting Chinese boxes should give some idea of the byzantine, secretive world of the Borsa: Tronchetti Provera now owns 53% of Gpi, which owns 55.1% of Camfin, which owns 29.6% of Pirelli and Company, which owns 100% of Pirelli and Company Luxembourg, which owns 27.7% of Pirelli S.p.A, which owns 60% of Newco, which owns 27% of Olivetti, which owns 54.9% of Telecom Italia which in turn controls 56% of Telecom Italia Mobile and 54.6% of Seat-Pagine Gialle, which is responsible for the seventh national television channel, now renamed 'the seven'. Looking at that empire, and it's much the most simple example of the genre, the usual pattern emerges. In a few family hands all the aces are held: telecommunications, publishing, mass media, offshore stop-overs and so on. None of which is, of course, illegal. It's simply that high-finance is like so much else: not exactly transparent.*

Italian investors, at least those outside the cosy 'salotto buono', were disinclined to invest money in someone else's Chinese boxes. There was for years an enormous export of capital abroad (an estimated three billion dollars in 1969, before the crisis had even begun). Once inflation did begin to go well into double figures, people realised that it was better to invest money in dollars, sterling, or even Parmesan cheese, than in the Lira. Foreign investment, too, was minimal (even in 1999 it was only one ninth of Britain's), largely due to the opaque quality of Italian finance. Transparency International, a company that analyses the corruption factor across the globe on behalf of potential investors, now ranks Italy bottom of all western European countries. On the world stage, it rates worse than Estonia and Botswana because its free-market is perceived as being besieged by 'dirty hands'.

Mani Pulite, *Clean Hands, was the name given to the pool of investigative magistrates who, in that brief period from 1992–94, caused the political and economic revolution. It was a period that marked the end of the First, the beginning of the Second, Republic. After fifty years, the music seemed to stop: the rules of that game of musical chairs (in which no seat had ever been removed, but politicians simply changed position according to the political music of the time) were suddenly rewritten. In their indignation the Clean Hands magistrates, overwhelmingly supported by the Italian public, removed all the chairs in one fell swoop. Entire political parties which had, for decades, been taking hefty kick-backs on the contracts they dispensed were brusquely rejected; the city of 'Tangentopoli' (meaning literally 'bribery city', referring first to Milan, but subsequently used for the entire peninsula) was razed to the ground by zealous 'revolutionaries' who fought to apply the letter of the law.*

What's strange reading the story with a foreigner's eyes is that everyone had always known that corruption was rife in Italy, many even had the evidence, but until the early 1990s nothing was done. It was politically or legally impossible. For years commentators had derisively talked about politicians' 'petrodollari' (the money they salted away in offshore accounts thanks to deals cut with the energy industry). Elio Vetri and Gianni Barbacetto had already published Milano degli scandali, *Giampaolo Pansa had written* Il Malloppo *(The Swag). The scandal of 1992–94, then, wasn't shocking because of the discovery of corruption; the real shock came in the fact that it was finally possible for the millions of long-suffering, law-abiding Italians to do something about it.*

The sudden crumbling of the First Republic looks, in retrospect, very much like the 'velvet revolution' of 1989. A system which had, since the end of the Second World War, been monolithic and menacing self-imploded within the space of a few, breathless months. There's more than imagery to link the two events. The collapse of the Soviet Union, and the end of the Cold War, had much sharper consequences in Italy than in other European countries. The credibility of the Italian Communist party obviously collapsed, but so did that of the Christian Democrats. Their winning card (and that of their junior coalition partners) had always been that they represented a dam against 'red terror'. Once that threat was gone, the dam looked rather unnecessary and – many finally dared to say it out loud – rather corrupt. At the same time, another international situation was bringing pressure to bear on the peninsula. The advent of the Exchange Rate Mechanism, and the monetary orthodoxy demanded by Europe in preparation for the Euro, meant that Italy needed

Clean Hands. The rules of the game were international, and Italy's record of inflation and budget deficits was being sternly criticised from both inside and outside the country. (At the time of the signing of the Maastricht treaty, Italy's inflation still stood at almost 7%, and 20% of all state revenue was going simply on interest payments for the public debt, which was itself over 100% of GNP.) What was new, at the beginning of the 1990s, was not that the bureaucracy was inefficient and discretionary (only useful to those with the right contacts), but that it was a luxury the country could no longer afford. The situation was exacerbated by the tradition of tax evasion which meant that, in order to recoup a percentage of the earnings of its citizens, various governments almost had to bribe them to buy into BOTs (government bonds) by offering absurdly high interest rates which the state, again, couldn't afford. 'The cake is finished' read one of the headlines in Corriere della Sera *at the time of the crisis,[5] as if to suggest that the system of corruption had collapsed not so much because of an outburst of righteousness but simply because there was nothing left to go round.*

Most importantly, Clean Hands happened thanks to the country's 'minoranze virtuose', *its moral minority: those 'recalcitrant elements obstinately convinced that the official morality of the Republic, its laws and constitution, couldn't be simply a fig leaf to cover non-codified practices'.[6] The pool of magistrates was made up of men of such steely integrity that the crude corruption of generations of politicians and businessmen was thrown into sharp relief. Head of the pool was Francesco Saverio Borrelli, the dignified* Procuratore Capo *of Milan; others included Gherardo Colombo and, most famously, Antonio Di Pietro. The latter was a gruff former policeman who became famous for his extensive computer database and his gruelling interview techniques. The word 'pool' had been borrowed from magistrates in Palermo, where another investigative pool was trying to perform exactly the same task as that in Milan: the application of the law after years of fudge and neglect. Indeed, those revolutions would often overlap, the southern one against the Mafia, the northern one against its white-collar incarnation.*

The revolution began on 17 February 1992. Mario Chiesa, a stalwart

of the Socialist party and head of Pio Albergo Trivulzio, an old peo-
ple's home, was filmed as he pocketed seven million lire, which was
half of the overall bribe, which was in turn exactly 10% of the agreed
contract. He had only been caught because a disgruntled contractor,
Luca Magni, had complained about the systematic extortion whereby
10% of any contract in Milan had to be paid back, under the counter,
to the people who gave out the contracts, be they for laundry, rubbish
collection, funeral services and so on. Chiesa, who had lowered the
blinds whilst taking the money, was caught red-handed. Twelve
billion lire were later discovered in his bank accounts. From that
simple, innocuous beginning, the whole system unravelled. Mario
Chiesa, languishing in prison and offended that the leader of his
party, Bettino Craxi, had nicknamed him 'Mariuolo' ('scoundrel'),
began to name names. From there the investigation snowballed,
although (and it's a vital point, since it would be one of the principal
accusations made years later against the revolutionaries) the Clean
Hands held back from investigating any politicians since there was
an election pending in April 1992.

After that General Election (in which the socialists lost only 0.7%
of the vote), the revolution began in earnest. Clemente Rovati, the
constructor responsible for the building of the third ring of the San
Siro stadium, was arrested. On 1 May 1992 Paolo Pillitteri, Bettino
Craxi's brother-in-law, and Carlo Tognoli, ex-Socialist mayor of the
city, were given 'avvisi di garanzia' (notice that they were under
investigation). Before long, there were lines of businessmen queuing
up to talk to the Clean Hands pool, keen to portray themselves as the
victims of extortion rather than parties to corruption. Notorious
businessmen and their political patrons were accused, arrested and
tried. The sophistication and calculation of the bribery system, it
emerged, was so precise that exact percentages were being given to
various parties. The kickbacks arising from contracts for work on the
Milanese underground, for example, were subject to an exact math-
ematical division: 36% to the Socialist party, 18.5% to the Christian
Democrats and the Communists/Democrats of the Left and so on.

Many accused politicians would later argue that such payments
were simply 'election funds'. The number of personal accounts held

offshore, however, awash with billions of lire, began to shock the public. The circumstances of the arrest of Duilio Poggiolini, head of the pharmaceutical department of the Ministry of Health, became emblematic for the corruption of an entire era. Billions of lire were found stuffed into a pouffe. 120 million dollars were found in three of his homes. He had fourteen Swiss bank accounts, sixty expensive paintings, diamonds, krugerrands, gold ingots stacked in shoe-boxes.

That, though, was to come later. In April 1992, after the general election, the country's politicians had to choose a new President of the Republic. They were on the eighteenth ballot of the tortuous process, with the usual names in the hat, when one of the anti-Mafia judges in Palermo was killed. Giovanni Falcone, his wife and his bodyguards, had been killed as they drove from Palermo airport to the city centre in an explosion which tore apart hundreds of metres of the motorway. The indignation against Italy's injustices reached new levels. The scenes from a funeral, in which one of the young widows of a bodyguard accused the church of containing mafiosi who would have to get on their knees if they wanted her forgiveness, were shown on live television. Bedsheets were hung out from balconies across Sicily, mourning Falcone and his escort. (Within months, Paolo Borsellino, another of the investigating magistrates, was killed as he visited his mother.) By then, it was obvious that the revolution was being fought on more than one front, and parliament was finally awoken to the acute danger of civilian disorder facing the country. 7000 troops were sent to Sicily, and a new President of the Republic, Oscar Luigi Scalfaro, was finally chosen: 'The abuse of public money,' he said,

is a very serious thing, which defrauds and robs the faithful, tax-paying citizen and shatters completely their trust: there's no greater evil, no greater danger for democracy, than the turbid link between politics and business.[7]

His indignation seemed shared by the rest of the country. The bitterness of ordinary Italians was prompted by the fact that the only tax in Italy that had been imposed with anything like systematic efficiency (the 'tangente') had been the one that vanished into private hands. The response was that the Clean Hands pool enjoyed an enormous *groundswell of support: people began wearing T-Shirts saying 'Milano ladrona, Di Pietro non perdona' ('Thieving Milan, Di Pietro is unforgiving'). Finally it seemed as if those words written in every Italian courtroom, 'La legge è uguale per tutti', 'the law's equal for all', were coming true. Endless graffiti appeared across Italy: 'Grazie Di Pietro', or 'Forza Colombo'. Over the ensuing months, Gianni De Michelis (the man who had written the book on the 'culture' of Italian night-clubs) was pelted with eggs and tomatoes in Venice. Bettino Craxi was showered with coins outside the Hotel Raphael in Rome: 'Do you want these as well?' chanted the mob.*

The human toll of the revolution wasn't only counted amongst Italy's magistrates. Throughout the next eighteen months, and as a 27 billion lire bribe, the biggest of all, was unearthed, a long list of suicides added to the list of illustrious corpses. Those deaths would change the symbolism of the revolution, turning it from a morality play into a national tragedy. As always, slaughters accompanied the upheaval. In May 1993, five people died when a bomb exploded in the Uffizi museum in Florence. In July five people were killed by a bomb in Milan.

By then, Carlo Azeglio Ciampi had replaced Giuliano Amato as the Italian Prime Minister. The lira had, like sterling, become the object of currency speculation, had duly lost 15% of its value and had been forced out of the Exchange Rate Mechanism. Parliament, which had traditionally benefited from immunity, had been handed over 600 requests to lift parliamentary privilege; Craxi himself was the subject of seventeen different investigations, and he would later flee to exile in Tunisia.

Thus, the most obvious consequence of Clean Hands was that there was a political 'voragine', an abyss into which almost anyone could step. The Christian Democrats ironically renamed themselves the Peoples' Party. The Communists had already changed their name to the Democrats of the Left. The Northern League, one of whose number had brandished a noose in parliament to publicise his revolutionary credentials, were gaining ground in the area of Italy above the Po river. The MSI, the neo-Fascists, had reverted to the more presentable Gianfranco Fini for leadership (Mussolini, he

famously claimed, was 'Italy's greatest statesman of the century').
The progress of those two fringe parties was shown in various elec-
tions in 1993. In June, Milan, traditionally the power-base of Bettino
Craxi and his Socialists, elected a mayor from the Northern League.
In the autumn, Gianfranco Fini was narrowly defeated in his bid to
become mayor of Rome (taking, however, 46.9% of the vote); later,
he would decide to rename the MSI the 'National Alliance'.

There was still, however, as one notorious businessman put it with
the usual football metaphor, a 'midfield' which was 'desolately
empty'. In January 1994, that businessman sent a video to Reuters,
RAI and his own television networks, announcing the formation of
a new political party, Forza Italia:

As never before Italy . . . needs people with heads on shoulders and a con-
solidated experience, capable of giving a hand, making the state work. In
order to make the system work it's indispensable that opposed to the cartel
of the left there be a 'pole of liberty' capable of attracting to itself the best of
a clean, reasonable, modern country. Around this pole there must gather all
those forces which refer to the fundamental principles of western democracies;
in the first place the Catholic world which has contributed generously to the
last fifty years of our history as a united nation.[8]

As rhetoric, that announcement was of unrivalled brilliance. Even in
translation, that combination of moderation, modernity, 'cleanli-
ness', statal good sense instead of a left wing 'cartel', is effective.
Berlusconi's popularity rested, not least, on his Midas touch in busi-
ness and on his whole-hearted endorsement of Antonio Di Pietro
(who he would ask to be his Minister for Justice): 'His [Di Pietro's]
moralising anxiety belongs to everyone. My newspapers, my television
channels, my group, have always been in the front line in supporting
the Clean Hands judges'. Another of the Clean Hands magistrates,
Tiziana Parenti, would later take her place on the Forza Italia
benches in Parliament.

The memory, though, is short. Only a few years after the Clean
Hands earthquake, the whole episode is already being assiduously
rewritten.

Every few weeks during the summer, my 'betrothed' and I make the spectacular journey across the mountains that takes us from the humid basin of Parma towards the warm, windy air of the Tuscan coast. At one point of the Cisa pass, as the road winds through the pine forests, the mountains loom into view. They appear snow-peaked because of the white quarries where huge blocks of marble are dynamited and lined up by the side of the roads. It's this white marble which, interlaced with black or green, makes Tuscan cathedrals – in Pisa or Siena – look like something squeezed from a toothpaste tube. Once last summer, we decided to stop in a little mountain town, Aulla, and eat a sandwich in the main square. Opposite us were two rhetorical monuments. One was to the fallen from the war, and described in one, long-winded sentence, the 'ardent hearth of vivid fire which at the beginning of Nazi-Fascist oppression released a spark which inflamed the children of the Resistance, who won fame with the legendary sacrifice of their women and their bloodied men who on an impassable path underwent atrocious slaughters, devastations and reprisals . . .'

Next to it was a small needle of white marble dedicated to the victims of the Clean Hands revolutionaries. 'Intolerance, like bombs, kills precious liberty', it says. 'When the word is feeble', read the words of one parliamentarian who committed suicide, 'there's nothing left but the gesture.' 'Let us remember in the dark of every injustice the victims and their executioners', are the words of the Aulla mayor engraved into the marble. There are billboards announcing that the town is a 'Di Pietro-free zone' and there's a cunning quotation in Latin: *Summum ius, Summa iniuria* ('the greater the law, the greater the injustice', which implies, I suppose, that the rule of law is not a particularly good thing). As ever, the roles of criminal and victim are so blurred and confused that no one can ever be sure whether Italy's 'Jacobin justice' is worse than the 'criminals' it prosecutes.

Having been (in his own words) in the 'front line' of support for Clean Hands in 1994, Berlusconi has also completely changed tack. Although he won that election in 1994, his government was dogged by accusations of corruption against his entourage. His brother, Paolo Berlusconi, and Marcello Dell'Utri were both accused of financial crimes: Paolo Berlusconi has, in various court cases, actually admitted paying bribes. In one case, he admitted paying a total of 1.335 billion lire, from 1987 onwards, to the town council of Pieve, in return for clearance to turn a castle into a residential building with a golf course. In court, he was fined the same total as the original bribe, and received a definitive, one year's suspended sentence. The accusation against Dell'Utri, head of Publitalia, is that he over-inflated the cost of advertising space on Mediaset channels. Part of that surplus money was then sent back under the counter to the people (over-)paying for the advertising. On appeal, a guilty verdict against Dell'Utri was upheld. He was sentenced to one year and ten months. Berlusconi himself, whilst ironically hosting a G7 summit at Napoli about organised crime, was served an *avviso di garanzia* (notice of investigation) in December 1994. His troubled government fell weeks later as the indignant Northern League withdrew its support from the coalition. Since then Berlusconi has been in opposition (an experience he describes, with his usual biblical sense of destiny, as the 'crossing of the desert'), fulminating against the judges who he once claimed as his allies.

Other investigations have begun, not least into the means by which, during the privatisation of IRI overseen by Romano Prodi, Berlusconi managed to block the acquisition of SME (IRI's food entity) by a business rival, and duly acquire it himself. The accusations centre on Cesare Previti, Berlusconi's Roman lawyer. (The two met when Previti was selling his client's estate at Arcore to Berlusconi back in the 1970s.) The accusation goes that Previti had bribed the Roman judge who 'refereed' the deal, thus allowing Berlusconi to complete the acquisition. For reasons unknown, the bid of Berlusconi's consortium was accepted, whilst that of Carlo De Benedetti was (despite agreement having been reached on the 497 billion lire purchase price) rejected. The means by which Berlusconi acquired Mondadori, Italy's largest publishing house, is equally mired in controversy. The accused deny the charges and both cases are on-going. It is, of course, impossible to know what to believe, especially since the man 'gazumped' by Berlusconi in both deals, Carlo De Benedetti, himself owns *La Repubblica* and *L'Espresso*, which means that parts of the left-wing media have no pretence of impartiality in reporting such 'scandals'.

Thus, Clean Hands is being rewritten, and the revolution has almost come a full circle. Those who once seemed to promise a cleaner future have been suspected of dirty pasts. The defence line of those accused is incredibly clever. The Second Republic, they say, is really very different to the First, and you can't judge one according to the rules of the other. Before 1992 corruption was so rife in the upper echelons of politics and finance that it was impossible not to collude in some way. Now that Clean Hands has taught us all a lesson, we should wipe the slate clean and start over again. Berlusconi's best defence, one which can only be deployed through hint rather than admission, is that he was only ever doing what everyone else was doing during the old days of the *salotto buono*. It's exactly the same line that Bettino Craxi used in 1992, when he deployed the classic Italian defence not that he was innocent, but that everyone else was just as guilty. Craxi admitted to 'an irregular system of financing', but underlined that 'all the parties took part in it'. According to that defence, the only difference between Berlusconi or Craxi and their electorates is the scale, rather than the character, of the crime; and if that's true, it's obvious that any punishment that is meted out appears excruciatingly selective.

Maybe Craxi wasn't any worse than any of us; maybe, the *Forza Italia* rhetoric goes, Berlusconi is no worse than us, and we're hypocrites if we pretend he is. Some Italian commentators, like Pietro Scoppola, have said precisely that: the lynching of high-ranking politicians was supported by the public since it represented some kind of vicarious absolution: we're all guilty and we needed 'illustrious' names to redeem us of our sins. When the revolution began to reach lesser names and impose 'cleanliness' instead of 'cunning', the bedrock of support for the magistrates collapsed.

Thus the fact that Berlusconi is under accusation only means that the magistrates are biased against him. He has, in fact, become a master of the art of *vittimismo*, complaining that every accusation against him is simply the work of those 'Jacobin judges'. Seven years after he offered Antonio Di Pietro a job, Berlusconi now says: '*Tangentopoli* never existed. Clean Hands was only a colossal conquest commissioned by the Communists and Democrats of the Left'. Thus, according to the man who most benefited from the whole affair, Clean Hands wasn't cleaning up Italian democracy at all, but actually strangling it. There was, say his supporters, an excess of *protagonismo*, in which a handful of judges suddenly appeared to enjoy rather too much their centre-stage; the leaks to the press about imminent arrests turned the judicial process into spectacular, televisual witch-hunts; the 'cautionary custody', which locked up politicians for months on end, was an abuse of judicial power, especially since white collar criminals pose no threat to society.

There are many responses to that 'restoration' defence. First, they portray all Italians as being as crooked as the billionaires with offshore accounts. Clean Hands, from what I can work out, happened precisely because noble men were prepared to risk their lives and their businesses to root out corruption. Since, at the most conservative estimates, that corruption had cost the Italian economy one trillion lire, those magistrates were supported by millions of Italians. They equated corruption not with 'backdoor capitalism' or harmless cunning, but with theft, pure and simple. They would be appalled to be put in the same bracket as the 'corrupters' and told that *così fan tutti*, 'everyone's up to something'. In fact the honesty of Italy's moral minority is all the more amazing because it comes in a context in which cunning and corruption are never punished. Luca Magni, the man who denounced Mario Chiesa, now says wistfully about the entire episode: 'From *Tangentopoli* I've had only problems, starting with the bankruptcy of my business, whilst he [Mario Chiesa] has been fined seven billion lire, but has kept another five billion. The moral of the Clean Hands fable is, as far as I'm concerned, that in this country those who are honest are losers.'

Second, there's a lazy use of terminology. Corruption is, as

I've said, like Parma's *prosciutto*. It's only a generic term. There's a difference between the corruption of 'irregular financing' (payments to political parties in return for the right contracts) and the corruption of personal bank accounts (which enrich politicians rather than their policies). There's a difference between those who (because of poverty or unemployment) earn 'in the black' and those businessmen throughout Milan who admitted paying billions of lire in bribes to politicians and police. Third, it's true that judges often appeared rather vain, long-winded, certainly not camera-shy; and it's true that 'cautionary custody' was a shock tactic which led to shocking suicides. But for years Italy's petty criminals, even its 'illustrious accused' like Sofri, had endured such treatment; and the argument that Sofri is more dangerous to society than white collar criminals is simply absurd. In fact, politicians only woke up to the procedural problems of Italian justice (they started talking about habeas corpus and human rights) once they were subjected to it, rather than exploiting it.

It was, by then, January 2001, almost exactly nine years after the arrest of Mario Chiesa. Berlusconi's face was grinning from huge posters across the country promising 'pensions' or 'work' to his electorate. Whilst I was trying to follow the unfathomable rhetoric of the election campaign, a tragic story began dominating the newspapers. A countess, Francesca Vacca Agusta, had gone missing from her cliff-top villa in Portofino, the jewel of the Italian riviera in Liguria. That was at the beginning of January. Only her dressing gown had been found bobbing in the Ligurian sea. Vacca Agusta was found two weeks later, washed up in France. It was to that countess that billions of lire were transferred in the spring of 1993, just as the Clean Hands operation was getting to the upper-ranks of parliament. Craxi had ordered one of his henchmen to empty his banks of billions of lire and transfer them to the countess as a 'dummy holder' of the money. She had duly fled to Mexico, only to return to Italy to endure 'house arrest'. Her death may well have been the tragic accident the inquest found it to be (she had apparently slipped during a late-night bout of hide-and-seek), but her central role in the Clean Hands enigma was yet another reason to revisit the revolution and ask where Craxi's billions had gone, if indeed they ever really existed.

By then, he had died in exile in Tunisia; 'they killed him' said his outraged daughter, with reference to the Clean Hands judges and their 'mob' supporters. Thus, as with most revolutions, the consequences had become somehow completely the opposite of what was hoped for. In its zealousness, Clean Hands had yielded its moral high-ground to the 'restoration' forces, headed by one of Craxi's closest friends, Silvio Berlusconi.

March 2001. I was sitting in the pub one night. It was the *Dubh Linn* just by the *duomo*. Giovanni was opposite me, lighting another Diana cigarette. He stared at the packet on the table and asked me if it was true that the British secret services had bumped off Princess Diana. He, like hundreds of my students, was convinced of it.

'No, no,' I said, suddenly offended that someone was slandering my country. Thinking about it, though, perhaps that's exactly what I was doing to his country: believing all the conspiracy theories, and understanding absolutely nothing . . . writing scurrilous essays which only showed Italy in the worst possible light. Maybe, I suddenly thought, all these tragic stories aren't real at all. Maybe they never actually happened, and I've simply fallen victim to Italy's most pervasive ailment: paranoia. It's so contagious, though, that everyone is as paranoid as they are cunning. No one in Britain really believes that dozens of the country's suicides and murders are linked, that they're the central strand of a sad national story. In Italy, there's barely anyone who doesn't think that. And no political party has a monopoly on the paranoia. Berlusconi himself is the most paranoid of all. In Italy everyone I spoke to, be they academics, journalists, politicians, judges or students, every book I read, seemed paranoid: uncertain of what was happening, but pessimistic about the unseen 'puppeteers' who pulled the strings or the triggers. As I wrote about the country's bitter historical debates, I found myself reflecting that pessimism. I didn't necessarily believe it all, but, I reasoned, to ignore that pessimism and paranoia would have been to edit out the emotional atmosphere of Italian life.

Giovanni, probably seeing that I was rather too deep in thought, decided I needed to get out of Parma for a while. He invited me to his house, hundreds of miles to the south, in Puglia. 'That's where Padre Pio lived,' he said, explaining that it was Padre Pio's face I kept seeing framed in shops, resting on endless mantelpieces, adorning key-rings or zippo lighters. His was the only face in Italy with more exposure than Berlusconi's. 'You need a pilgrimage,' he said, stubbing out his cigarette.

7

Miracles and Mysteries

Italy is a land full of ancient cults, rich in natural and supernatural powers. And so everyone feels its influence. After all, whoever seeks God, finds him . . . wherever he wants . . .
  Federico Fellini

At the beginning of the twentieth century, San Giovanni Rotondo was a tiny village in the rugged Gargano mountains of Puglia, the region that forms the heel and spur of the Italian boot. Even forty years ago it was linked to Manfredonia (the nearby port) only by a mule track that zigzagged down through olive trees to the Adriatic. Now, though, San Giovanni Rotondo is Italy's most-visited tourist spot, welcoming more than six million visitors a year. It has overtaken Lourdes as Europe's most popular destination for Catholic pilgrims. It has more than a hundred *alberghi* and hotels, and will soon have a new cathedral designed by Renzo Piano. There is also an imposing new hospital, one of Italy's largest and most modern.

Behind all this is San Giovanni's most revered son, and one of the best-known Italians of the twentieth century: Padre Pio. When he was beatified on 2 May 1999, most of the country became immersed in preparation for the big event (even the Serie A game between Roma and Inter was postponed to the following day). Pope John Paul II celebrated a televised mass in St Peter's, and then travelled down to San Giovanni Rotondo to celebrate mass there. The million *pellegrini* in attendance were transported by more than 5,000 coaches (100 from Poland alone) and 19 special trains. 1,000 chemical toilets were set up in the village and big CCTV screens surrounded its two main squares.

Long before San Giovanni Rotondo became famous, another nearby village, Monte Sant'Angelo, was a place of pilgrimage: the village formed the end of the medieval pilgrim 'Route of the

Angel', which wound its way from Normandy to Rome and beyond. The reason for its fame is a mixture of local lore and millennial angst. The story goes that, in 490 AD, a local man went up into the mountains, searching for his prize bull. He found it at the entrance to a cave, way up on the most precarious promontory. The bull was reluctant to move, so the man shot an arrow at it: the arrow turned in the wind and embedded itself in the man's forehead. The Bishop of Siponto was called on for advice, and when he arrived at the grotto he received a visitation from the Archangel Michael, who ordered him to consecrate a Christian altar on the site. It's not known what happened to the man with the arrow in his forehead, but the result of his misadventure was the famous *Santuario di San Michele*. In 999 AD, the Holy Roman Emperor, Otto III, made a pilgrimage to the sanctuary, and prayed that the apocalypse prophesied for the end of the first millennium wouldn't happen. A thousand years later and the same worries, together with the beatification of Padre Pio, prompted a sudden *risveglio*, or reawakening, of religious piety and pilgrimage.

I'm met off the train at Manfredonia by my friend Giovanni whose family live in the town. It's almost midnight and he drives me to my hotel. By the reception desk there's a cabinet of Padre Pio mementos – letter-racks, mirrors, diaries, plates, each one bearing his by now familiar image: a high forehead, grey beard and bushy eyebrows, deep-set eyes above a slightly bulbous nose. The set of his mouth makes him look as if he is wincing. He seems kindly but austere. A sleeve, or more usually a fingerless glove, covers up the reason for his fame – his stigmata. Giovanni says it's a farce: 'This used to be one of the poorest parts of Italy, but it has suddenly become very wealthy, simply because of Padre Pio.'

Padre Pio was born Francesco Forgione in 1887 in Pietrelcina, a small town half-way between Naples and Manfredonia. He was ordained into the order of Capuchin monks in 1910 and moved to San Giovanni Rotondo in 1916. He stayed there, almost always within the *Chiesa di Santa Maria delle Grazie*, until his death, at 81, in September 1968. Almost exactly fifty years before, on 20 September 1918, he became the only Catholic priest to have received stigmata. A month after the wounds appeared, he wrote to his spiritual adviser, Padre Benedetto, describing what had happened:

After I had celebrated Mass, I yielded to a drowsiness similar to a sweet sleep. All the internal and external senses and even the very faculties of my soul were immersed in indescribable stillness. Absolute silence surrounded and invaded me. I was suddenly filled with great peace and abandonment which effaced everything else and caused a lull in the turmoil. All this happened in a flash . . . I became aware that my hands, feet and side were dripping blood. Imagine the agony I experienced and continue to experience almost every day. The heart wound bleeds continually, especially from Thursday evening until Saturday. Dear Father, I am dying of pain because of the wounds and the resulting embarrassment I feel in my soul. I am afraid I shall bleed to death if the Lord doesn't hear my heartfelt supplication to relieve me of this condition. Will Jesus, who is so good, grant me this grace? Will he at least free me from the embarrassment caused by these outward signs?

Between the wars, Padre Pio's fame grew, thanks to the stigmata and the endless stories about his miracles: there were tales of bilocation (being in two places at the same time), inexplicable cures, celestial perfumes, instant conversions and prophetic visions. Every Italian seems to have a favourite anecdote: he blessed a pile of envelopes brought to him, but refused to bless one (when it was opened it was found to contain coupons for the football pools); he knelt to pray for George VI before his death had been announced; he appeared in the cockpit of an American aircraft during bombing missions in the Second World War. His most celebrated feat was to have picked out a letter from Poland, which pleaded for his intercession on behalf of a mortally ill woman. 'We cannot say no to this one,' Padre Pio is supposed to have declared. The woman recovered and the Polish priest who had written on her behalf, Bishop Wojtyla, subsequently became better known as Pope John Paul II.

Until recently, however, Padre Pio's relations with the higher echelons of the Catholic church were strained. Doctors were repeatedly sent to inspect his wounds, and there was an attempt to have him transferred to Spain (averted only by the intervention of the Ministry of the Interior). But Padre Pio's admirers have included Gabriele D'Annunzio, who was one of his correspondents; the TV presenter, Luciano Rispoli, at whose marriage he officiated; the show-girl Lorella Cuccarini likes to drop his name in interviews. The magazine *Gente* – a cross between *Hello!* and the *Catholic Herald* – regularly runs new anecdotes about him, and offers readers cassettes of 'his actual voice'. Abroad he's just as popular: the Padre Pio Foundation of America has a doting website, and there's a bookshop entirely devoted to him in Vauxhall Bridge Road in London.

In November 1969 it was decreed that he had died in *odore di santità* (the 'scent of saintliness') and the case for his beatification was formally put by the Bishop of Manfredonia. The process is a tortuous one: first, the *Tribunale Diocesano* gives its verdict, then the matter is passed on to the *Congregazione per le Cause dei Santi* in Rome. The theologians and cardinals on this committee reexamine all the relevant writings and testimonies and, if they are satisfied that someone deserves to be recognised as a *beato*, medical evidence is called on to demonstrate that miracles occurred as a result of his or her intercession.

The day Giovanni and I arrive in San Giovanni Rotondo it is raining heavily and the town – with its roads and woodlands disappearing into the low clouds – resembles a new ski resort. There are cranes everywhere, constantly gyrating as they lift lumps of concrete into place for the next huge hotel. Opposite the façade of *Santa Maria delle Grazie* are a series of staircases that rise high into the hills, flanked by statues of the Padre and the Madonna. Nearby, a portakabin serves as the studio of the official radio station, *La Voce di Padre Pio*.

There is normally a three-hour wait to get into the *Chiesa*, though we get in quite quickly thanks to the rain. The hushed queue snakes round the monastery, past strategic notices and collection boxes. You can get objects blessed every fifteen minutes and a line of people has already formed with wedding rings or car keys at the ready. The Padre's tomb is a massive marble edifice, surrounded by wrought-iron railings and boxes into which photographs and letters can be posted. Some two hundred people are gathered round it, lighting candles, falling to their knees and whispering prayers.

There's a spontaneous outburst of Hail Marys as we approach Padre Pio's sealed-off cell, above which are written Thomas à Kempis's words from *The Imitation of Christ*: 'Worldly honours have always sorrow for company'. Through the glass you can see every book, painting, photograph, as well as his comb, perfectly preserved. The bed is made, and by it are his size-nine shoes, purple-black and almost as wide as they are long because of the bleeding and swelling. In the nearby chapel a plaque marks Pio's seat, and the exact location in which he first received the stigmata. Facing the *piazza* outside, still teeming with pilgrims, is a narrow window. It was here that, like the Pope, Padre Pio used to bless his visitors, raising his hands so that everyone could get a look at his bandages.

Back outside in the rain, every shop is offering *articoli religiosi*, from paintings and postcards of the man to statues costing as much as four million lire. With an embarrassed smile, Giovanni tells me that his father built a house here for an old lady – it had a large garden, three storeys and a lift – whose income derived entirely from the sale of these trinkets. I come from a Methodist background, and I'm uneasy with icons and relics, but my objections here are mainly aesthetic: too many semi-naked women releasing a dove to the heavens where, of course, the famous Capuchin priest is sitting.

We walk towards the hospital, the *Casa Sollievo della Sofferenza*, or House for the Alleviation of Suffering, which dominates the town with its massive white façade topped by a statue of St Francis. In 1940 Pio decided that a hospital should be built. Legend has it that he single-handedly sought funding for the building from his visitors, placing donations in his handkerchief every day, and emptying out the coins onto his bed every evening (in fact, the hospital also received 250 million lire from the UNRRA in 1947). A protein used to treat diabetes was discovered in the hospital's laboratory, adding to its renown, and – peculiarly – visitors are offered guided tours round its theatres and wards. On the anniversary of Pio's death, tens of thousands of pilgrims gather to walk round the hospital through the night, keeping a candle-lit vigil.

We return to Giovanni's house in Manfredonia. His father shakes his head when we begin talking about the town: he knew Padre Pio and describes him as *scontroso*, surly. (Similarly, Rispoli, the TV presenter, says that Padre Pio was *burbero, ai limiti della scortesia* – 'gruff, on the verge of discourtesy'.) Everyone seems sure that he would not be pleased with what now goes on in his name. Certainly the town bears very little resemblance to a description of it by another priest in 1915, the year before Padre Pio's arrival. 'Only a deep silence is around me,' he wrote, 'sometimes interrupted by the sound of a bell hung on the neck of some sheep or goat which shepherds take to graze on the mountain behind the convent.' Now the *Frati Cappuccini* have a website, urging exorbitant contributions to the new cathedral and quoting by way of encouragement the implausible last words of Padre Pio: 'Make it big.' There's the constant noise of cranes and cement mixers, and I think of the words of the priest in *La Dolce Vita*: 'Miracles are born out of solitude and silence, and not in chaos like this . . .'

The following day is warm, the sky entirely clear. We are going to visit the sanctuary at Monte Sant'Angelo, the place of the man with the arrow in his forehead. Giovanni, though, refuses to drive there: the village is very dangerous, because of a feud between two families that started fifty years ago when some livestock was stolen, and the two sons of the offending family were killed and dumped in the town. It's not a place Giovanni wants to leave a smart car, so we take the coach. The scenery, as we rise away from the sea, is spectacular: hairpin bends take us towards whitewashed houses where linen, hung from every balcony, billows in the wind.

The town seems older than San Giovanni Rotondo: the streets are narrow and steep, with labyrinthine flights of steps leading to the medieval quarter. The red-tiled roofs you can see from the top of the mountain are huddled together at odd angles. From here you can see clean across the Adriatic to the coasts of Albania and Montenegro. Even the local delicacy reflects the influence of the Catholic church: *ostie ripiene*, literally 'stuffed hosts', are two large, obviously unconsecrated, communion wafers around a filling of almonds and honey. Lining many of the pavements are religious stalls: next to the tiny bottles claiming to contain the *Profumo di Padre Pio* are ashtrays inscribed with a word of advice to users: *Stronzo, smetti di fumare* ('idiot, give up smoking').

The *Santuario di San Michele* is carved into the mountain. 'This,' it says in Latin above the entrance, 'is the house of God and the gate of heaven.' Legend has it that the Archangel Michael left a footprint here, which has prompted thousands of pilgrims to scratch the outlines of their own hands and feet into the stone slabs. Some, those in the prime positions, have become templates into which other people have placed their own hands. And I do have some sense of a gateway, even if it's not a strictly religious sense – more the feeling that centuries of pilgrims, millions of them, have put their hands in the same spot mine is now, and that their touch has gradually eroded and smoothed and humanised the hard stone. It's like cathedral steps hollowed in the middle after centuries of use.

As we look at the initials and dates, I realise there's something very reassuring about antiquarian graffiti; about the fact that people over a thousand years ago were making this journey with miracles and the millennium in mind. Two centuries after Otto III, St Francis of Assisi visited the *Santuario*, but – feeling himself unworthy – didn't enter it. We, of course, do, and admire the Byzantine Madonna of Constantinople and the filigree, crystal cross (a gift from Frederick II) which is said, like so many others, to contain wood from the True Cross.

We emerge from the cold *Santuario* and sit on a wall overlooking the sea. There are gulls soaring in the breeze and way below we can just see a fleet of fishing boats setting out from Manfredonia. Eating my *ostie ripiene*, I feel, if not the piety of the pilgrim, at least the serenity of the pilgrimage.

Catholicism is Italy, and vice versa. Even for a non-believer, being Italian implies absorbing the mores and morality of Roman Catholicism. It doesn't offer a set of beliefs or liturgies to which a rational adult can chose to adhere; it offers a way of life, and of death. It's a cradle-to-grave religion that isn't only devotional, but political and social and aesthetic. It seeps into every corner of the country, into every stage of every life. 'I know,' Federico Fellini once said, 'that I am a prisoner of 2,000 years of the Catholic Church. All Italians are . . .' Or, as Hyppolite Taine put it: 'Italians are entirely accustomed to Catholicism. It is a part of their eyes, their ears, their imagination and their taste.'

The connections between the country and its Catholicism are most obvious in the language. One hardly ever hears the words 'Christian' or 'Christianity' in Italian. The words, even the concepts, have been almost entirely replaced by 'Catholic' and 'Catholicism'. People talk not about the Christian (let alone Jewish) commandments, but the 'Catholic commandments'. Even Catholicism sometimes goes unmentioned, and is replaced by 'The Church', as if it's already understood that we're talking about an indivisible concept: Roman Catholicism.

I used to get irritated by that dogged belief in *Extra Ecclesiam Nulla Salus*: that no one outside the (Roman Catholic) church can possibly be saved. Bishops still talk of the Catholic Church as the only true church of Jesus Christ, dismissing all other strands of Christianity as heretical. Many cardinals mention millennia of Judaism or centuries of Protestantism with an acid sentence, and you begin to see why the country is so amazingly homogenous: nothing other than the Church will be tolerated. It's 'Catholic or nothing' in Italy. It's an argument I've had many times, and one which presents a relentless, circular logic: 'Of course,' I'm told, 'Italy's mono-cultural. Until five years ago there was no religion other than Catholicism.' Why not? 'Because Italy is Catholic.' I know, but why? 'Because it doesn't have other religions.' Why not? 'Because we're Catholics!'

What irritated me was the ignorance of, and intolerance towards, anything outside the Church. 'You're Protestant?' people would ask me, nervously, 'does that mean you can't eat pork?' The intolerance not just to other religions, but to other types of Christianity, is unfortunately fostered by the upper echelons of the Church. In August 2000 a Church declaration (called *Dominus Jesus* and endorsed by the Pope) announced that the Catholic Church represented the only 'valid' and 'genuine' Christian episcopate. Any other type of ordination – either Anglican or Non-Conformist – was simple heresy. Even to many Catholic onlookers it appeared like something from the Middle Ages. The inspiration for such announcements is invariably Cardinal Joseph Ratzinger, a man who heads what is called the Congregation for the Doctrine of Faith (an organisation that acts as the guard dog against pluralism and tolerance).

It doesn't take long to realise that Roman Catholicism is excruciatingly conservative and – like Italy itself – acutely hierarchical. An obvious consequence of that is a visceral anticlericalism. In Emilia-Romagna there's even a shape of pasta called the 'priest-strangler'. I'm frequently asked by the army of anticlericals what my most creative British blasphemy is. The disappointment, not to say disbelief, when I'm unable to produce a decent blasphemy is tangible. 'Our priests,' I always have to explain, 'simply aren't powerful enough to make us want to blaspheme. You would have to go to Ireland for that . . .' Because of that power of the priesthood, the role of intermediaries and go-betweens is especially important. Nowhere else had I seen a congregation so distant from the deity. There are so many Madonnas ('Dolorific Mary' from one parish, 'Honoured Mary' in another), there are so many saints, that something as democratic as a direct relationship with God is unthinkable. The priest always gets in the way. The actual business of the Bible, and what it says, seems left behind. When the Bible is involved, excerpts are read by priests: for example the entire Passion story is read for 45 minutes each Palm Sunday.

The congregation in Catholicism is entirely recipient rather than participant. Particularly so since the vernacular liturgy was adopted very late by the Church (masses are still said in Latin in some churches). The one thing that really got me thinking was the fact that entering a Catholic church is the only place in Italy I'm guaranteed not to hear singing. Or I might hear singing, but not the joyful, uplifting arias you can hear just walking along the street. It's more timid, doleful. The Church is the only place, other than the post offices or the banks, where everyone is suddenly submissive, fretting quietly until their turn comes.

The other thing that strikes you is the fudging of right and wrong. In part it's the result of the Church's noble and unbending beliefs. Certain things are right, others wrong, and the man who decides is infallible. But after centuries of theological and catechismal accretion, its teachings are so specific that everyone inevitably falls short. The trouble is that the very strictness of the Church means that there's a yawning gap between what's preached and what's practised. The fact that Italy has the lowest birth rate in Europe is simply the crudest example. Divorce, like contraception, isn't allowed by the Church; therefore marriages, tens of thousands of them, are simply annulled each year as if they had never happened.

Once my initial irritation began to subside, however, I started to appreciate how wrong I had been about certain things. When you start talking to believers about what Catholicism really means to them, it appears – like all religions – beautiful and bizarre. The sacrament of 'confession' I had always understood simply as a way to keep sheep in the Catholic fold after (probably Protestant) apostasy; but I began to see that it wasn't a substitute for punishment, but rather the result of a different notion of 'grace'. It might be true that the dark confessional is in some ways responsible for the habitual impunity of Italian society, but it's also, I thought, true that it contains an admirable sincerity. As for the iconography of the mother of the son of God, I began to admire it the more I saw of it. Not artistically, but symbolically: the kneeling, meek, mourning, very virtuous Madonnas, never glimpsed in any church

I had ever worshipped in, seemed to express the epic suffering of centuries of mothers. And as indignant young girls started telling me about what their village Madonna meant to them, I began to see the first cracks of light to suggest the existence of feminism in Italy. It's completely unquantifiable, of course, but the Madonna is probably the reason that some notion of the family as a 'sacred unit', having evaporated elsewhere, still exists in Italy. It's certainly the reason that maternity has such an exalted status.

As for other sacraments, I finally understood why eating has such an important place in the country's ceremonial set-up: the Mass. In church it's called 'communion' or 'eucharist', but also the 'holy dinner'. 'Do Protestants have holy dinners?' someone once asked me, as if convinced that a combination of northern European food and Protestantism precluded the possibility. And the saints, all those saints who I had never heard of and who are so high on the heavenly pecking list, I began to warm to them because devotion in their name invariably coincided with culinary delight. In Emilia-Romagna, for example, San Giovanni is remembered in July by the eating of *tortelli*, wraps of pasta containing pumpkin or potato or ricotta and herbs. Then, once you've eaten, it's traditional to sit with friends in a garden or in a field until the dew arrives the following morning. Eating is, I realised with pleasure, Italian Catholics' answer to the 'work ethic'.

A more serious, social side of the Church is the amazing work of hundreds of thousands of volunteers who, through Catholic organisations, dedicate entire weekends, or entire summer holidays, to helping immigrants or the ill or the aged. Their work is the flipside of the hierarchy's intolerance. Whenever I spoke to those volunteers, they would always urge me to read not encyclicals from the Vatican, but the liberation theology from the Second Vatican Council (1962–65). That theology, they said, talked about a social rather than authoritarian religion and represented the true Church. The Second Vatican Council was an attempt at a modern Magna Carta, an attempt to involve bishops, even the laity, in the decisions of the Church. Many would say that its objectives have by now been entirely defeated by the Church's extraordinary conservatism, but the documents from Vatican II stand out for their lyricism and tolerance. In *Nostra Aetate*, for example, the Church announced its 'sincere respect for those ways of acting and living, those moral and doctrinal teachings which may differ in many respects from what she holds and teaches, but which none the less often reflect the brightness of that Truth, which is the light of all men'.[1]

In fact, I began to enjoy precisely what, for centuries, had been the butt of jokes by northern Europeans and Americans: the ritualism. From Henry James to Charles Dickens, there's one word that always seems on the tip of their Protestant tongues: paganism. James described one Pope as 'that flaccid old woman waving his ridiculous fingers over the prostrate multitude'; he eventually 'turned away sickened by its absolute obscenity . . .'[2] Charles Dickens was no less scathing. Churches, he said, looked like a 'Goldsmith's shop' or a 'lavish pantomime'; 'I have been infinitely more affected in many English cathedrals when the organ has been playing.' For their tastes, Catholicism was all too visual, tactile, the air was too thick with incense. Dickens couldn't stand the 'perfect army of cardinals and priests, in red, gold, purple, violet, white, and fine linen.'[3] But that folkloric side, the blood-and-earth atmosphere, the glint of gold and the clicking on and off of electric candles, is exactly what I began to enjoy. It's a religion that is felt rather than thought. Seeing and touching and smelling has become integral to believing, which is why churches are museums, houses of both high-art and the desperately kitsch. Their centrepieces are often relics which can be glimpsed through narrow grates: a fist of earth from Calvary containing Christ's blood (in Mantova), San Gennaro's blood which occasionally liquefies (in Naples), the remains of St Nicholas (at Bari). Relics, if you're imaginative, are just morbid, meditational prompts in the Church's sensuous assault on its believers.

There's also a belief – as with the *misteri* of the Italian state – in the intervention of unseen, inexplicable powers. A miracle happens every time mass is celebrated. The communion isn't a metaphor of a united church, it's actually the literal flesh and blood of the deity 'transubstantiated' by the interventionist miracle of the presiding priest. And people really do believe in the direct power of the Madonna, or various saints, to alter earthly reality. Even I, having been sceptical about weekly news reports about miracles, began to listen to the stories (you don't, I suppose, have to believe in the miracles to believe in other people's belief). And when, every Easter, a local monk would ring my doorbell and ask to bless my flat with his holy water, I would always ask him to come in. I was supposed to read a prayer (which mentioned loyalty to the local bishop, of course, before God even entered the equation), and then he started blessing the flat. I even found myself ushering him towards certain objects – computer, football boots – that need all the holy water they can get.

The bullet that, on 13 May 1981, was fired at Pope John Paul II is now lodged in the crown of the Madonna of Fatima in Portugal. The Pope's desire to place the bullet there was the denouement to the story of Catholicism in the twentieth century. For someone used to the whitewashed walls of Methodist chapels, where religion appears simple, cerebral, occasionally austere and sometimes dull, the story of Catholicism and the Vatican in recent years appears completely the opposite: colourful, confusing, gripping and always mysterious.

Fatima, like Lourdes or San Giovanni Rotondo, is an important place of pilgrimage for modern Catholics. On 13 May 1917 (exactly 64 years before the shooting of John Paul II) three young peasants in Fatima in Portugal received visions from the Madonna. The revelations were in three parts. The first warned of the condition of hell for transgressors against God. A few months later, the second revelation was more temporal: 'If my requests are not granted,' the godhead revealed to the children, 'Russia will spread its errors throughout the world, raising up wars and persecutions against the Church.' The political message, on the eve of the Bolshevik revolution, was understood and widely publicised. Strange, specific observances were apparently required of true believers: the necessity of the Rosary, the wearing of the brown scapular. On 13 October, just days before Lenin took power in Russia, 70,000 believers gathered in the small Portuguese village, where the children had promised a miracle to testify to the truth of the message. Observers described a moment in which the sun seemed to 'dance' and change colour in the sky (an event now classified by the Church as 'a veritable miracle').

The third 'secret' was written down in the 1940s, but remained unrevealed for the entirety of the remaining twentieth century. Only in 2000, at the ceremony in which two of the Portuguese peasant children – Francisco Marto and his sister Jacinta – were beatified, did John Paul II make the third secret public: speaking of the killing of a 'white bishop' by enemies of the faith, it was interpreted as a prediction of the assassination attempt against the Pope himself. The shooting had occurred in 1981, on the day the Church calls the Feast of Our Lady of Fatima. Karol Wojtyla, with his grey hair and white cassock, was being driven slowly through the crowds outside St Peter's. A Turk, Mehmet Ali Agca, stepped forward and fired. The Pope (the first non-Italian pontificate since 1523) collapsed, apparently whispering 'Mary, mother of mine' as his entourage rushed towards him. The Pope, though, has never shown any interest in who, apart from Agca, was responsible for the shooting. Rather, he's constantly emphasised who it was who saved him: 'One hand shot, another hand guided the bullet,' he once said. On the first anniversary of the shooting he went to Fatima to give thanks to the Virgin and place the actual bullet in her crown.

John Paul II is, few doubt it, an honest and humble figure besieged by the realpolitik of the Vatican. He genuinely seems to fight, with shrewd political calculation, for religious causes which, inevitably, spill over into the temporal. He has always urged peaceful resolutions. He has acknowledged Judaism as Christianity's 'older brother'. Under his command, the Catholic church has also partially apologised for its own intolerance during the Counter-Reformation. Now a bowed figure shaking with Parkinson's, he still relentlessly travels the world, angrily admonishing those who fail to heed his slurred words. He has sometimes tried to promote the unity of Christianity and urge ecumenicalism. Against the wishes of both the Catholic hierarchy and the Greek Orthodox church, he visited Greece in 2001 and pleaded that the 'Western Church' and the 'Eastern Church' become the left and right lungs of a united Christianity. He also apologised for the horrors committed by Catholics against the Orthodox church during the Fourth crusade. That brave decision to apologise was seen as a wooing of not only the Greek Orthodox church but also the Russian one. As a Pole who suffered under Soviet rule, in 1984 he dedicated the Soviet Union to the Immaculate Heart of Mary (as was commanded by the Virgin in the revelations at Fatima). He has publicly made it his dying ambition to be admitted to Russia, though has so far achieved it only via satellite.

Critics of John Paul II claim that he is like a Pope from the Middle Ages. He has actively promoted the Catholicism of interventionist saints and miracle-workers. During his pontificate he has beatified more people (798) and made more saints (280) than were given the honour during the previous five centuries. He has also halved the number of miracles necessary to make a saint. Padre Pio's double-quick procession to sainthood was announced only two years after the beatification. Such criticisms, though, are unthinkable within Italy. The country now identifies so wholeheartedly with its pontiff that it's hard to imagine that the Vatican and its papacy were once the enemies of the Italian state. In fact, the lack of Italian patriotism is probably in large part thanks to the hostility of that other country called the Vatican. After the Risorgimento, the attitude of the Vatican to the new nation was one of suspicion. The Vatican demanded from its devotees a veto of the new-born Italian state. Catholics were urged not to participate in elections (on pain of excommunication), and were warned in apocalyptic terms of the dangers of the lay state which was besieging the 'saintly seat'. Until 1920, the papacy forbade foreign (Catholic) heads of state to visit Rome, fearing that it would give the Italian state undue recognition.

Only with Mussolini's Lateran Pacts of 1929 were diplomatic relations established between the two states, allowing the two to begin their loving, sometimes suffocating, embrace. The Church's collusion with Fascism barely seemed to affect its post-war prestige (apart from the agreement with Mussolini, there had been a Concordat *with the Nazi regime, and Pope Pius XII remained eerily silent on the Holocaust). A former Vatican librarian, Alcide De Gasperi, became the leader of the newly formed Christian Democratic party which duly won the vital 1948 election. (Alcide De Gasperi's wily young secretary was Giulio Andreotti; an old joke went that when De Gasperi went into the church and closed his eyes to pray to God, Andreotti got up and went to sort things out with the priest.) Other Catholic organisations like Azione Cattolica (which by 1954 had a membership of three million) were to provide other historic leaders of the Christian Democrats like Aldo Moro.*

The intricate system of spiritual blackmail and bribery (excommunication of Communist voters, for example, was announced in 1948) has meant that the Catholic church has since then always been able to nudge and knead Italian political life. Traditionally, for example, Madonnas started weeping around election time, especially if it looked as if the left was on the brink of victory. In 1948 in Naples, when the Communist party looked likely to assume power, no fewer than 36 Madonnas began to shed tears. It's a good example of the strange, clandestine control the Catholic Church has over Italian politics, of its uncanny ability to let the interior, spiritual side of life well-up and overflow into the purely political. Although abortion and divorce were tortuously legalised in the 1970s, there are still strange laws that hint at the reach of the Catholic Church. Premarital contracts are illegal. A percentage of income tax (eight lire for every thousand) can be directly offered to the Church (although you're now allowed to specify alternative destinations). Until 2001, blood donors had to sign a clause of 'non-homosexuality,' a law that was necessitated more by morals than anything medical.

The Vatican, in fact, is viewed by even the most devout Catholics as a country of purple finery, of power and prestige which seems the antithesis of Christianity. In 1563, the Venetian ambassador to Rome described the atmosphere of the Vatican: 'Here adulation is dressed up as honesty, a con as courtesy. Every vice appears masked. Simulation is the soul of the court . . .' It's a judgement that has been repeatedly echoed. Free-masonry (what John Paul II's predecessor, Paul VI, called the 'smoke of Satan . . . penetrating and fogging the temple of God . . .') is, apparently, ubiquitous. According to anonymous priests who recently published an insider's critique of the Vatican, 'pretence in the Vatican becomes second nature, which has the end of dominating the first [nature]. The hypocrites are flatterers and tutors of all the faked virtues, whilst they defame and persecute the truth'.

The Vatican, in fact, had by the 1980s become a willing protagonist in Italy's post-war scandal par excellence. A suave American bishop from Chicago, Paul Marcinkus, had risen to the top of the Vatican's 'bank,' the so-called Institute for Religious Works (the 'Istituto per le Opere Religiose,' or IOR). Roberto Calvi, another ambitious banker, had meanwhile risen through the ranks of the Banco Ambrosiano in Milan. It was traditionally a bank for Catholic investors; even the name was taken from Milan's patron saint. When the two were introduced by a Sicilian tax expert, Michele Sindona, they worked out an intricate banking scam in which the Vatican would be the conduit for the exportation of huge sums of capital. The IOR's secrecy, as well as the respectable front it offered Ambrosiano, made it the ideal accomplice.

Throughout the 1970s, Calvi shifted billions of lire into offshore accounts in Luxembourg, Nicaragua, Peru and Nassau. The transactions were so complicated that when the money returned to Italy, propping up shares in the Banco Ambrosiano or falsely inflating other investments, the provenance was never certain and no one could prove that the IOR and Calvi were simply engaged in a very profitable paper-chase. By the late 1970s, the bank had debts of $1300 million to businesses that were little more than addresses in the Caribbean. As the sums loaned became ever-larger, the Bank of Italy – which oversaw the 1,060 banks on the peninsula – began to investigate. The businesses of Michele Sindona, the Sicilian tax expert, were already creaking, as many began to suspect that his 'golden touch' was nothing more than false-accounting and spurious share issues. The man sent in to study Sindona's accounts, Giorgio Ambrosoli, was first threatened, then murdered in July 1979. The man sent to investigate Calvi's own bank, Emilio Alessandrini, was also murdered by a terrorist outfit (Alessandrini was also linked to the investigations into Piazza Fontana, having been one of the first to incriminate Pino Rauti and his Ordine Nuovo). There was also an attempt to frame managers at the Bank of Italy, and a new governor, Carlo Azeglio Ciampi, was chosen to head the difficult, and dangerous, investigative operation.

Magistrates investigating the murder of Ambrosoli and the strange, faked kidnapping of Michele Sindona kept coming across references to one Licio Gelli. Gelli was a former Fascist, having fought in Mussolini's volunteers in his teens, and was to become – alongside Andreotti – the most mysterious figure of post-war Italy. One journalist described him with the following, evocative words:

[Gelli] understands more than he lets on, he's courteous, metaphorical, allusive, slippery. He weighs his words, doesn't raise his voice, he measures his gestures. Nothing seems to upset him . . . never have we been caught up in an enigma more enigmatic, in a sibyl more sibylline.[4]

The investigating magistrates decided to raid his various addresses: his suite at the Excelsior hotel in Rome, his Villa in Arezzo, an old business address in Frosinone, and the Giole textile factory in Castiglion Fibocchi. At the latter, a safe was found containing a mass of documents and a list of 950 names: members of what emerged as the register of Propaganda Due (P2), a masonic lodge that included 52 officials of the Carabinieri, 50 army officers, 37 members of the Treasury Police, five government ministers, 38 members of parliament, fourteen judges, ten banking presidents and various journalists and editors. In short, the most powerful men in Italy appeared linked into a secretive, occasionally murderous, organisation whose manifesto was called 'A Plan for the Rebirth of Democracy'. That manifesto, discovered in the briefcase of Gelli's daughter at Rome airport, included a rewriting of the Italian constitution, control of the mass media, the removal of parliamentary immunity and the suspension of union activity. Gelli was the 'venerable maestro' of a masonic lodge that seemed to link, albeit without explanation, coups and bombings and murders throughout the 1970s.

The startling revelations about P2 seemed to explain much about the underbelly of Italian life. It was an event that, in the words of one *historian, 'touched one of the deepest constants in post-war Italy, and one that it is most difficult to write about with any degree of historical certainty. Behind the surface of Italian democracy lay a secret history, made up of hidden associations, contacts and even conspiracies, some farcical and others more serious'.[5] The discovery of P2 was a moment that, as it was poetically described to me by one politician, was like the effect of approaching and grasping the aerial of a cheap television: suddenly the interference and blurred picture comes into focus, and you can finally see, hear and understand what has been going on. Retrospectively, it was possible to see connections between cases, and understand various mysteries. It began to look as if the paranoia about a parallel state, a shadow government that controlled banking, business and the media, might not have been misplaced after all. Not for the first time, the Italian media was caught up in, rather than just reporting, the news: the Rizzoli family, owners of the* Corriere della Sera *and at the time a quarter of all other Italian newspapers, was heavily compromised by its proximity, and that of its journalists, to P2.*

Recent revisionism of P2 in Italy has suggested that the aspirations of the lodge were purely financial, and that very few of those involved knew of the lodge's more sinister operations. Others suggest that the whole lodge, looking so sinister from the outside, was, from the inside, a chimera that many 'P2ers' didn't even realise they had joined. Whatever the truth, the traces of Gelli and his P2 are evident in every iconic crime from Borghese's 'coup' of 1970 until the Bologna bombing of 1980, which claimed 85 lives. The subsequent parliamentary enquiry wrote: 'This committee has reached the reasoned conclusion, shared by several courts, that the lodge . . . established on-going links with subversive groups and organisations, instigating and countenancing their criminal purposes.'[6] Terrorist groups had been prompted and nudged, the report said, by P2.

As for the Banco Ambrosiano, as the investigative net closed in on Calvi, the rogue banker, he escaped to London. There he was found hanged under Blackfriars bridge in June 1982. Calvi's secretary, Graziella Corrocher, had also fallen to her death in what, by contrast, appeared a genuine suicide. When Sindona was arrested and *imprisoned he was passed a poisoned coffee by 'ignoti,' unknowns, an act that only fulfilled his prediction that he would be murdered in prison. The Banco Ambrosiano, saddled with epic debts and no returns, duly collapsed. The most obvious beneficiaries of the whole affair were the Vatican and the political parties. There was no major political party that wasn't on Calvi's pay-roll: the parties – the Christian Democrats, the Socialists, the Communists – received as much as 88 billion lire from him throughout the 1970s. Craxi's name, and the number of his Swiss bank account credited with $7 million by Calvi, was amongst Gelli's documents. The Vatican, for its part, displayed a reticence to excuse or even explain itself. The creditors asked Paul Marcinkus, the American bishop, for a return on their investment, but were met with only silence. The IOR, responsible for creaming off millions in mysterious deals, washed its hands of the dirty affair.*

I mention the whole episode not because it's in any way representative of Italy or Catholicism, but because three of the sub-plots from the 'Calvi case' and P2 all re-emerged onto the scene twenty years to the day after the shooting of John Paul II: it was 13 May 2001, the day of the Feast of Our Lady of Fatima. The noble banker from the Bank of Italy, a man who had fought as a partisan in the 1940s before becoming the Prime Minister in the 1990s, was by then President of the Republic. Carlo Azeglio Ciampi was, on this election day, expected to oversee the smooth, constitutional handover of power. The man expected to become Prime Minister was once on the roll-call of P2 members, and is the epitome of the lodge's avowed intention to 'rebaptise Italian democracy' through control of the mass media and the rewriting of the constitution: Silvio Berlusconi. Meanwhile the Pope, twenty years after the shooting, is celebrating mass in St Peters.

In the morning's newspapers I see that the son of Roberto Calvi is now claiming that his father had confided in the Pope. Calvi, before his 'suicide' in London, had told his son that he had spoken with John Paul II, and that the shooting of the Pope was organised by the same people who were hounding and threatening Calvi himself. The Vatican was so intimately involved with Calvi, went the son's theory, that the Pope himself almost became another victim of the banking fiasco and its masonic connections. The entire story was, as ever, so sinister, so confusing and secretive, that I just shrugged and decided to ignore the whole, sordid affair in favour of something 'simpler': the General Election.

8

An Italian Story

In any self-respecting democracy it would be unthinkable that the man assumed to be on the verge of being elected Prime Minister would recently have come under investigation for, among other things, money-laundering, complicity in murder, connections with the Mafia, tax evasion and the bribing of politicians, judges and the tax-police. But this country is Italy . . .

The Economist

Three months before the General Election, the last Queen of Italy had been laid to rest. It was the beginning of February 2001, and the ceremony was taking place at Hautecombe, in France, because the male line of the Italian royal family – the *Principi Savoia* – were still barred from entering Italy. They had been exiles ever since the 1946 referendum in which the country voted to become a republic. Prior to that, Maria Josè, the matriarch then being mourned, was Queen of Italy for little more than a month.

Her funeral was the occasion for the Savoia's press relations to go into overdrive: the family wanted to return to Italy, and the funeral, just a few months before a General Election, was the perfect opportunity to publicise their case. It was a bizarre spectacle. Most of European royalty, bar the Windsors, turned out in support: the Bourbons from Spain, the Romanovs, the Prince of Monaco, Luxembourg's Grand Duke and Duchess. Outside the church there was a huge screen conveying the service to the gathering of a few hundred Italian royalists who had arrived from Turin and Milan. Some were singing the March of the Savoia: 'Sound glad trumpets, beat the drums: vivailrè, vivailrè!'

The funeral was, to say the least, rhetorical. 'Nothing's beautiful like my country' intoned an Alpine regiment. Later, when chatting to journalists, Prince Emanuele Filiberto's phone went off. It didn't ring, though: it beeped out the Italian national anthem, the *Inno di Mameli*. His father, the ruddy, jowly-cheeked Vittorio Emanuele, is always a little less adept with the media. 'We'll see you in Naples in four months,' he said optimistically. Does that mean, asked one of the journalists in a huddle around the 'monarch', that he's prepared to take an oath of loyalty to the Italian republic? 'No, no, I don't want to talk about that, absolutely not,' he snapped. His wife leant towards him and whispered something in French. 'Yes, yes, of course,' he then said stiffly.

In the still before its election storm, Italy underwent a mini Savoia revival. There was, not for the first time, much discussion about changing the Italian constitution (which currently decrees: 'For the former king of the House of Savoia, his consorts and male descendents, entry and sojourn in national territory is forbidden.') For most Italians, though, the Savoia are the cause of the darkest days of Italy's twentieth century. What democratic instincts King Vittorio Emanuele III possessed quickly folded in the face of Mussolini's 'March on Rome' in 1922; years later, in 1938, he signed the country's anti-semitic race laws. The king swiftly swapped sides in 1943, after the Allied landings in Sicily, thus starting the Italian civil war between Fascists and partisans which raged until April 1945 and, some would argue, way beyond. In exile, Vittorio Emanuele has become one of Europe's major arms dealers, and in 1978 he accidently shot and killed a German tourist from on board his yacht.

It's a strange 'first family': the now *capofamiglia*, Vittorio Emanuele, is usually decked out in jeans and brogues, and is always irascible. His wife, Marina Doria, is the daughter of a biscuit magnate, and was four-times world water skiing champion in the 1950s. She's often photographed as she slips back into Italy for a shopping trip. Most visible of the three is their son, Emanuele Filiberto, whose lanky hair and unshaven face is used to promote various products, and who occasionally commentates on Juventus matches for Italian TV from his house in Geneva. The family were a small, side-issue to the election, but in many ways their cause touched all the key issues involved. The election was to become largely about attitudes to immigration, with the right desperate for tougher measures against everyone bar the Savoia. Welcoming back the royal family would in itself require the rewriting of the constitution; once work was then started over-hauling the country's key democratic document, many suspected that it would continue far beyond simply allowing the Savoia back into Italy. Finally, that promise radically to alter the consti-tution reminded many of a particular masonic lodge of which both Vittorio Emanuele and Silvio Berlusconi had once been members: P2.

A few weeks after the funeral I received a book in the post. I hadn't ordered it, certainly hadn't paid for it. It just arrived one morning. It was called *Una Storia Italiana*, *An Italian Story*. It was distributed to about twelve million Italian homes by Berlusconi's publishing house, Mondadori, at an estimated cost of some eleven billion lire. The name of the author wasn't on the cover. Instead there were, on the front and back of the book, a total of 114 photographs of the same man. Balding, smiling, shaking hands, cheering football teams, greeting world leaders, blessing the Pope: Silvio Berlusconi. The vanity of the book was nothing as compared to its contents. It opened, of course, with that Italian obsession – the horoscope – as if to suggest that Berlusconi's destiny was written in the constella-tions. Silvio, I was told, was born a Libra, and is thus 'a commu-nicative person, capable of strong passions and profound loves. Charismatic, thanks to great adaptability and innate talent, he stands out in the activities which he brings before the great pub-lic, has optimum ability to judge, analyse and synthesise, con-structs every reasoning with stringent logic managing to confer clarity on every debate . . .'

Berlusconi had previously published a collection of his speeches called *The Italy I Have in Mind* (a text which was interrupted by repeated parentheses to indicate where the audience had broken into 'prolonged applause'). Reading *An Italian Story* was even better, like reading a rags-to-riches fairy-tale, and just as enchanting. It was impossible to put the thing down. After the horoscope, came the opening chapter, describing Silvio's family, his love for his mother, his 'spiritual exercises' in Bermuda where he retires with his friends to read the great classics of the western canon. The text was easy to read, because between every paragraph was a photo: baby Silvio, Silvio at school, Silvio singing on a cruise ship accompanied on the piano by someone called Fedele Confalonieri (now Chairman of Mediaset). It was also almost impossible to read the book and not think 'I want to emulate this man, I want to become like him, or at least follow him, certainly vote for him': his life is a dream, a childhood fantasy. He's been a musician, a businessman, a TV impresario, he has a beautiful wife, good-looking children, houses and gardens and cruise ships and private planes. Most of all, he adores football, his team actually wins things, he wins things. He wins everything. Now, of course, he wants to win an election.

For many, however, *An Italian Story* was nothing more than that: a story. It was an incredibly vain, slick, seductive story, a glossy piece of propaganda. Many found it ridiculous and rather embarrassing. Friends of mine in Parma, during a rally of environmentalists, decided to put out a large bin, offering any of the passing twelve million Italians who had been sent the 'story' the opportunity to throw it away for recycling. 'For a clean recycling' read the banner. To anyone with a sense of irony, the allusion was obvious, and much repeated over the ensuing months: *riciclaggio*, recycling, was to become the key word of the election.

'Recycling' is an issue which has dogged Berlusconi for decades, and it came back to haunt him during the election. The allegations that his humble beginnings were aided by epic *riciclaggio* – money laundering on behalf of the Mafia – dominated the campaign; Berlusconi denied all the accusations. A rival 'Italian Story', *L'Odore dei Soldi*, was published two months before the electorate went to the polls. Its claims were equally fantastic, and received ample publicity on those television channels (of the state RAI network) still outside Berlusconi's reach. The book was based on an interview with an anti-Mafia judge, Paolo Borsellino, shortly before he was killed in 1992. During the interview Borsellino had hinted that the Mafia, having at its disposal vast sums of money made from drugs-smuggling, laundered it through companies in the north, including (according to the authors) Berlusconi's Fininvest holding company. The title of the book was particularly apt. The crime of Mafia collusion in Italy is called, evocatively, *odore di Mafia* (literally 'the whiff of Mafia'). The book was called *The Whiff of Money*.

According to the authors of *L'Odore dei Soldi*, Berlusconi had, throughout the 1970s, profited from collusion with organised crime. The allegations went that Berlusconi was a prime example not of the peasant, murderous Mafia in Sicily, but something more sophisticated exported to the north. This was something much larger, more sinister and more disguised: the 'White Mafia' of financial scams, money-laundering and international invest-ment rackets. The book quoted the old notion that you enter the arena of democratic politics by leaving 'your wallet and your pistol at the door'. The implication was not just that Berlusconi would bring his wallet into government if he won the election (some $14 billion); the allegation also went that he had friends in Sicily with some very sizeable holsters.

Both stories, Berlusconi's own and that of his enemies, were gripping. *An Italian Story* and *The Whiff of Money* formed a per-fect symmetry, one full of implausible, heroic achievement, the other full of improbable accusations. As with the country's press and television, there was no room for the middle-ground: Berlusconi was either a saint or a sinner, and the ordinary voter was confronted by two versions of his career both so incredible that it was hard to know what was reality and what fantasy. If, as was probable, the truth lay somewhere between the two stories, no one was willing to say so. I didn't know what to believe. Enrico Deaglio, the editor of one political weekly, told me bluntly that he believed every word of the accusations against Berlusconi. Marcello Veneziani, a columnist on Berlusconi's *Il Giornale*, told me that the whole thing was 'obscene and absurd'. Was it too incredible to think that Berlusconi really did have connections with Cosa Nostra? Where, after all, was the evidence?

I tried, not for the first time, to understand Berlusconi's origins. Complication and confusion, as it should by now be clear, are the smokescreens of Italian life, and Berlusconi is a master of the art. When he began building the 3,500 flats on the outskirts of Milan in the 1970s, he created endless financial Chinese boxes which were entirely unfathomable to outsiders. Bizarre businesses were set up under *prestanomi* ('nicknamed' accounts with dummy holders) and furnished with billions of lire from businesses in Switzerland. Or else money arrived through the Banca Rasini where Berlusconi's father had worked and which has been frequently cited in Mafia trials in recent years. Then Fininvest, the empire which was later to become the driving force behind *Forza Italia*, was set up with 22 'holdings' and mysterious offshore companies like 'Group B' and 'All Iberian'. It would take an accountant an eternity to understand what was going on. To many the Chinese boxes seemed a suspiciously complicated way of building a few blocks of flats.

The story of one of Berlusconi's gardeners on his Arcore estate is equally bizarre. Berlusconi had bought the estate after two murders, a crime of passion, prompted the owner to sell the property in the mid-1970s. Berlusconi, having moved in, employed someone called Vittorio Mangano, a *mafioso* later handed down two life sentences for murder and heroin trafficking. Berlusconi had no involvement in Mangano's crimes, but it was certainly extraordinary company to keeep. Apart from being resident on Berlusconi's estate, Mangano was also on close terms with Berlusconi's business-partner and *Forza Italia* general, Marcello Dell'Utri (currently on trial in Palermo for 'association with the Mafia'). Maybe it's all just coincidental, maybe not. 'For me,' Mangano said during a prison interview in July 2000, 'Berlusconi was like a relative. The trust he had in me was the same as that I had in him and his family. I like Berlusconi, still do. He's an honest person, write it!' Is a compliment of honesty from a convicted murderer an asset? Does that mean he really is honest? The extraordinarily complicated facts are all out in the open, hundreds of thousands of dubious transcripts and transactions (dubious because they cast doubt in both directions: towards both the investigators and the investigated). It's only the interpretation that differs.

Berlusconi's response to the (hardly new) accusation of being a closet *mafioso* was to be indignant, aggressive and bullying. 'Contain yourself,' he screamed to one RAI presenter whose programme he had interrupted with a live telephone call. The programme in question was Michele Santoro's *Il Raggio Verde* on RAI 2 (the channel which had originally publicised the book). *Forza Italia's* general, Marcello Dell'Utri, the man at the centre of the scandal, was later given a chance to defend himself. For once an Italian studio was silent rather than noisy; instead of the usual revolving glitter-ball, the lighting was low. The advertising breaks were announced by a string quartet. It takes courage for a journalist from Palermo to hint live on national TV that a man of Dell'Utri's power was possibly guilty of collusion with the Mafia: 'You really are a heedless Palermitan,' said the journalist, Saverio Lodato, 'who has been very unfortunate in his choice of friends. In those years [1970s] one smelt the Mafia. Any Palermitan sensed it.' At the suggestion Dell'Utri, I thought, whitened visibly, his skin tightening in disbelief at the arrogance of the suggestion. 'Not even in my dreams', he stuttered, caught off-guard by the frankness of the frontal attack, 'did I smell the Mafia.'

Thereafter, Berlusconi refused (temporarily) to appear on the RAI TV channels, as did those in his coalition. They retreated to the safety of Mediaset journalists. His allies spoke of cleaning up the ranks of RAI after the election. Others urged Italians to refuse to pay their licence fees to RAI, since it was clearly Communist. Berlusconi's own Mediaset television channels resorted to impassioned pleas not to believe the allegations: on 'Rete 4', for example, the newscaster Emilio Fede couldn't contain his outrage, banging his fists on his desk as he denounced the dirty tricks of the left. Each time he tried to introduce another story he couldn't do it, he started frowning, almost on the verge of tears, and returned to defend his boss, Silvio Berlusconi. Not for the first time, the nation's television channels became, like the country at large, polarised into shrill declarations of love or loathing for Berlusconi. The actual issue, of whether there was any truth in the allegations, of whether Berlusconi really was dangerously close to collusion with organised crime, became lost in the hysteria.

Some saw sufficient grounds to indict *Il Cavaliere*, suggesting that suspicion really is 'the antechamber of truth' as far as the Mafia is concerned. Weeks before the election, the cover of Britain's *The Economist* showed a photograph of Berlusconi, with the headline 'Why Berlusconi is Unfit to Govern Italy'. The article, which caused an even bigger storm than the *The Whiff of Money* book, duly proceeded to list the crimes for which *Il Cavaliere* had been recently investigated: 'money-laundering . . . connections with the Mafia' and so on. 'The public's acquittal,' the magazine warned, could become 'a terrible condemnation of the electorate.' The reply from *Forza Italia* was the same as usual: a conspiracy of left-wing intellectuals had it in for the honest, family-man, Silvio Berlusconi. *The Economist*, far from being a sober organ of financial analysis, was a 'Communist publication,' edited by wannabe Stalinists. (*The Economist* was swiftly issued with a writ for damages in Italy. The publication is currently fighting a libel action brought by Berlusconi arising from the cover article. Over a year later, in May 2002, both Berlusconi and Marcello Dell'Utri would be acquitted by the Palermo courts of any involvement in the murder of Paolo Borsellino and Giovanni Falcone; the judge noted, however, as he 'archived' the case, that 'links have been ascertained betweeen companies which are part of Fininvest and people who are in various ways linked to Cosa Nostra.' Those links, wrote the judge, meant that the accusations of penitent *mafiosi* who had implicated Berlusconi were 'not entirely implausible'.)

Italians of eighteen and above elect 630 *deputati* (aged 25 or over) of the parliamentary camera. Those of 21 and above also elect 315 *senatori* (40 or older) in the *senato* (there are nine 'senators for life', the equivalent of life peers, either former Prime Ministers or Presidents, or else dignitaries like Gianni Agnelli, head of FIAT, Juventus, Ferrari and so on). The eventual make-up of the parliament is decided both by a first-past-the-post system (75%) and by proportional representation (25%).

On the surface, the election was a presidential show-down between – on the left – the former mayor of Rome, Francesco Rutelli, and – on the right – *Il Cavaliere*. Dozens of political parties were lined up in one coalition or the other. The bucolic left-wing coalition was called 'the olive' and was made up of 'the sunflower' (greens and socialists), 'the daisy' (Democrats, the Popular Party, the Union of Democrats of Europe, a former Prime Minister's 'Dini list'), 'the oak' (the former Communist party, now called Democrats of the Left), and one half of the Communist party proper (The Italian Communists). The 'Pole of Liberties' was Berlusconi's rival, right-wing coalition, made up of his own *Forza Italia* party, the 'post-Fascist' National Alliance, and the separatists/federalists of the Northern League. Other parties supporting him were from the 'White Flower', made up of the two broadly Catholic parties, the CCD and the CDU. Various fringe parties (the Refounded Communist Party, the 'Di Pietro list', the Radicals) refused to adhere to either coalition, preferring to go it alone and barter with their votes in the aftermath of 13 May.

Given that confusing plethora of parties, few ordinary voters understood those coalitions, let alone what they stood for. It was hard even to know what had happened in the last five years: during the 13th parliament of the Italian republic (1996–2001) 158 politicians had changed political allegiance, and the country had had three different Prime Ministers (Romano Prodi, Massimo D'Alema, and Giuliano Amato) presiding over four different governments. Political debate and front page scoops had often simply been about who was building or breaking which coalition, about who was redesigning their party flag or currently reinventing themselves as a politician of the right, or of the left. Smears, scandals, accusations and court-cases had piled up. During the election, leading politicians were arrested or investigated: one Democrat of the Left in Tuscany was arrested for taking bribes; a *Forzista* in Calabria was sentenced to five years for collusion with the local Mafia; another *Forzista* in Milan was arrested, accused of extortion.

The President of the Republic, Carlo Azeglio Ciampi, appealed for dignity, but the strange, hysterical campaigning continued.

Short, always wearing a double-breasted suit, smiling and sun-tanned, Silvio Berlusconi was obviously viewed by the left as a very Faustian figure, and his probable victory on 13 May was seen in apocalyptic terms. Even cultured political commentators on the right, however, were dismayed. Italy, they said, had never produced a 'normal' right-wing party. Mussolini's Fascism, the Christian Democrats' 'Christian Democracy' were both, by any-one's reckoning, highly unorthodox political movements. Berlusconi's *partito-azienda*, his business-political party, appeared, if anything, even more idiosyncratic. Indro Montanelli was a right-wing, nonagenarian writer who many saw as the soul of Italian journalism (he used to be editor of Berlusconi's paper, *Il Giornale*, before resigning because of editorial interference). In the weeks before the election he called the *Forza Italia* leader a 'systematic liar', someone whose methods are 'of the truncheon ... akin to those of Fascism'. (Berlusconi didn't directly answer the accusation, although his defenders did suggest that Montanelli, by then in his 90s, was simply senile and embittered.)

That, indeed, was the next accusation: that the Pole of Liberties was an umbrella under which many closet Fascists were gathered. The National Alliance is simply the new name of the *Movimento Sociale Italiano*, the post-war Fascist party. Its leader, Gianfranco Fini, is a chess player, and always appears measured, calm and cerebral. In the ranks of his party, however, are many who have dark pasts, former Fascists who, according to the accusations, took a very active part in the country's *anni di piombo*. The grand-daughter of *Il Duce*, Alessandra Mussolini, is another of the party's 'big names'.

More extreme, and more maverick, was Umberto Bossi, the gravel-voiced leader of the Northern League. He's always decked out in the party's green livery and its symbol: a wagon wheel. He's the prime example of what is called *qualunquismo* – 'everymanism' – a term for crude, vote-grabbing populism. His electoral base is the rich, industrialised north which views Rome and the south as the epitome of all that's wrong with Italy. ('Garibaldi didn't unite Italy, he divided Africa' goes the rhetoric.) When a piece of land at Lodi was recently set aside for a mosque, Bossi's *Leghisti* protested, marching under banners proclaiming 'our pigs have urinated there'. It was Bossi who, withdrawing his support from the government, caused Berlusconi's downfall in 1994.

Meanwhile, Francesco Rutelli toured the country in a specially designed 'Olive' train (he is, after all, a former green). Next to the cult of Berlusconi, Rutelli – youngish but greying hair – appeared well-meaning, efficient, but lacklustre. Nor could anyone remember quite what the left had done in five years of government. Rutelli, for better or for worse, wasn't even part of that government, but mayor of Rome. Many incumbent government ministers (Tullio De Mauro, the Minister for Education, Umberto Veronesi, the Health Minister) weren't even standing for re-election, prompting the suspicion that they were abandoning a derailed train.

It was hard to know quite where and why it went so wrong for the left. When Romano Prodi won the 1996 election, it seemed that Italy's *bipartitismo imperfetto* (with the Christian Democrats, or the right, permanently in power, and the Communists, or the left, permanently excluded) had finally, after fifty years, come to an end. In power, however, those Communists (or, as they're now called, Democrats of the Left) and their allies proved to be strict monetarists, determined to prepare the country very painfully for entry into the Euro. In their five years in government, net borrowing as a percentage of GDP had fallen from over 7% to 0.3%; the national debt had fallen, as had inflation. Only taxes were increased, or new ones introduced, like the 'tax for Europe'. Most suggest that Prodi's government, and those which followed, had been very successful financially and fiscally. The consequence, however, is that they were, politically, a disaster.

The left's greatest blunder, however, was simply tactical. Raising the spectre of Berlusconi's conflict of interests should have been the Olive coalition's winning game plan, but having ignored the problem for five years in government, they were unable suddenly to argue that it was a pressing problem. Massimo D'Alema, the man who replaced Romano Prodi as Prime Minister once the Refounded Communists withdrew from the coalition, had effectively been 'made' by a handful of votes from Francesco Cossiga (a former Christian Democrat, and a coalition partner even less reliable than Bossi). In an attempt to strengthen his hand, D'Alema, an astute, intelligent but old-school politician, had been locked in bipartisan, bicameral constitutional debates with Berlusconi. The intention was to give Italy once and for all a powerful executive and a presidential leader, no longer hostage to the small PR parties. As leaders of the country's two largest polit-ical movements, D'Alema and Berlusconi clearly had interests in common when it came to the constitutional talks. Meetings (480 hours of them) dragged on for years, during which time legisla-tion against Berlusconi was unthinkable. D'Alema, apparently desperate to pass a new electoral law, had thus leant over back-wards to accommodate his rival in order to reach an accord. Having appeared so cosy with the leader of *Forza Italia* in the late 1990s, D'Alema's subsequent suggestion – after the constitutional talks had collapsed and as an election loomed – that Berlusconi really *was* a Faustian figure after all lacked any credibility.

The difference between the two presidential candidates was underlined at a rally of *Confindustria* (the equivalent of the CBI) in Parma. Rutelli, as desperate as all the other politicians to appear *anglosassone*, stumbled through an economic analysis in English which no one understood. The next day, Berlusconi (relayed live on Mediaset channels) was the usual slick showman: relaxed and jokey, a man at ease amongst his fellow-businessmen. He invoked 'Signora Thatcher', and promised sweeping tax-cuts (he announced his intention to reduce the top rate of income tax from 50% to 33%, and to slash inheritance tax). He received ecstatic applause. Watching him, one could understand the attraction. He is, like Bettino Craxi before him, a charismatic leader amidst a sea of grey politicians and confusing coalitions. Former members of Craxi's socialist party subsequently endorsed *Il Cavaliere* and his post-Fascist and federalist allies.

Berlusconi also benefited from the fact that the anti-establish-ment vote in Italy is always influential. Politicians are held in such low esteem that anyone who appears outside the old guard is immediately more appealing than the incumbent government. (One politician from the centre-left coalition admitted recently that any politician who denied taking backhanders was a *bugiardo matricolato*, an 'out-and-out liar'.) So it was one of Berlusconi's strengths to be able to portray himself as the non-politician, lead-ing a party of entrepreneurs not politicians. (About 90% of the parliamentary intake of *Forza Italia* deputies in 1994 had never been in parliament before.) From that perspective, Berlusconi's $14 billion private wealth became an asset, not a hindrance, to democracy: he openly argued in the run-up to the election (and one can see his point, if not necessarily believe it) that he was so rich that he was perfectly placed to become a statesman (meaning, no one could bribe me or buy me, so I can be trusted). Poor politi-cians are corrupt, the argument went, rich ones don't need to be.

Another advantage was that, as Machiavelli recognised, Italy seems ever to be 'waiting to see who can be the one to heal her wounds . . . See how Italy beseeches God to send someone to save her from those barbarous cruelties and outrages; see how eager and willing the country is to follow a banner, if only someone will raise it . . .' There is, in Italy, a yearning for a redeemer, for a politi-cian who will raise a new banner and 'cleanse those sores' arising from years of misrule. That was the appeal of Mussolini in 1922, or of the Christian Democrats in 1948. Each new political regime is seen as a bright dawn before being furiously rejected when that dawn appears as false as the last (which, naturally, only increases the yearning for another redeemer).

Beyond the symbolism of the non-politician healing wounds, Berlusconi's bed-rock of support came from the business com-munity. Even the most left-wing commentator would accept that Italy's labour laws beggar belief. Contracts run on for 'time immemorial', and it is virtually impossible for any company with more than fifteen employees to lay anybody off. Wages might be measly, but at least they are still guaranteed for life. Companies are then forced to pay hefty pension contributions for any full-time employee, a figure that, given that anyone can claim a state pension at 56, is crippling to Italy's small businesses. (No one mentioned that pensions would fall, and the retirement age rise, if Berlusconi's reforms were put in place.)

He was promising to untie the red tape, slash taxes, reform labour laws. As a man whose business acumen has never been doubted, Berlusconi appealed even to the traditionally 'red' areas of Italy, in the richest parts of the centre and the north. His slogan was the 'three i's' – *internet*, *inglese*, and *impresa* (business). New English words began peppering the political debates, as both sides tried to show how Anglo-Saxon (and therefore Thatcherite) they were: words like 'flexibility' and 'new economy'. All of which only made Berlusconi more indignant when he came under attack from those organs – the *Financial Times* and *The Economist* especially – who he thought shared his business vision.

And for all the criticisms of Berlusconi, he certainly has vision. His leadership is extraordinary and magnetic, and the fierceness with which people defend him bears witness to his charisma. His closest friends, lawyers from the 1970s or his pianist from the early cruise ship days, are still sworn allies and are now in parliament or heading arms of the business empire. His political offices are so slick that I almost forgot, phoning them occasionally to check facts or quotations, that I was really in Italy: they were polite, efficient, always helpful. That, *Forza Italia* voters kept telling me, was all they wanted from the Italian parliament: quick decisions, clarity, less red-tape. Berlusconi, they said, was good for business. 'He's on our side.'

Another appeal to the electorate was a bizarre, entirely Italian affair. The leader of *Forza Italia* was presented as a *garantista*, a defender of civil rights against the witch-hunts of the Italian judiciary. Having suffered first hand the legal attacks, Berlusconi promised a complete overhaul of the magistrature. Whatever Berlusconi's motives, it was a winning line. Everyone knows that the legal system is excruciating here. 40% of those in prison are still awaiting trial; not just for a few days, but for years. The accused, according to one book by a *Forza Italia* deputy, are being effectively sentenced even before their trial. Thus the country warmed to a politician who promised radically to reform the whole judiciary. (The irony, of course, was that the perception of judicial corruption cut both ways: for Berlusconi's admirers the judges were corrupt because they were persecuting Berlusconi; for his enemies, they were corrupt because they believed Berlusconi's personal lawyer, Cesare Previti, had corrupted them with hefty bribes, an accusation for which he is currently standing trial in Milan).

Berlusconi's other great vote winner was the immigration issue. Italy, for decades one of the world's largest exporters of human beings, had in the space of a few years become a net importer. The country has invariably been the first port of call for refugees from the Balkans, Eastern Europe and North Africa. For a society which is so homogenous (socially, if not politically), and one with, significantly, the lowest birth-rate in Europe, the sudden influx had been traumatic. The problem of immigration was compounded by the much more serious problem of 'illegal immigration': the number of *clandestini* in the country was estimated to be nearing half a million, and every day more *extracomunitari* were arriving, thrown out onto the shores of the Adriatic from inflatables.

None of which, however, was really mentioned. Berlusconi, as the journalist Montanelli had realised, had become the 'millstone that paralyses Italian politics'. Issues and ideas weren't even debated. The election had become, in the words of Umberto Eco, nothing more than a 'moral referendum' on the leader of *Forza Italia*. It was simply a case of 'for' or 'against' one man. It was an experiment in saturation advertising: the brand was Berlusconi and the simple slogans were 'liberty' and 'democracy'. By late spring few were in any doubt about the 'morality' of Silvio Berlusconi. It only remained to be seen whether the electorate even cared; whether –as *The Economist* had predicted – the public would acquit *Il Cavaliere* and thereby vote him into office.

April 2001. Little more than a month to go until the election and another two bombs appear. The first explodes in the early hours in Rome, outside the offices of the Institute for International Affairs and the Office for American–Italian Relations. Half a kilogram of TNT had been detonated by a mobile telephone: the door is blown away and its steel jambs left twisted like crossed fingers. Another bomb, which didn't go off, was placed outside the former offices of Fiat in Turin.

The bomb in Rome is claimed by the 'Nuclei of Revolutionary Proletarian Initiatives' in a 36-page message emailed to newspapers via a mobile-phone modem. 'With this attack,' the group explained, it was 'taking up a position with the strategic objective of constructing a combative anti-imperialist front.' The targets at the Rome address where the bomb went off were chosen because 'they orient positions of bourgeois imperialism . . .' For pages and pages it continued, invoking the proletariat against 'war-mongers' and 'landowners', and warning that a Berlusconi government would 'represent the substantial identification between state institutions and land-owning interests.' The document was dedicated to four members of the Red Brigades killed by police in 1980.

Both bombs were minor but there was, not for the first time, a neurosis that Italy was witnessing a return to her dark, terrorist past. Giovanni Pellegrino – President of the Slaughter Commission and by now a rentaquote for opinions on Italian terrorism past and present – claimed that elections are like a 'little wind which rekindles the flames'. And, absurd and inconsequential as the new terrorist groups seemed, they were strangely mimetic of party politics, fractured into tiny groupings of alphabet soup, each using pages (36 in all) of pompous prose to explain themselves.

Then, days before the electorate went to the polls, Berlusconi produced a brilliant piece of theatre. Sitting at an elegant, cherry-wood desk in a (RAI) television studio, he signed a contract with the Italian people. He promised to create a million new jobs, to increase pensions. He assured voters he would walk away from politics if at the end of his first term his promises hadn't been met.

***

The day of the election, and the weeks that ensued, were tragi-comic. Everyone had expected a low turn-out, a lot of disillu-sioned absenteeism from the voters on the left. Instead people flocked to the polls. Italy has always had one of the highest voter turn-outs in the west. During the electoral show-downs between Communists and Christian Democrats, voters were well-drilled and turnout was invariably about 95%. The 2001 election was like a return to the old days. People clearly felt strongly and over-whelmed the polling booths. Thus, when closing time was sup-posed to be called at 10 p.m., there were still thousands of voters, impatiently waiting in queues which snaked around entire sub-urbs. The (soon-to-be-out-going) Minister of the Interior duly went on television to say that the 'urns' would remain open into the small hours. It was all very familiar. It was like so many scenes I had seen during previous years: the queueing, the slowness with which things move, and, most of all, the changing of the rules half way through the game. 'But this never happens,' said my 'betrothed', offended that I was laughing at the chaos. 'This is honestly the first time there have ever been queues at an elec-tion.' The advantage, of course, was that whatever the result, the country's new Prime Minister would have an overwhelming democratic endorsement.

Berlusconi won by a landslide. The interregnum was over, the restoration complete. The tactic of demonising Berlusconi had badly misfired. The more he was seen as under attack from pointy-heads on the left and financial journalists on the right (especially foreign ones), the stronger and more patriotic he appeared. In the 'moral referendum' the majority had chosen the 'immoral option'. *Forza Italia* was voted for by almost 30% of the electorate. The left was decimated (only Rutelli's 'Daisy' coalition didn't wilt, claiming 15% compared to 9% five years earlier), and the few independent parties (Di Pietro's 'Italy of Values' party, the ambiguous Radicals) failed to make the 4% minimum required for a parliamentary seat from the allocation of PR votes. Even so the election might have been a close finish had the Refounded Communists, full of pomp and principle, been allied to the

'Olive'. In the new, two-coalition politics, the Communists' 5% of the vote would almost have guaranteed a hung parliament. Outside the coalition, however, that 5% simply translated into eleven inconsequential seats in the lower house.

There were, of course, anomalies: Parma and its province, centre of 'communist-chic', returned five out of five candidates from the Olive coalition. The night after the election result, I was invited to the studio of a local TV station in Parma. The presenter was a staunch *Forzista*, and asked in all seriousness if there existed a conspiracy of foreign journalists aligned against Berlusconi. I denied it, and the assembled heads of all the left wing parties smiled at me and nodded in agreement. The next question was what the British press made of the result. 'The feeling is that it won't last,' I stuttered. With Italy having had 57 or so governments since the war, it seemed like a safe reply. But all the big-wigs, the entire horseshoe of local politicos around me shook their heads, either with glee or despair. The feeling was that Berlusconi was set to remain *Il Presidente* for a very, very long time.

The Italian election, then, was on 13 May. The British one was on 7 June, almost a month later. Yet the new British government was chosen and sworn in before its Italian counterpart. That gives an idea how long it takes for things to move. Once elected, it wasn't enough for Berlusconi to pay a visit to the President of the Republic and get to work. There had to be 'consultations', everyone had to speak to everyone else. Deals had to be cut. Defeated powers had to be received and soothed by Ciampi. Berlusconi had to choose which 'armchair' to give to which party. For weeks there was speculation about who would get what. Finally, the team was assembled: the *Leghista* Roberto Maroni went to the Welfare Ministry; Maurizio Gasparri, a man who to my eyes behaves like a barking Fascist, was given the job of Minister of Communications (the ideal candidate to 'clean up', as predicted, RAI channels); Pierferdinando Casini, former Christian Democrat and now of the Catholic CCD, became the speaker of the lower house. To keep things 'in the family', Letizia Moratti, the cousin of the

President of Inter Milan football team, became Minister for Education; although Count Montezemolo, head of Ferrari and favoured son of Agnelli, turned down the offer of an armchair. (Another trusted Agnelli stalwart, Renato Ruggiero, became Foreign Secretary.) Umberto Bossi, leader of the Northern League, became the Minister for Reforms. Gianfranco Fini, boss of the National Alliance, was the government's vice-president.

The priorities of the new government quickly became obvious. Most things take years and years in Italy but, when there's something of overwhelming importance, it's done with lightning speed (*direttissima* is one example, when petty criminals are speed-sentenced within days of the crime, in sharp contrast to the grinding progress of 'sensitive trials'). By the summer, one of Berlusconi's first significant acts of legislation had been proposed. It directly affected his own business manoeuvres. The crime of *falso in bilancio*, of cooking the books, was decriminalised. The legislation was, admittedly, begun under the previous government, but the new amendments which suddenly emerged were tailored to Berlusconi like a bespoke suit. The very crime of which Berlusconi had so often stood accused was, in his first foray in government, turned into a minor infringement (or, in the technical phraseology, it was changed from being a crime of 'danger' to a crime of 'damage').

Basically, in future, corrupt businessmen will face fines instead of prison and only if denounced by their own shareholders. It was a perfect example, according to the defeated left, of what is called a *colpo di spugna*, a clean-up job with the 'sponge'. As always with Berlusconi, the only thing to admire was the audacity. At the same time that extremists from the Northern League were talking about their idea of making *clandestinità* (illegal immigration) a full-scale crime, Berlusconi's government was giving accounting irregularities the all-clear. Thus, an impoverished immigrant risking his life to reach the shores of the Italian peninsula might face jail, whilst multi-billionaire businessmen who fiddle their tax returns will, from now on, simply face a fine or, more probably, a pardon. According to the left, it was *salva-ladri* (save-the-thief) law-making at its finest. (Berlusconi had pulled a similar stunt during his first, brief period in power in 1994. As prosecutors were on the verge of arresting several executives from his Fininvest empire, and as Italy was absorbed in the World Cup in America, his government hurriedly tried to pass through parliament the *Decreto Biondi*, making it impossible to arrest defendants accused of white-collar crimes.) The actual amendments were conceived by the Judicial Affairs Committee. The Chairman of the Committee, Gaetano Pecorella, and another of its members, Niccolò Ghedini, both double as defence lawyers for Berlusconi in various trials.

The false-accounting legislation had two very clear implications: since prison terms were drastically reduced, the Statute of Limitations – the practice whereby a crime is no longer a crime after a certain period – was reduced from fifteen years to seven and a half. That simple amendment would mean that all those white-collar crimes dogging Berlusconi, from Clean Hands to Dirty Feet, would be washed away, no longer subject to legal investigations or prosecutions. The second implication was even more far-reaching and more indicative of the new *Presidente*'s intentions. Since false accounting was only a crime if denounced by affected parties (a shareholder or creditor), it was obvious that something as mundane as the state, trying to impose taxes on company profits, would be impotent. For me, it was the first indication that the country was now at the service of *Il Cavaliere*, rather than vice versa.

It's part of the rewiring process of living in Italy that, as one experienced journalist described it to me, 'it's entirely useless to think in terms of left and right. Politicians swap so often between the two that that will leave you utterly confused'. To understand what goes on in the country, it was explained, the only possible definitions for slippery politicians are 'pre-political' ones: not 'right' or 'left' wing, not historical dinosaurs like 'Fascist' or 'Communist', but old-fashioned judgements like 'honest', 'law-abiding', 'tax-paying' or simply 'moral'. Given those definitions, the politics of Berlusconi were thrown into sharp relief: the man who had so earnestly painted a picture of himself as a free-marketeer in the Thatcher mould, was actually nothing of the sort. With his first legislative act he had – it seemed to me – removed one of the foundation stones of capitalism: probity with the accounts.

Berlusconi wasn't the only one who found himself with a mild conflict of interests in the government. The newly promoted undersecretary at the Ministry of the Interior, Carlo Taormina, continued practising as a defence lawyer for someone accused of 'external collusion with the Mafia'. 'That's not, of course,' a left-wing politician explained to me, 'to say he's a *mafioso*. Simply that it's absurd to have an undersecretary at the Ministry of the Interior,' he repeated it in disbelief, 'the *Ministry of the Interior!*, who doubles as a lawyer for someone accused of "external collusion with the Mafia". You can't be part of the State and the anti-State at the same time. Can you? Here you can. You can be on both sides . . .'

The left-wing press were understandably indignant about the government's new, ambiguous approach to law-abiding:

The principle, let's admit it, is revolutionary. Thinking about it, it could be extended to other fields. An unscrupulous person robs a bank? The regional authorities send him a taxi and reimburse him for the balaclava. A *mafioso* kidnaps a northern industrialist? The regional authorities pay for the transfer and send an accountant to negotiate. A robber cleans out a supermarket? The regional authorities busy themselves with the stock-taking and provide an alibi to the burglar. The rule is clear: who does wrong goes unpunished, gets helped, understood, encouraged . . .

Within months of the election, two historic sentences were handed down by the courts. After almost eighteen months, on 30 June 2001, the judge and jury in the Piazza Fontana trial reached a decision on the bombing which had taken place 32 years previously. The announcement of three life sentences, for Delfo Zorzi, Carlo Maria Maggi and Giancarlo Rognoni, was greeted in court by applause from the families of the bomb victims. The verdict barely raised a stir in the press. By then we were all suffering from scandal-fatigue and over-exposure to contrite *pentiti*. The revelations that the Italian state machine colluded with Fascist bombers decades ago was either, given the farcical court case, unbelievable, or else was so obvious already that it wasn't even news. What was news was the fact that Gaetano Pecorella, one of Berlusconi's judicial advisers, had also been the defence lawyer for Zorzi; Taormina, the undersecretary at the Ministry of the Interior, had previously acted as defence lawyer for Maggi. 'The outcome of political show-trials is already written at their inception,' Pecorella wearily told the cameras outside the court, before pouring more scorn on the judiciary of which he had become one of the political heads. 'History is being rewritten with a red pen,' said Taormina.

The other court case which came to a conclusion during the same month was the trial of a judge accused of collusion with the Mafia. The judicial career of Corrado Carnevale had been for decades typical of the insinuation of organised crime into the upper echelons of the Italian state. Throughout the 1980s and early 1990s Giovanni Falcone and Paolo Borsellino (the two mag-istrates murdered at the outset of the Clean Hands revolution) had gathered evidence about the Mafia and its tentacles across the Italian peninsula (rehashed interviews with Borsellino were, of course, the foundation for the accusations against Berlusconi). The research and prosecutions began by Falcone and Borsellino resulted in major, spectacular convictions against hundreds of *mafiosi*. With startling regularity, however, when the cases against *mafiosi* came up for appeal, they were often thrown out on grounds of an absurd technicality or by the convoluted logic of the judge Carnevale.

Carnevale (president of the 'first section' of Italy's Supreme Court) was 'like Homer's Penelope in the Odyssey',[1] unravelling the threads of the diligently assembled tapestry. His was a career indicative of that so-called 'White Mafia': the export of Cosa Nostra to the *gangli*, the 'ganglions', of the Italian state. As he overturned convictions, and released hundreds of *mafiosi*, Carnevale became known in the press as the *ammazza-sentenze*, the 'sentence-killer'. In June 2001 he was sentenced to six years in prison. Dozens of *pentiti*, repentant *mafiosi*, had come forward to witness that for decades Carnevale had been a 'guarantee' of a legal let-off for the Mafia. Carnevale, a man who appeared the true incarnation of the corrupt legal system, much more sinister than the zealous

Clean Hands investigators, was however swiftly defended by the government. As with the convicted Fascists from Piazza Fontana, government ministers leapt to his defence. The phrase of 'Communist justice' was again trotted out. The conviction was hailed as just another instance of the work of 'red togas'. More than simply taking sides in legal cases, the government always seemed to be on the least savoury side. After the fall-out from the two trials, one newspaper carried a bitter cartoon. Two people were discussing politics. 'The lawyers for the Fascists and *mafiosi* are all in government' said one. 'That,' replied the other, 'is because they've followed their clients there.'

Meanwhile, throughout that summer, miles of newsprint were dedicated to comparisons between 1969 and 2001. Many government ministers whispered anxious warnings that the country was sliding back towards its terrorist past. The left, meanwhile, promised a 'hot autumn' (the phrase used in 1969) if, as predicted, Berlusconi's government began rewriting the 18th article of the Workers' Charter, thus tampering with workplace rights and pay. Not since the 1960s or 1970s, I was told, had the country been so clearly divided down the middle: one half denouncing 'Communist delinquents', the other fretting about the 'Fascist government' and its swaggering, aggressive statements.

The tensions came out into the open in July. The month before the G8 summit in Genoa in July 2001 the Italian media spoke about nothing other than the threat of riots and terrorism. £300 million had been set aside to organise the summit, and 15,000 'forces of order' had evacuated the streets of the city at the height of the tourist season. The country was whipped into a frenzy as it was treated to back-to-back broadcasts showing police and rioter rehearsals for the confrontation (truncheons and tear-gas for the former, gas-masks and cardboard shin-pads for the others). Manu Chao, a popular and politicised French/Spanish singer, went on stage to lend his support to the *Tute Bianche* (the 'white overalls' anti-globalist lobby). Looking like astronauts, they joined him on stage days before G8, raising their left fists in their meaningless 'anti-global' salute.

For anyone with a sense of history, the Genoa venue was ominous. It was there that, in 1960, the neo-Fascist party, the *Movimento Sociale Italiano*, attempted to organise a conference. It was to have been chaired by the former (Italian) prefect of the city when it was under Nazi occupation. On 30 June 1960 the city saw riots which were, at the time, unprecedented, and which were intended to prevent the inclusion of the Fascists in government. Within days the riots spread elsewhere, particularly to Reggio Emilia, the 'red' town a short drive east of Parma. There, five protestors were killed by police, raising to 94 the number of strikers and 'rioters' killed by the Italian police between 1945 and 1960. That memory of martyrs from 41 years before, and the history of trigger-happy policing, meant that the G8 summit was becoming a cause for acute concern.

Shortly before the summit, bombs appeared across the country. As usual they were 'minor'. Many didn't go off, and others were paltry packages with simply a dusting of dynamite. Benetton, Fiat, an office for 'temporary work' were all targeted. (Employment agencies are seen as an affront to the 'time immemorial' job, and are thus as much a target of Italian anti-globalists as is McDonalds.) Emilio Fede, Berlusconi's favourite newscaster, was sent a bomb which did explode, hospitalising his secretary. The hysteria about terrorism and the G8 reached ridiculous new levels.

What actually happened in Genoa is well known. There were the usual looters and car-burners (the so-called 'black block') amongst the quarter of a million protestors who marched around the outskirts of the city. The 'white overalls' protestors had been infiltrated, according to Berlusconi's Mediaset channels, by a sinister new terrorist outfit. All one could see were a few dozen people dressed in black, banging drums and throwing bricks into shop windows; hooligans certainly, but hardly the 'terrorists' the government said they were. (One was decked out in blacked-up cricket pads, which hardly seemed to me like the livery of a dangerous revolutionary.)

Much more serious was the behaviour of the police. The problem of Italian policing (as at the football stadia) is that it's a combination of the incompetent and the very heavy-handed. The one exacerbates the other: the greater the incompetence, of course, the greater the need for heavy hands. If those hands are carrying loaded weapons that are fired at point-blank range it seems fairly obvious that there will be casualties. The £300 million spent organising the summit wasn't enough to prevent an armoured car being 'attacked'. Defending himself from a fire-extinguisher being thrown towards his vehicle, one *Carabiniere* opened fire and killed the twenty-year-old Carlo Giuliani. But even that tragic and unnecessary death was surpassed a day later. The *Carabinieri* then conducted a night-raid on the Diaz school where many journalists and protesters from the Genoa Social Forum were staying. The brutality of the *Carabinieri* overshadowed anything that had happened before. It was thuggery at its crudest. Pictures the next day showed teeth strewn across the floor of the school. There were bloodstains at head height on many of the walls. 93 people were arrested and others were taken to the temporary barracks at Bolzaneto, outside Genoa.

There, various protesters suffered beatings to the accompaniment of the Fascist hymn, *Faccetta Nera*. One *Carabiniere* later confessed to *La Repubblica* newspaper what his colleagues had done to the journalists and protestors: 'They lined them up and banged their heads against the walls. They urinated on one person. They beat people if they didn't sing *Faccetta Nera*. One girl was vomiting blood but the chief of the squad just looked on. They threatened to rape girls with their batons . . .' Bones were broken. The injuries of the British alone were obscene: broken ribs, punctured lungs, ruptured spleens, broken wrists, severe head injuries. Months later many people, both Italians and indignant foreigners, were still imprisoned and awaiting charges, let alone a trial from the government of 'civil rights'. The Italian press compared the behaviour to that of militarists in Pinochet's Chile, and for once the rhetoric didn't appear overblown. 'This,' said my normally reticent flatmate, 'is just the beginning. It's a calling card from the Fascists in government.'

A few days later, I was back in Parma drinking a coffee in the town's main square, Piazza Garibaldi. I heard a chorus coming from outside the bar and, accompanied by the jovial policeman who had been at the bar, I went outside to see what was going on.

There were about two or three hundred people of roughly student age, shouting 'Justice! Justice!' and marching under a banner (a painted sheet) saying 'Forces of Order = Fascist Murderers'. The protesters walked up to the dozen *Carabinieri* in attendance and pointed their middle fingers in their faces, shouting 'murderers'. It was, of course, impossible to reason with the marchers, as they walked past with left fists raised defiantly. It was pointless trying to point out that not all 'forces of order' are Fascists, in the same way that (despite government rhetoric) not all protesters were *teppisti, delinquenti* or *deficienti* ('hooligans,' 'delinquents' or 'half-wits'). It was bizarre. Parma, whilst fiercely political, is normally blissfully peaceful. Here, though, was Genoa writ small: visceral hatred between Italy's 'two halves'. The friendly policeman from the bar looked as bemused as me.

Within a few weeks, the Justice Minister, Roberto Castelli, was confronted with a request to offer a *grazia* to Adriano Sofri to allow him to leave prison. The *guardasigilli* ('keeper of the seals') turned down the appeal, saying that it would be 'inopportune' to pardon a police-killer 'considering the climate' of the times, and the recent 'confrontations with the police' in Genoa. Sofri, not surprisingly, was downcast. 'I will die inside' said the 58-year-old who isn't due for release until 2017.

Just as the Genoa tragedy reached its conclusion, the nonagenarian journalist Indro Montanelli died. To the last he had continued his vehement criticisms of Berlusconi, claiming that the methods of *Il Cavaliere* were 'akin to Fascism'. Since he had never been a figure who endeared himself to the left (he had been a dedicated anti-Communist and old-fashioned authoritarian who had, in the 1970s, been kneecapped by the Red Brigades) his dying pronouncements were all the more powerful. No one could convincingly dismiss his criticisms as the whingeings of a 'Communist'. His death, coinciding with 'Year Zero' of the new regime, was thus quickly seen as a metaphor for the closing of one chapter of 'The Italian Story' and the opening of another, much stranger, one.

9

Concrete Problems

It was the houses: all of these new buildings that were being put up, tenements from six to eight storeys high, their white mass like a barrier shoring up the crumbling slope of the coast, opening up as many windows and balconies as possible on to the sea. The concrete fever had got hold of the Riviera: over there was one building already lived-in, with its geranium tubs, all looking similar, on the balconies; here was a recently finished development, its window panes marked with snaky chalk squiggles, waiting for the little families from Lombardy eager to go to the seaside; further on, a castle of scaffolding and, under it, the turning concrete mixer and the estate agent's sign advertising the new flats on sale . . .

Italo Calvino

Sicily. The scene looked like something from a war. There were women wailing. Some occasionally collapsed with grief and an ambulance was called. It arrived dramatically with sirens blaring, in full view of camera crews. There was an indignant priest, shaking his head at what was going on. On the other side were armed police and military, huddled around heavily defended jeeps and holding large weapons. The *terapia delle ruspe*, the 'therapy of the bulldozers', was a new front in the very strange Italian civil war. It was a shock therapy, and one which few Sicilians ever expected to see: the military were bulldozing their houses.

That was in the spring of 2001. The therapy of the bulldozers was the sting in the tail of the out-going left-wing government, an attempt to raze to the ground the various houses and hotels which had been built illegally around one of the country's beauty spots. The war on *abusivismo* – illegal building – was a side-issue during the bitter election campaign; there were so many other accusations against the Pole of Liberties that the suggestion that they were firmly on the side of the concrete profiteers came very low down the list. And yet left-wing politicians, *Legambiente*, *Italia Nostra* (Italy's environmental pressure groups), and northern Italians in general have constantly denounced *abusivismo*. The practice of erecting enormous hotels and houses without planning permission might sound innocuous until you realise the scale on which it happens. In Sicily 4,780 illegal houses sprang up in 2000 alone, which represented another 717,000 square metres of cement poured out around the island's besieged beauty spots. Those figures simply represent the illegal building in one part of the country. Legal and illegal houses combined now mean that Italy has a higher per capita consumption of concrete than any other country in the world. In the last five years another 163,000 illegal houses have sprung up, invariably in Italy's south, and especially in Sicily. By now the country has a very unusual housing problem: there are simply far too many of them for a declining population. Two and a half million houses aren't even lived in, whilst hundreds of thousands more are built every year. It's a particularly poignant problem for Italians because it's not only an affront to ethics but also aesthetics. *Abusivismo* is more than just another example of the hazy attitude towards law-abiding and the authority of the state. Its importance lies in the fact that it's the one instance in which illegality is very clearly ugly. Critics of *abusivismo* consequently denounce not only the illegality, but also the visual impact of the rampant building, suggesting that Italy, traditionally the *bel paese*, the 'beautiful country', is at risk of extinction.

The most important front of the war against *abusivismo* is the country's beauty spot par excellence: Agrigento. On the southern coast of Sicily, it's an ancient town squeezed between the mountains and the sea where the Greeks, in the fifth century BC, built temples out of ochre limestone. Most of them are still standing, and are referred to as Agrigento's Valley of the Temples. It's Agrigento that the Greek poet Pindar once described as 'the finest city among those inhabited by mortals', a place where, he wrote with uncanny prophesy, people 'lived their lives as if they were supposed to die the next day and built houses as if they were immortals'. Despite Sicily's reputation as an island that is secretive and impenetrable to outsiders, it's hard to disguise what's going on in Agrigento and the Valley of the Temples. It's a strange story, though, and one which could have been written by Agrigento's most famous inhabitant, Luigi Pirandello: nothing is quite what it seems, everyone contradicts each other, and you're never certain quite what to believe.

The town is only a couple of hours on the train from Palermo. The railway snakes across the island, past Corleone – where *The Godfather* characters came from – and onwards between rugged hills and golden wheat fields. Every now and again you can see, from the window, the concrete shell of some abandoned construction project. Agrigento is the end of the train line from Palermo, and it feels like it. Rubbish has been uncollected for weeks, the pavements smell of rotting fruit and fish. There are stray dogs and sun-bleached posters promoting parties for last May's general election. Electricity cables are slung casually from one house to another, barely above head height. When I walk down the main street I'm almost knocked over by two men on two mopeds who are somehow carrying a double mattress between them. But the town is eerie and beautiful. It's on about the same latitude as Tunis, and is set on a steep hillside. People sit outside their houses on the pavements, just waiting and talking and shouting jokes to their neighbours. If you ask someone for directions to your hotel, they will either ignore you, or else actually walk you there themselves.

When I finally arrive in my prison-like hotel, the jovial, sedentary maitre d'hotel is watching television. As he shows me my cell, I ask him what he makes of *abusivismo*. He just laughs, and cryptically, improbably, quotes Constantine: 'With the sign of the cross we will win.' When night falls, you can walk to the edge of the town and see the temples a mile away: rows of floodlit orange pillars. Beyond them is the sea. It's also a place of mournful and austere Catholicism. One of the town's tiny squares is called Piazza Purgatorio. When I go into a bar, an old woman, surprised to hear a foreign accent, offers me a glow-in-the-dark rosary and a picture of the Madonna (stamped with 'ecclesiastical approval' from the Archbishop in Palermo). Her advice for my travels is a mixture of the medical and the Catholic, a sort of prescription devotion: 'Say two Ave Marias before breakfast, and a Gloria to this blessed Madonna before you go to bed.'

The next day, *Legambiente*'s Sicilian lawyer, Giuseppe Arnone, arrives in a large jeep. He opens the passenger door for me, before driving through the steep, narrow streets, saying nothing. We stop outside the courtroom, its two guards armed with submachine-guns and sunglasses, before driving towards the outskirts of the city. Eventually Arnone pulls up on a blind bend on the road, and points at a building which looks like a large doll's house sawn in half: all the interior walls and floors are showing. To the left, on the outer and under side of the blind bend, is the rest of the building. 'The law limiting the building craze came after this landslide in 1966,' says Arnone, speaking for the first time. 'It was caused, of course, by over-building on a fragile hillside. By now, that landslide and the reasons for the protective legislation have been forgotten, and the whole process has started again.'

Within minutes we are at the temples. We walk onto the narrow ridge of the hill between the city and the sea. There's a forest of columns – the Temple of Hercules, the Temple of Concordia, the Temple of Juno and the rest. Linking them there's a wide path, lined on each side by cacti. Many of their large, flat leaves engraved with declarations of love or of political opinions: 'Pachu loves Sabri' or else 'Communists are the shit on your shoes'. Like Agrigento, it's all both beautiful and depressing. The sun is so hot it blurs the near-distance: you can just make out, within a few hundred metres of the proud, crumbling temples, a motorway on massive concrete supports. Huge *palazzi* hem in the area, and there are nearby cranes heaving new (illegal) breezeblocks into place. Agrigento itself, about a mile away on the hilltop inland, is a wall of white concrete.

'The therapy of the bulldozers,' says Giuseppe Arnone, 'is a physical as well as political battle. It's the cranes against the bulldozers.

And it's a race to save one of the most important archaeological areas in Europe.' He explains how the economics of *abusivismo* work: despite being a stone's throw from the temples, agricultural land in the area is worth very little. Growing wheat or grapes has a very low and very long-term yield. A hotel built there, however, would be incredibly lucrative since tourists and academics arrive from all corners of the globe. So people build on their land, and the profits are so great that they can be shared out with the 'local authorities', who thus give them the retrospective go-ahead for the building.

During the 2001 election, Italy's most popular novelist, the Sicilian Andrea Camilleri, tried to persuade the inhabitants of Agrigento to get out of its 'tunnel of illegality and *abusivismo*'. The trouble is that the people in Agrigento aren't used to thinking in terms of the Italian state. Many are so poor that they care little for archaeologists, novelists, lawyers and high-brow politicians from northern Italy who wag their self-righteous fingers. But the strange thing about the Agrigento story is that it's not the poor who are building houses (the traditional defence of illegal building), it's the wealthy, political classes; precisely those people who are supposed to be most bound by the law are above it. 'Here,' says Arnone, 'anyone with money can do what they want. There's a seriously criminal administration and a class of politicians who are simply thieves . . .' It's not the poor and pious who are building their sumptuous *palazzi* a stone's throw from the Greek temples, but a different class of customer: the rich and powerful, like the former mayor of the town.

I go to see the new villa of the former mayor of Agrigento, Calogero Sodano, recently elected to parliament as a deputy for Silvio Berlusconi's coalition. It's an imitation of the temples, built (illegally, according to the prosecution) in the same, ochre limestone. The gates are now chained up, with a notice announcing that it has been 'sequestered for investigations'. It was Arnone who 'denounced' the new member of parliament. 'Sodano presented himself as the face of change, the bright new Italy of Berlusconi, but it's just typical *gattopardismo* [Lampedusa's 'leopardism'], in which everything appears to change, but remains exactly as it always was. Sodano has been involved in this racketeering business for years: massive invasions of concrete, profits shared round the political classes and so on.' Giuseppe Arnone is a man so reticent that he's almost impossible to interview. He doesn't say much, only hints occasionally at what is really going on. What is clear, given those long silences, is that Agrigento is a very dangerous place for a law-abiding lawyer.

I have often read in newspapers that Agrigento is the *zoccolo duro*, the 'hard hoof' of the Mafia. That's why, the more you understand it, the more *abusivismo* seems not chaotic lawlessness but precision profiteering. 'Nothing,' says Arnone, 'ever gets done here without the correct clearance.' There's clearly nothing in Agrigento that money and connections can't achieve: all the illegal houses have running water, telephone lines and electricity, even though they don't, on paper, actually exist.

Meanwhile, the week that I'm there, the bulldozers are poised to go to work on new houses. In Licata, a few miles east along the coast, the order has just been given to raze another eighty houses. But in Agrigento and Licata nothing is happening. The troops are back in their barracks on standby. There seems to be a truce. Andrea Camilleri had already understood which way the wind was blowing: 'Demolition work has been stopped. There are no bulldozers anymore, they've retreated in orderly fashion. That's a very beautiful indication of the way things are going in Italy . . .' The reason is that, since the spring offensive against *abusivismo*, Silvio Berlusconi has become *Il Presidente*. More than that, he was the first man in the history of Italian democracy to win 61 out of the 61 directly elected parliamentary seats in Sicily. The implications are obvious. The therapy of the bulldozers had given offence, and Berlusconi isn't going to repeat the error. He knows which side his political bread is buttered, and it's widely predicted that he will now do everything he can to encourage the cranes instead of the bulldozers. *Figuriamoci!* laughs one person I speak to, which (given the tone) translates as 'but of course!'

Few people really expect the bulldozers to win the war anymore.

[211]

The new houses will be 'sanitised' and therefore given the *condono*, the 'official pardon'. That *condono* only encourages more illegal housing. It's the magic wand of Italian illegality, repeatedly waved often over criminals in return for a fine. Avowals are made about being tougher in the future, which never discourages others from attempting the same scam. 'Every hypothesis about an official pardon,' says *Legambiente*'s president, Ermete Realacci, 'will only serve to increase new abuses and further degrade the few corners of our coast which have remained uncontaminated.' The practice of pardons, it's obvious, just encourages more of the same: if you're not supposed to build on a particular site, you build anyway and then pay a paltry fine and sanitise the illegality. Every few years, the Italian government, strapped for cash, agrees to recognise thousands of new constructions in return for a little investment: 207,000 houses, originally illegal, were sanitised in that way between 1994 and 1997. It doesn't matter if you've broken the law: it will be changed to accommodate you and your accommodation.

The most frequent question any foreigner is asked in Italy is 'isn't it beautiful?' 'Yes, absolutely' is the obvious, expected answer. The standard reply I now give (having been asked the question three or four times a week for the last four years) is that of course Italy is the *bel paese*, but that it has aged like someone who has lived life in the fast lane, someone who has abused themselves and has the lines and scars and stories to prove it. Because Italy, as is obvious to anyone who looks out of the window of a train, is big on building. Since the war the country has seen half a century of ceaseless construction – be it at break-neck speed or more usually in snail-pace developments. (All 'works-in-progress' have billboards announcing the law and the architect which have allowed building to begin, accompanied by a projected completion date which is usually long-since passed.)

La Speculazione Edilizia, basically 'real-estate gambling', was the novella which Italo Calvino considered his best work. It describes the 'new social class of the post-war years', the 'improvising entrepreneurs without scruples' and the way in which they caused the 'squalid invasion of cement'. The book was written during 1956–57, but could equally be applied to the entire post-war period in which money flowed as fast as the concrete. It's a trend that was captured in the opening shots of Francesco Rosi's *Le Mani Sulla Città* ('Hands Over the City'): all you can see from the window of a helicopter are tons and tons of white concrete. In one long and uninterrupted take, the camera shows Naples and all its rampant redevelopments. The buildings look the same: tall white cubes with tiny windows, stretching for miles and miles over the hills and towards the port. When the camera looks directly down, you can see the grid of the city, the narrow streets between the new buildings and, as it zooms in, the lean-to shacks between the motorways.

The film, made in 1963, was similar to Rosi's other films: a plea to battle against the abuses and illegality of society. It was a nightmare vision of the new Italy: the collapse of a *palazzo* isn't used to slow down development but to speed it up. The 'Party' (the Christian Democrats) get rich by assigning building contracts to *mafiosi*, who in return guarantee the politicians their votes. The city council's one honest politician, a Communist, is powerless to stop the speculation, and is reduced to traipsing from office to office looking for proof of illegality which doesn't exist. As far as the law goes, *tutto è in regola*, everything is 'by the book'. The lawless has been legalised. The commission of inquiry can reach no conclusion. Politics is reduced to the buying and selling of votes, made possible by the vast amounts of money slushing around the construction business. Besieged by angry women, the mayor unfolds huge notes and passes them around. Looking over his shoulder he smiles and says 'Consigliere, see how democracy works?'

If building residential properties is lucrative, *appalti* are even more so. *Appalti* – governmental contracts – are the gravy of the Italian economy. Before the Clean Hands prosecutions against bribery, it was normal for politicians to get a hefty kickback from the recipient of any contract. As the system became habitual, huge factories and refineries were built simply to make the politician and the constructor a profit, regardless of whether there was any need for them. Once a particular project had served its purpose (injecting a bit of cash in the right directions), it could be shelved and forgotten. Many now lie abandoned half-way to completion, as people have realised that there was never the necessity. There are, all across the south, roads that lead literally nowhere. Those abandoned, useless constructions are called the 'cathedrals in the desert', and look like something from *Ozymandias:* 'trunkless legs of stone' in the sand.

Since Clean Hands, people are more aware of the problem of government oiling the wheels of big business, and politicians therefore benefiting. But it still goes on and is, many have suggested, making a comeback. Eyebrows were raised after the election of 2001 when a building entrepreneur from Parma, Pietro Lunardi, was made 'Minister for Infrastructure and Road-Building'. Lunardi's role in his engineering and construction company, Rocksoil, would provide yet another potential conflict of interests for the government since he would be responsible for spending a 100 trillion lire war-chest on everything from the high-speed rail link between Milan and Rome to the long-projected bridge which might finally unite Sicily with the mainland. What if Lunardi's Rocksoil had interests in the bidding? Quizzed on the matter by a journalist, the politician's defence was the invincible 'family' argument – 'Why should one hundred families have to be turned out of house and home just to please I don't know who?'

Then, a few months later, the minister made a comment that sent out a very clear message about his intentions: 'One needs to get along with the Mafia and the Camorra [the Napolitan Mafia]. Everyone should resolve problems of criminality as they see fit . . . the Mafia has always existed, always will . . .' If anyone was still in any doubt, his words were a chilling indication of who the government was prepared to accommodate. It was, wrote one newspaper, as if the martyred anti-mafia judges had never existed, as if all the mourning at their deaths had suddenly been forgotten. One cartoon in the (left-wing) *L'Unità* newspaper spelt it out:

'The government says we should get along with the Mafia,' says one character. 'Judging by the election results in Sicily,' replies the other, 'someone's getting along with them very nicely.'

The fact that the scandal blew over after a few days' indignation is typical, because fear about construction corruption is so widespread that it isn't news. The consequences, though, for the country at large are hugely damaging: tax-payers feel, rightly or wrongly, that a cut of all their taxes is paid back into the politicians' pockets (I've never met anyone in Italy who isn't convinced of this); thus tax-dodging comes to appear a form of honest resistance; the costs of public works are artificially high, because it's in the interests of both parties to up the prices; finally, nobody outside the loop is likely to get a look-in. The best company making the most financially competitive bid rarely comes out on top.

The cost, unfortunately, isn't only financial. When I first arrived in Italy, in the spring of 1999, there was a short news flash: a block of flats had collapsed in Foggia in Puglia. 71 people died. I was astonished, not just by the fact of what had happened (the flats, constructed at the cheapest costs conceivable, had just caved in to gravity), but by the fact that a few days later it wasn't even mentioned. It was, I was told, a not uncommon occurrence. Three and a half thousand people have been killed since the war in landslides alone. Part of the reason is that Italy has a uniquely sensitive ecosystem: 6,400 miles of coastline, two mountain ranges, tectonic fault-lines, volcanoes. Britain appears geographically very gentle by comparison. Many reports from around the country, whatever the season, are about the physical battle for survival. Earthquakes flatten entire suburbs, landslides obliterate villages, fires rip through ancient forests and volcanoes spit out molten lava. The elements, given the sheer number of human lives they claim, seem simply crueller than elsewhere. But the problem is compounded by the human desecration of the landscape, and the deaths often seem an almost biblical revenge for the violations of the land.

The tragedy of Vajont was Italy's worst civilian disaster of the post-war period. For years, until a 'protest-play' by Marco Paolini was broadcast in 1998, it was simply forgotten. Now the valley in the Dolomites has become a place of lay-pilgrimage, where thousands of people from across the country visit and pay their respects. The atmosphere there is like that at the former trenches from the First World War in France and Belgium. As you walk around the rough scrub you know that here, in the earth, lie thousands of people swallowed up by the soil. In October 1963, Mont Toc, a mountain of porous rock, gave way under the weight of a man-made lake whose capacity had been endlessly increased despite the warnings of every visiting expert. As the mountain collapsed into the lake, fifty million cubic metres of water slopped like a tidal wave over the edge of the dam. The water fell vertically for hundreds of metres before ripping through the villages below. Two thousand people lost their lives.

Another – this time on-going – man-made disaster is the car culture. Car-production is the foundation stone of the Italian economy, and the country now has a higher per capita ownership of cars than any other country in the world (it overtook America in the late 1990s). No other country in the world is as obsessed by its cars and their possible speeds. Driving is a white-knuckle ride: everyone seems embarrassed by being anywhere other than the fast lane (the slow lane is known as the *corsia della vergogna*, the 'lane of shame'), so it thus gets slower. Then impatient drivers overtake on the inside, slaloming between the other cars and flashing their lights to persuade a lorry to pull onto the hard shoulder. Many are simultaneously talking on telephones, or else gesticulating to a driver in the adjacent lane who is going too slowly. Even on narrow streets in the *centri storici* of medieval cities, four-wheel jeeps career like large bobsleighs through the shoppers, the drivers shouting wildly if someone holds them up. The consequence is a mortality rate that is nearer something from a war zone: in the last decade, 72,000 people have died on Italian roads. News reports are invariably dominated by the latest multiple crash on a motorway. At the same time, levels of smog throughout the plain of the Po are suffocating. Often the traffic in Milan has to be literally halved, meaning that only odd or even numberplates are allowed into the city centre in order that pedestrians might breathe.

The response of the new government to the car problem was to announce plans to notch up the speed limit by another 20 kph, to 150 kph on certain roads. For the first time since emigrating to Italy, I felt completely disgusted by the whole situation and desperate to go home. More people, I repeated aloud to myself, have lost their lives in the last decade on Italian roads than America lost in the entire Vietnam war . . . seventy-two thousand people. And yet the solution is to increase the speed limit. As with *abusivismo*, the new government appeared on the side of the lawless bandits and the *menefreghisti* (the 'I couldn't carers'). Any rules or laws were by now nothing more than an affront to individual freedoms, and were to be ignored or done away with. That lawlessness might sound vaguely attractive unless you've seen it first-hand: hundreds of miles of beaches replaced by concrete slabs, cars which career onto the pavement and into prams and which never stop after an accident, residential buildings which give way like sandcastles at sunset.

After a few days watching immobile bulldozers in Agrigento, I decided to make my way back to Palermo. Most of the other journalists had already left weeks before. Waiting for the train in Agrigento's railway station I went into the little chapel. Under a little image of a Madonna were the words: 'Monsignor Montucci decrees that whosoever pronounces four glorias in front of this shrine shall receive one hundred days of indulgence.' It's that, I suppose, that lies at the heart of the moral conundrum of *abusivismo* in Sicily: transgressors are indulged rather than punished, and everyone's sins are forgiven as long as they say the right prayer, or else pay the fine to the politicians' coffers.

I left the railway station's chapel and decided instead to hitch-hike back to Palermo along the coast. I had little optimism, given the rude grunts I had received in many bars and hostels. By then, though, I knew that each time I was exasperated by life in Italy, an act of breathtaking civility was only just around the corner to restore my faith. Within five minutes a man stopped. The car, like most in Sicily, was so dented that it looked like aluminium foil folded over a leg of lamb. There were already seven in the car. The driver had just stopped to explain why he couldn't pick me up. *Auguri*, he said. 'Best wishes'. Another soon stopped to explain he had to turn off. It's inconceivable that something of the sort would ever happen in the north. Two rich kids predictably stopped slightly ahead of me. One step towards them and they sped off, laughing. Then a baker picked me up. 'I'll take you to where there are a lot of girls. You're still up to that at your age aren't you? You American then?'

'British.'

'Myself, I've never been to the continent,' he said, examining me as he overtook a lorry loaded with lemons. I wasn't sure if he meant 'continent' as in Italy or Europe.

'Britain's not really the continent either. It's a collection of islands like Sicily . . .'

The baker then delivered a soaring, eloquent monologue explaining exactly what he had intended by the word 'continent': 'For me,' he said, 'the continent implies anything that creeps onto this island, that tells me what to do. I don't care whether that's Rome or London, if you come here and want to be my boss, you're the continent.' He went on for an hour, summarising his notion of autonomy from any authority. Each time his voice sounded stern about the 'continent', he would offer me another of his *arancini*, his balls of fried, orange rice. He left me at a beach full of adolescents, including the two, now-sheepish, rich kids who had driven by earlier. 'My house is over there if you ever need anything,' the baker said extending his flour-dusted fingers.

That was in Marsala, a town whose name implies in Arabic 'the port of God'. It's famous as the home of the sweet dessert wine and as the landing place of Garibaldi and his 'thousand men' in Sicily as they exported the unification movement to the south. I sat on the beach watching the huge rollers crash against the coast, splashing the private deck-chairs which everyone has to hire. (Even in Sicily the beaches have all been privatised.) Huge speakers blared out Europop. Stunningly beautiful girls, their fluorescent bikinis flattering their dark skin, were throwing frisbees to each other, seemingly hoping that they got taken in the wind to the deck-chairs where the single men were sitting.

I looked at the sea and beyond, trying to catch sight of the north African coast. Sicily, I suppose, has always been held up as the epitome of what's wrong with Italy. And yet, sitting there in the sunset, it also seemed exactly what's right: despite poverty, the generosity is instinctive. Despite daily reports about murders and kidnappings, it also appears blissfully peaceful and serene. Things might be serious, but I had never heard so much laughter. In fact, behind the stereotypical lawlessness is hidden what many consider the real, earthy intellectual caste of Italy. Sicily has been the cradle of some of the country's greatest writers: Giovanni Verga, Luigi Pirandello, Giuseppe Tomasi di Lampedusa and Leonardo Sciascia. Reading them, you get an idea of the sheer aridity of the island. Always in the background there's a sense of mortality amidst the dust. Grandiose concepts like dignity and honour still dominate the moral and immoral spectra. And because everything is a hall of mirrors, in which nothing is ever quite understood, words are always carefully chosen, no utterance is ever idle.

Sicilians are admired because, as Sciascia wrote, they 'little love to speak', their lives are 'made up more of silences than words . . .' A friend from Parma who now teaches at Palermo university talks admiringly of Sicilians' *flemma serafica*, their 'seraphic phlegm', which enables them to put up with poverty whilst watching the profiteers. Another friend from Parma, a middle-aged man whose son spent a long time on the island recovering from heroin addiction, says that Sicilians are the most noble and intellectual of all Italians. 'They have,' he says, 'the perfect combination of hardness (*durezza*) and refinement (*raffinatezza*). You see it in all that studied politeness, the dutiful examination of their own behaviour . . .'

After a few idle days at Marsala, I went to Mozia, which is, along with Agrigento, one of the southern Mediterranean's richest archaeological sites. It was here that an Englishman named Joseph Whitaker began painstakingly retrieving bits of boats and weapons and burial sites from the shallow waters around his off-shore island, San Pantaleo. In his villa you can still see marine charts, tracing the Carthaginian sailing routes between southern Sicily and Spain, north Africa, and Greece. Nearby improbable windmills sit in the shallows, sucking in the sea to produce hill-sides of glistening salt.

When I got back to Palermo it was July 14, the day of *La Santuzza* or Santa Rosalia, the patron saint of Palermo. The city centre is still largely as it was after the Allied bombing raids from the Second World War: some houses have no front walls, so you can peer in and see abandoned cookers and a tree sprouting in the kitchen. Lone walls rise up and lean randomly without any pur-pose. There are still piles of mortar and horizontal doric columns where the bombs fell over fifty years ago. Against that backdrop, *La Santuzza* appeared beautifully, elegiacally pagan. Loudspeakers were hung from street corners to relay the voice of a husky French actress which was alternated with the stern tones of the *Arcivescovo* of Palermo. 'I am *Santuzza*,' said the actress, 'I am the city, I live between the mountains and the sea.' Meanwhile beautiful, busty girls mounted on huge iron horses were wearing twelve-foot dresses and lighting extravagant fires. Fat, topless men were looking bored as they pushed the oars of the float, occasionally stopping for a cigarette when the man in a suit at the front received an order from his walkie-talkie. The air smelt of lighter fuel and incense. Behind me a Vespa screeched to a halt inches from my calves. The guy took off his helmet, excused himself, and made the sign of the cross.

Within weeks of returning to Parma there were more bombs, this time more professional and consequential. One blew apart Venice's marketplace outside the city's tribunal the day before Berlusconi was due to arrive. Another, a few days later, at Vigonza (again in the Veneto) targeted the headquarters of the Northern League. After the bombing, the outside wall of the headquarters looked like a spider's web – the masonry and plaster cracked into interconnecting lines. The response was, again, paranoia that the country was slipping back towards the irrational reprisals of the *anni di piombo*. Berlusconi responded by trying to knit together another 'historic compromise', drafting the left wing onto his side to denounce and isolate the 'terrorism'. No one really bought it though. Everyone realised that Italy was nowhere near the violence and terrorism of the 1970s. It was much shallower, more superficial, and no one really thought, however tragic his death at the hands of the forces of order, that Carlo Giuliani was going to become a new Pino Pinelli, the Anarchist who suffered the 'accidental death' back in 1969. There was, certainly, a strange nostalgia for the *anni di piombo* amongst a tiny minority, in the same way that in the 1970s there was a yearning to recreate the Resistance. But all the vital ingredients that made the 1970s so bloody were entirely lacking. The government, however, appeared to enjoy the *anni di piombo* comparison more than anyone else. Given the twin threats of Communism and terrorism, the Christian Democrats were for decades electorally invincible. Berlusconi was trying the same tactic, talking up both threats in the hope that his politics and his past could be ignored. From July onwards, any opposition to Berlusconi would be labelled 'terrorism', and protesters were likely to feel the full force of the forces of order.

Francesco Cossiga, a former President of the Republic, was once described as playing 'a Pirandellian game of double truth and double lie . . . [he was] even fantastic in his wish for rationality filtered through ambiguity'. That ambiguous reputation arose because of the suspicion that he knew more about the country's terrorism than he let on. (There was, in the early 1980s, an attempt to indict Cossiga when he was Prime Minister because he lied about tipping off terrorists about imminent arrests. The indictment failed.) Now, though, Cossiga is nicknamed 'pick-axe' because of his violent, provocative outbursts. Having witnessed the terrorism first-hand in the 1970s, he has frequently urged peace negotiations between Italy's warring sides. In the aftermath of the G8 and the bombings of August 2001, however, he changed his attitude. As the country was worrying about the next international conference (due in Rome in November) Cossiga outlined his advice to Berlusconi:

> If I were Berlusconi, who has changed a lot since 1994 . . . I wouldn't even put one policeman in the piazzas, I would let those kids break every window. I would let them do it: go ahead with iron and fire . . . your tango. I would want these kids to vent their anger. And then: Bang! Armoured vehicles on the streets . . . you would see that even today, exactly as in my era, the left invokes the police, the hard hand . . . This autumn will be 'hot' because the target is a big one. People will beg us to stop them. And we will stop them with armoured cars and with loaded guns, authorised to shoot and also to kill . . . And we will clean up the piazzas.

As a synthesis of strategic, Christian Democratic advice to the government it was breathtaking: let a few hooligans riot, and then truncheon them into submission (or worse). The very politician who had tried to bring the two halves of the country together was now advocating the settling of some old scores with the left. Given Italy's history it wasn't surprising that many Italians, going into another 'hot autumn', were mildly paranoid.

Such was the atmosphere in Italy immediately prior to the terrorist attacks on America. The Allied response to 11 September was a mixed blessing for Berlusconi. They allowed him to play the patriotic card and, according to his supporters, to add to his stature in the international arena. For one half of the country, Italy could finally be proud once more. After years of feeble government, they said, the country at last had a leader who could strut the international stage. There was a tangible upsurge in patriotism. The national anthem, the words of which are notoriously unknown by most Italians, was even played before a local derby in Verona. Tricolour flags were hung out over balconies and little lapel-badges of the red, green and white were dusted off by television presenters and politicians. Italian troops were offered to the Americans and were, to the delight and surprise of the patriots, actually accepted.

For the other half of the country, though, what was happening was worrying. Television, as usual, was the first to register the subtle changes. Dancing troupes began wearing military outfits: khaki bikinis or mini-skirts made up of stars-and-stripes. In another toe-curling show, a group of girls danced dolefully in burqas before the band struck up Yankee Doodle and they stripped off to the all-Italian sequin underwear. Films about the Crusades were shown repeatedly throughout September, and government ministers began going on air to denounce Islam and any other religion not subject to the Vatican (one of the Catholic leaders likened Bin Laden to Luther). Berlusconi, at the end of September, told journalists in Berlin about 'the superiority of our civilisation' over Islam. It was, he said '1,400 years behind'. It was the first signal that his presence on the world stage was to be an awkward, blundering one. What appeared swashbuckling bravado in Italy looked like ignorance abroad. Every Western government distanced itself from his comments: 'It's clear that Berlusconi's remarks were offensive and offence has been taken,' David Blunkett observed the next day. Realising that he had made a mistake, Berlusconi then denied ever having made the comments. The unfortunate phrases were, said Berlusconi, the malicious inventions of Italian Communists.

When the war on terrorism found a 'financial front', his position became evermore unfathomable. As the international community began taking an ever-tougher line on the movements of unsourced money, Berlusconi's domestic legislation was going in exactly the opposite direction. With the eclipse of the Italian currency, the Lira, just around the corner, his government passed legislation which was little more than a licence to launder money. In return for a fine of 2.5% of the sum involved, illegally exported (or earned) capital would be allowed to return to Italy. It was called, simply, *rientro dei capitali*, and was introduced as a sly amendment to a vote on the introduction of the Euro. Apart from the international derision that the legislation incurred, the government won on both counts: financially the Treasury would benefit from the fines and the influx of funds, and politically *Il Presidente* seemed to have honoured his side of the dark bargain struck before the election. Stashes of illegally exported cash could now, for a small fee, be put through the governmental washing machine. Such was the unease at the legislation that, only months after coming to power, the government was forced to make the 're-entry of capital' legislation a vote of confidence in the government.

Meanwhile, a parallel piece of legislation seemed, in the face of international efforts, even more perverse. The government had added two amendments to a treaty agreed between Switzerland and Italy in 1998, and which was only now being ratified in parliament. Those amendments were effectively bureaucratic spanners in the wheels of international investigations into financial fraud. They rendered useless any documents used in on-going trials for banking irregularities unless they met rigid and improbable conditions (adherence, for example, to a raft of laws from February 1961, which ratified the Convention of Strasbourg). It seemed apparent that certain trials would have to be postponed, or begun again from scratch. By that time, the Statute of Limitations would take effect, and further prosecution would be impossible. The Director of Public Prosecutions in Geneva, Bernard Bertossa, spoke of his 'impression that this disgraceful law has a clear objective: to do away with certain evidence to neutralise certain judicial processes in Italy.'

Even on the government benches there was outrage at the legislation. For the first time, 27 *franchi tiratori* ('snipers' from Berlusconi's own Pole of Liberties coalition) took advantage of the secret ballot to vote against the government. As the legislation was passed, there were physical fights on the floor of the parliament. It was described as a *rissa*: not exactly a punch-up, but a lot of pushing and shoving between opposing politicians. Indeed, as the amendments were being passed, opposition parliamentarians held up posters with the name of Cesare Previti (Berlusconi's lawyer currently on trial in Milan) and the number of his Swiss bank account.

It became very obvious that the backlog of court cases against Silvio Berlusconi and his allies was the main reason for the autumn's rushed legislation. He intended, it seemed, not to defend himself *in* the various trials, but to defend himself *from* them. Even the Northern League, which at the beginning of the 1990s had appeared a minor party intent on rooting out the corruption of Rome, had become entirely co-opted to the cover-up. The Justice Minister, the *Leghista* Roberto Castelli, repeatedly inveighed against the 'dirty togas'; Carlo Taormina, the Sicilian lawyer, went further, saying that any magistrates who continued to prosecute Berlusconi should themselves be prosecuted. Each time he went abroad Silvio Berlusconi desperately tried to explain himself to his allies: Italy had 'Jacobin judges' he said in Spain. 'For the last ten years,' he said in an interview with one of his own magazines, 'there has been a civil war in Italy.' In a move which seemed intimidating, and whose full significance would only be understood months later, protective escorts for magistrates were drastically cut back. By the beginning of December, after weeks of relentless attacks, the entire committee of the 'National Association of Magistrates' resigned en masse, the first time it had done so since 1924.

Days later, the partners of the European Union met to discuss plans for a European arrest warrant for 32 of the most serious crimes: terrorism, arms-trafficking, paedophilia and so on. It was expected to be a straight-forward meeting, but Italy unexpectedly, and for the first time in her post-war history, had suddenly cooled on the idea of the European Community. The Italian delegation refused to sign the agreement. The motives for Italy's reluctance to introduce a European arrest warrant were baffling. Others, though, suggested it was only natural: at a time when the Italian government was intending to stitch-up its domestic judiciary, it wouldn't then go and create an international noose for the presidential neck. Roberto Castelli, the Justice Minister, returned from Brussels wearing his green, Northern League neck-tie, and duly announced to a rally in Milan that a European arrest warrant was a sure way to guarantee Communist justice; nobody, said Umberto Bossi – the Minister for Reforms and leader of the League – would have been safe from the left-wing 'executioners' had the legislation been signed. An agreement was eventually reached, but only once many of the crimes under discussion had become subject to 'dual incrimination': the arrest warrant would only be valid if the crime was legally a crime in both the country requesting extradition and the extraditing country. As Graham Watson, the Chairman of the European Parliament's Justice and Home Affairs Committee, later told me: 'The whole episode raised further questions in Brussels about the cleanliness of Berlusconi's government. That a Prime Minster should go so far to guarantee what is effectively a veto against the arrest of criminals is very worrying. I should say that I don't think he was trying to save his own skin, but that of his friends and allies.'

Within a week, the European governments met for another summit, this time at Laeken in Belgium. The Italian contingent was, again, cantankerous. The Italian government pulled out of the military transport project, refusing to finance the purchase of any of the A400M aircraft. (Germany had purchased 73, France 50 and Spain 27.) The summit was also intended to decide the destination of various European agencies, but even agreement on that couldn't be reached since Italy vetoed any distribution of the agencies that didn't guarantee Parma, the 'food capital of Europe', the seat of the European Food Safety Agency. Helsinki had been the rival for the food agency, and Berlusconi was quick to ridicule Finnish cuisine: 'They don't even know what *prosciutto* is. I gave a strong "no". I even had to raise my voice.' The summit finished amidst bitter recriminations. The Italian Mario Monti (European Competition Commissioner) said that the Italian government's behaviour had been 'adolescent'.

The rise in Italian patriotism, previously such an unseen sentiment across the peninsula, clearly meant that the country's leader had begun to distance himself from the European Community only weeks before the vital launch of the Euro. Many suggested that the shift in policy had, paradoxically, been prompted by the rabid Northern League (a party which is actually opposed to the Italian nation state, and whose opposition to Europe is therefore entirely political, rather than patriotic: it's simply too left-wing). The one government minister of truly international stature, Renato Ruggiero (former head of the World Trade Organisation and Foreign Secretary under Berlusconi) had repeatedly made clear his concern about Italy's new-found Euroscepticism (called by the government 'Eurorealism'). At the beginning of January 2002, after months of fractious criticism from his own colleagues, Ruggiero resigned in dismay. Berlusconi immediately appointed himself Foreign Secretary, the head of Italian diplomacy: 'Who better than me?' he asked journalists, who obviously didn't offer any alternative suggestions.

By then, even Gianni Agnelli appeared edgy. He had consistently defended Berlusconi in the run-up to the election, rounding on foreign journalists who used phrases like 'banana republic'. Once 'his man' in the government, Ruggiero, had been humiliated, Agnelli said: 'Banana republic? Italy doesn't even have bananas. All we've got here are prickly pears.'

Italy, it was obvious, was subtly changing. The best barometers of the change, as always, were the politicised plaques, memorials and graffiti. Throughout 2001 there was clearly a new symbolism emerging as an assiduous renaming of streets began (one to Benito Mussolini in Catania, two to Giorgio Almirante, the historic leader of Italy's post-war Fascism). In Friuli, in the north-east of the country, a plaque bearing the Fascist slogan outside a secondary school was restored to its former glory: 'Believe, Obey, Combat' it read. In Benevento, the name of the central square, Piazza Matteotti (Matteotti was a socialist MP murdered by Fascists in 1924) was changed to Santa Sofia. All the mayors responsible for the new urban appearances were from the ranks of the National Alliance. As was the mayor from Latina (a town built from scratch by Mussolini), who decided to replace the marble plaque on the town's modern bell-tower (it had been removed after the Second World War): 'Peasants and rural people should look at this tower which dominates the plain and which is a symbol of the power of Fascism'. It all reminded me of a paragraph from Moravia's *The Conformist*:

At one street-corner a group of people had put up a long ladder at the corner of a building, and a man who had climbed to the top of the ladder was hammering vigorously at a stone which bore the name of the regime. Someone said, with a laugh, to Marcello: 'There are Fascist signs everywhere . . . it'll take years to efface them all.' 'It certainly will,' said Marcello.

Little by little the landscape of the country was altering. The changing of the political guard didn't imply only new policies, it implied the complete overhaul of every institution: the magistrature, the television, the street names, the syllabus. Even the dignified President of the Republic, Carlo Azeglio Ciampi (in what could only be interpreted as an attempt to maintain the fragile sense of national unity), said publicly that the '*Ragazzi di Salò*', those Fascists who fought the civil war to the bitter end in 1945, at least had the merit of fighting for a unified Italy. He was rounded on by the left, who accused the former resistance fighter of offering yet another *sdoganamento* ('customs-clearance') for Fascism.

The strange thing is that, despite the hysteria, the government of 'black shirts' and 'white collars' isn't about the return of Fascism. It's about something much more subtle, much more amorphous. It's about a style of government based upon crude power, using as its motto the old Sicilian proverb *potere è meglio di fottere* ('power is better than screwing'). It's nothing to do with ideology, with Fascism or anti-Communism, it's simply about power and realpolitik. One of Mussolini's political slogans used to be 'ideas not men'. It expressed the idea that policies were more important than the politicians. Contemporary Italian politics, though, is the inversion of the slogan. For all the talk about Fascists and Communists, it's really about 'men not ideas'. The culture is one of *clientelismo*, the habit of mutual backscratching. A politician sits at the top of his pyramid of clients, looking after their needs as he tries to out-manoeuvre opponents. It's an organic supply-and-demand of favours that, given the size of the public-sector work force and the reach of political appointments, runs through all levels of society. A new government implies a clean sweep through the ranks of RAI, it implies new magistrates and new teachers, all chosen upon the basis of their personal allegiances.

That's why any notion that one might voluntarily remove a conflict of interests is anathema. It goes counter to every notion of realpolitik. Days before the General Election, Berlusconi had melodramatically signed his 'contract with the Italian people'. He promised that within one hundred days of entering office, he would resolve the anomaly of a politician whose telecommunications empire dominated domestic broadcasting. Eight months later, and nothing had been done. The conflict of interests had become blatant that autumn when an American offer of 800 billion lire for a 49% interest in the RAI infrastructure was bluntly turned down by the government's Minister for Communications. As soon as the lucrative deal fell through, Mediaset shares soared on the stock exchange.

In fact, rather than resolving the RAI-Mediaset conflict by selling Mediaset, Berlusconi was instead attempting to colonise RAI. One Sunday afternoon in December 2001, *Quelli Che Il Calcio* (a football programme on RAI 2) ran a satirical sketch about the 'post-Fascist' Minister for Communications, Maurizio Gasparri. As everyone knew, Gasparri was about to sack the head of RAI (present in the studio) because he represented the old-guard appointed by the former left-wing government. As soon as the sketch (a very gentle parody about political interference in television) was finished, the Minister for Communications unintentionally proved the point. He was immediately on the telephone, his booming voice interrupting the live broadcast of the country's favourite television programme. The studio fell silent, everyone looked nervously at their shoes as the Minister berated them. He didn't, he said, approve of the wrong kind of satire, and he hinted darkly that RAI should have known better since he, Gasparri, was now effectively its boss. That is just one, mundane example of Italy's 'vertical' structure, in which power drips imperiously from above, rather than surges from below.

January 2002. I was in a bar watching a late-night football match. In one corner I recognised a blond guy I had taught almost two years before. Marco was one of those silent types who very rarely spoke in the lecture hall. When he did, it was normally a memorable put-down to one of his fellow students. He wasn't superior, just very studious, a little sarcastic and aloof. I liked him a lot, though I didn't really know him.

'Zio Tobia!' He called me over to his table and I sat down opposite him. 'Are you still writing that book?' he asked.

'I'm afraid so,' I replied.

'What are you writing about now?'

'The government.'

He looked at me and went quiet. Then he began shaking his head, grimacing. '*Ma tu, non ti rendi conto*?' he hissed. ('Don't you get it?' said as if he were accusing me of something.) And he was accusing me of something, however indirectly. 'You foreign journalists are so facetious and condescending. You only write about how terrible our country is.'

'But I'm only repeating what you all tell me. And it's true, it is terrible.'

'I know. But that's exactly why you foreign journalists fuck me off. You come here and laugh at the farce, not realising that for us it is a tragedy. You come here with your British patriotism and laugh at us peasants before going back home. If you want to stay here, you mustn't laugh anymore,' he said. 'This is a terrible country and Berlusconi is a tragedy for Italy. It's all an unbelievable tragedy. Italians are *coglioni* [pillocks] who elect the first person they think will make them richer. Berlusconi only speaks to the *pancia* [the belly]. But you mustn't laugh about anything anymore. You must write that there's another side to Italy.' He was exceptionally angry, tears rolling down his cheeks as he prodded his finger against my chest. 'You must write that there's a completely different country which hates Berlusconi and all his corrupt *giannizzeri* [flunkeys]. Life for us will be very difficult from now on. You don't understand, but you will . . .'

We sat in silence for five minutes, ignoring each other and just pretending to watch the game. He was right, of course. By then, after three years abroad, I longed to go back home. I was sickened not just by what was going on, but by the acceptance of it all.

Saturated by Mediaset television, everyone seemed indifferent. I, by contrast, was feeling vitriolic and very foreign. It didn't even feel like I was living in a democracy anymore. Marco, though, somehow knew that I would be staying, and he knew that there was still 'a different country', one outside the reach of *Il Cavaliere*, which I had ignored.

He caught me looking at him and began to apologise. 'Excuse me, Zio Tobia,' he said finally. 'Excuse me. It's just that Berlusconi brings so much shame upon our country, and you mustn't add to that. You must write about the other country, about the resistance.'

'I will. I promise, Marco, that's what I'll write next. And I didn't mean it's all terrible here. I love it here, it's just that . . .'

'It's terrible,' he nodded, smiling.

10

I Morti

Now that I have seen what a civil war is I know that, if one day it finishes, everyone will have to ask themselves 'And what to do with the fallen? Why did they die?' I wouldn't know what to reply. At least not now. It doesn't seem to me that the others know. Maybe only the dead know, and only for them is the war really over . . .

  Cesare Pavese

Writing a book, however obliquely, about Silvio Berlusconi is rather like going to Britain to write about hooliganism or like going to Ireland to write about 'the troubles': there's a danger that, as you try to explain a tragic phenomenon, a very nasty niche of the country comes to obscure all else. Admittedly, having given myself the task of taking the temperature of Italy's body politic, I couldn't then fudge the issue and pretend that that body wasn't suffering from a very serious and unappealing infection. And yet, identifying Berlusconi entirely with his country is an unnecessary compliment to the former, and definitely an unkind slur on the latter. Italy is not a single entity but rather a country of two opposing sides. The country is, in fact, probably as divided now as it was during the civil wars of the 1940s or the 1970s. There's the same visceral loathing between two halves of the country. This mutual hatred and disdain might not have overspilled into another civil war, but there is once again a very obvious civil stand-off in which one half of the country looks with absolute contempt at the other. That cleavage within the country is as obvious to Italians as it is to a foreigner. As Angelo Panebianco, a journalist for *Corriere della Sera*, wrote in January 2002:

[There is] a type of 'battle between civilisations'. On one side are those who retain that the current government is a sort of infection, a repository of wickedness and illegality, and on the other are those for whom that same infection can be seen in the relationship between the political left and the magistrature. The division between the two Italys is radical. It's a division about values and principles which cancels any possibility of communication and of compromise . . .[1]

I don't suppose that in the preceding chapters I have particularly disguised my own position as regards that division. Yet in writing almost exclusively about that 'wickedness and illegality' I recognise that I have narrated only one, small part of the country. There obviously exists, within the physiology of the peninsula, a completely different heart: one disdainful of oligarchical football presidents, critical of corruption and unbounded construction, dismissive of a Prime Minister who now controls six out of the seven national television channels. It's hard to underline the passion and vehemence with which they talk: some begin to cry, others bang their fists on the table. Most, like Marco, look around at their fellow countrymen (the other half) and spit out the word *coglioni*, 'pillocks'.

Throughout the spring of 2002, the stakes between the two halves of the country were exponentially raised. For the first time, commentators started talking about the 'regime' and the 'resistance'. In January, at the opening ceremony for the new judicial year, the *Procuratore Generale* of Milan and former head of the Clean Hands pool, Francesco Saverio Borrelli, took the microphone. The reduction of protective escorts, the attacks on the magistrature, the new laws which interfered with on-going court cases – all, said Borrelli, carried the stamp of an authoritarian regime. He urged his colleagues and the Italian public in general to 'resist, resist, resist' Berlusconi's government. Having invoked the Resistance, he then also invoked Italians' brave First World War defiance on the Piave front. His rhetoric was warmly applauded, and magistrates removed their ermine and red robes to mourn in black ones instead. Gerardo D'Ambrosio, the Milanese *Procuratore*, echoed the sentiments. About Berlusconi's government, he said ominously: 'This is the night of Italian democracy.'

A month later, on the tenth anniversary of the start of the

Clean Hands revolution, a huge rally was held by the legal lobby in Milan. 40,000 took part, holding candles for justice, carrying banners demanding that the law be 'equal for all'. The crowd was mostly middle-aged and middle-class. It was one of a number of spontaneous protests that had emerged across the country. They were called *girotondi* (ring-a-ring-a-roses); they were simple gatherings of Italian citizens who held hands around buildings whose independence appeared threatened by the new government (mostly courtrooms and television studios).

The response from the regime was swift. Two days after the Milan rally, a bomb exploded in the middle of the night on one of the streets outside the Home Office in Rome. Mopeds were blown across the road, green plastic skips were torn apart. Berlusconi, linking the attack with the gathering of the legal lobby in Milan and the snowballing opposition movement, said that the left should 'lower the tones' of its meetings, because terrorism was the result of incautious criticisms. Other government ministers said that the phrases used by the legal lobby were 'words of lead', an obvious suggestion that any criticism of the government would be construed as terrorist talk akin to the *anni di piombo*. At the same time, the regime began deploying its one, invincible argument to defend the government's incursions into all corners of the state. Berlusconi was democratically elected, and therefore his actions were the expression of the wishes of the people. He was – like Thatcher before him – a beacon of democracy, audaciously attacking left-wing cartels within the media, the unions and the judiciary. An equally important weakness of the resistance was the fact that, after a decade of exceptionally complicated legal wrangling, most people outside the legal lobby dreaded hearing the word 'justice'. It was Berlusconi's good fortune to be involved in court cases so complicated and so boring that most Italians switched off from the debates and switched on their televisions instead.

Television, in fact, became the next theatre of the encounter between the regime and the resistance. When the conflict of interests bill was finally introduced to parliament, politicians once again screamed abuse at each other. 'Shame' or 'Pinocchio' chanted the left, standing and shouting like a group of football fans before abandoning the parliament in a walk-out. The tone of the editor of *Oggi* was more sober: 'This law on the conflict of interests isn't honourable. It's laughable. In fact, it's disgusting.' The main cause for complaint, days after Berlusconi had appointed a new 'advisory commission' for RAI, was the bill's second article. It stated that 'mere ownership' of a business wasn't sufficient to preclude taking up governmental office. The conflict of interests existed, effectively, only for those concerned with the day-to-day running of the business. Berlusconi wasn't even subject to the legislation.

Days later, Roberto Benigni, the Oscar-winning actor and comedian, made a live appearance on the closing night of the San Remo music festival. Millions of people watched Benigni's scatty, clever performance. He was part-clown, part-sage as, quoting Dante, he began taunting the government. He ridiculed Berlusconi and his supposed resolution of the conflict of interests. 'Please Berlusconi,' urged the actor, 'please do something that, when we go to bed at night, will make us all proud to be Italians.' The implication was that *Il Presidente* had prompted only shame, rather than pride, amongst most citizens.

By April, it was becoming obvious that criticisms of that sort would no longer be allowed. When on an official visit to Bulgaria, Berlusconi began listing the journalists who he wanted to see sacked from RAI. He mentioned three in particular who had been 'criminal' in their use of the state channels. All three – Daniele Luttazzi, Michele Santoro and Enzo Biagi – had cast doubt upon his integrity in the previous year's election. 'The precise duty of the new management,' said Berlusconi, 'is to make sure that this doesn't happen again.' It's difficult to exaggerate the impact of those comments: from Sofia, the man who doubled as both Prime Minister and Foreign Secretary, someone who owned three TV channels and had just appointed the management committee for the other three, was publicly listing inconvenient journalists who should be sacked. The mention of Enzo Biagi was particularly odd. A hugely popular, owlish man in his mid-80s, Biagi presents a ten-minute evening slot on RAI 1 debating the issues of the day. His only crime had been to interview Roberto Benigni on the eve of the 2001 election, allowing the comic to make a few jokes at Berlusconi's expense.

In an article on the Sunday after Berlusconi's outburst, the normally measured Biagi made a comparison with Hitler on *Corriere della Sera*'s front page. Even *Il Foglio*, a bizarre newspaper which is in part funded by Berlusconi's wife, called the Prime Minister's comments 'a political error and an abuse of power', and conceded that Berlusconi 'seriously risks compromising his political career'. Another of the threatened journalists, Michele Santoro, opened his weekly programme on RAI 2 by singing *Bella Ciao*, an old song from the Resistance.

By the end of April all the new directors of the RAI channels had been appointed. Only RAI 3 remained in the hands of the left-wing opposition. RAI 1 was headed by Fabrizio Del Noce, a *Forza Italia* stalwart; RAI 2 went to Antonio Marano (Northern League). The news programmes on those channels were to be headed by Clemente Mimun (*Forza Italia*) and Mauro Mazza (National Alliance). The sister of the leader of one of the Catholic parties in the Pole of Liberties coalition was given responsibility for all local news. Even the most pessimistic hadn't expected Italy's notorious spoils system to be used so ruthlessly. Umberto Eco, days later, wrote about the only type of resistance left: 'To a new form of government,' he wrote in the pages of *La Repubblica*, 'a new form of political reply. This really would be an opposition . . .' It was the kind of proposal that, from the outside, seems surreal: Eco was proposing a veto of all the products advertised on Mediaset channels:

One doesn't reply to a government-business with flags and ideas but by aiming at its weakest point: money. If the government-business then shows itself sensitive to this protest, even its electors will realise that it's nothing more than a government-business which survives only as long as its leader continues to make money.[2]

But by far the most serious and sad conflict was over Article 18.

It was, in some ways, Article 18 that had started Italy's cycle of violence more than three decades ago. Guaranteeing various work-place rights, Article 18 was written and passed in 1969. That legislation was perhaps one of the reasons for reactionaries to plot the brutal bombing at Piazza Fontana. Now, years later, a sinister symmetry emerged: the attempt to repeal the legislation caused more terrorism, and further loss of life.

Marco Biagi, a university professor who had written the government's White Book of proposed changes to employment law, was shot and killed at point-blank range as he returned to his house in Bologna. The scene under the arches outside his house presented a familiar picture: puddles of blood, the Red Brigade's five-pointed star etched onto the wall, numbered cards propped up on the asphalt where the bullets had been found. It was the one side of the resistance that everyone, especially those in the peaceful opposition, had dreaded. The killing was claimed, in a 26-page manifesto sent to an internet news agency, by the BR-PCC, the 'Red Brigades–Combatant Communist Party'.

'After such a terrible event,' said the speaker of parliament's lower house, 'we need to rediscover a spirit of concord.' Instead, the murder brought all the poison of Italian politics to the surface. Berlusconi has said that the killing was the result of 'the chain of hate and lies' aimed at himself and his government. 'I won't yield to the pistol and the *piazza*,' he later said. 'Democracy is being blackmailed,' replied an editorial in the left-wing *La Repubblica*.

Many, in fact, claimed the government was partly to blame for the murder: in reducing protective escorts, it had left one of its most controversial figures dangerously exposed. Nor was the danger unexpected. Only one week before, Berlusconi's magazine, *Panorama*, had cited an intelligence leak which suggested that Biagi was high on the terrorists' hit-list. 'My husband was terrified,' Biagi's widow said. 'He knew he was a target.' She bitterly refused the offer of a state funeral in protest at the way her husband had been abandoned to his fate.

To many, then, the death seemed almost foretold. The Employment Secretary Roberto Maroni, Biagi's boss, said wistfully after the murder: 'I can't say I'm surprised.' 'It's an endless chain of blood,' said Romano Prodi, one of Biagi's closest friends. 'It's a long obscure line which has been with us for many years.' In fact, in 1999, another governmental advisor on labour reform, Massimo D'Antona, was also killed (by, it now emerges, the same pistol which killed Biagi). As always, conspiracy theorists went to work, especially when the man investigating that previous murder was himself found dead days after Biagi was killed. It looked like suicide, but many had their suspicions.

One of the biggest unions, CGIL, duly organised a protest – against both the repeal of Article 18 and against terrorism – in Rome. Two million turned out. Red flags made the Circo Massimo, site of the Roman chariot races, look like an ocean full of masts and sails. The flags bobbed up and down in the sun, billowing and then going slack. The city even sounded like a marina: that sound of cloth twisting and clapping in the wind. 'We are here to join the fight against terrorism and to defend our rights,' said Sergio Cofferati, leader of the union.

I spent the afternoon wandering across the capital. Every hilly street was crammed with flags and banners against Berlusconi. Small bands played music on street corners. Kids kicked footballs from pavement to pavement. People were passing round flasks of wine. Everyone had their own theory of what was going on. 'Italy,' one wizened old man told me, 'has always been like this: one third ruled by the Vatican, one third by foreign powers, and one third by our home-bred tyrants. But the reason we have tyrants is the reason we survive them: we're completely lawless.'

One shop-owner told me how he hated these protesters: 'I'm from the National Alliance and I've got absolutely nothing in common with those idiots,' he said. 'I think Article 18 should be repealed. Of course it should. Here it's impossible to sack anyone. It's like having marriage without a divorce. A lot of what the government wants to change is for the better: it wants an elected president, chosen by the people not by parliament. It wants to reform the judiciary and RAI. All that is fine. It's just that,' he began rocking his hands in the imploring praying position, 'it's just that if there was one man in the entire country you wouldn't trust to reform all those things, the one man you shouldn't let near the whole project, it's Berlusconi!'

On the train back to Parma I read Shelley. Writing about the long history of Italian tyranny, he spoke about the 'viper's paralysing venom' (the snake was the symbol of the Visconti family). 'Lawless slaveries' and 'savage lust,' he wrote, trample 'our columned cities into dust.' It's much the same language that the country's left wing is now using: apocalyptic and pessimistic, convinced that democracy is in peril. Is it a hyperbole to say Berlusconi is a dictator? Is '*Forzism*' really a twenty-first century, televisual version of Fascism?

It's certainly true that the authority of the boss is unquestionable. He is above the law and criticism of him will be punished. Protest marchers will be dispersed by bullet and baton. Magistrates who rock the boat are themselves threatened with prosecution. Six out of seven channels of communication are dominated by the government. What passes for programming is really propaganda or else cheap pornography. The outcome of elections, at least in certain regions, seems certain to be levered in the government's favour. Any diversity in Italy, any criticism of *Il Presidente*, is now identified with terrorism. It is seen as an incitement to violence and will be duly quashed by the authority of the state. It reminds me of Primo Levi's definition of democracy: 'Dissension, diversity, the grain of salt and mustard are needed,' he wrote; 'Fascism does not want them, forbids them.' The trouble is that there's something slightly absurd about accusing Berlusconi of being a Fascist. It's ridiculous to say that Italy isn't a democracy. Then again, it seems equally ridiculous to say that it *is*.

Il Presidente is such a unique political model, he's so *sui generis*, that it's impossible to compare him with anyone else. Perhaps only a fictional creation captures the idea. Shortly after all the TV channels fell into Berlusconi's hands, there was a satirical email doing the rounds. It succinctly expressed the way in which Berlusconi has become the Orwellian Big Brother:

Hi, my name's Mario Rossi and I live in Milan in a building built by the

Prime Minister. I work in a company who's main share-holder is the Prime Minister. My car insurance is provided by the Prime Minister. I stop off every day to buy a newspaper owned by the Prime Minister. In the afternoon I go shopping in a supermarket owned by the Prime Minister. In the evening I watch the Prime Minister's TV, where the films (often produced by the Prime Minister) are continuously interrupted by adverts made by the advertising company of the Prime Minister. Then I get bored and go surfing on the internet using the Prime Minister's service provider. Often I look at the football results, because I'm a fan of the Prime Minister's football team. On Sunday I stay at home and read a book from the Prime Minister's publishing house . . . obviously, he's governing exclusively in my interests, not his own . . .

The only other useful comparison for the bizarre political model is a religious one. It's a comparison which Berlusconi himself has often made, comparing himself to either Moses or Jesus. That's exactly what watching him feels like: he can be caring, gentle, smiling. Then suddenly he will become stern, strict and critical of all around him. He seems to think he has a monopoly on moral guidance; he's followed by millions of the faithful, some because they believe him, others because they might need him. He appears to own the land we walk on, and to watch our every waking move. Shortly after the Euro arrived, I received a currency-converter in the post with a letter from *Il Presidente* saying 'Dear friend, our dear old Lira is to be substituted . . .' It had been sent to everyone in Italy, 'with the most cordial good wishes'. Everywhere you look, you realise that Berlusconi is involved. It reminds me of those hymns about how 'The Good Lord Made It All'. You can't escape, anywhere on the peninsula, his presence and his produce. Everyone is agreed that he's a prophet, only as yet no one knows if he's a false one or not.

Late that spring, I was back watching football. It was an international match and the tinny trumpets were rasping out the national anthem, the *Inno di Mameli*. For some reason I found it intensely moving. I sang the melodramatic words with the rest of the stadium. They seemed to express the immense suffering and bravery in the country: 'We're ready for death! We're ready for death! Italy has called!'

I realise I have become something I never thought possible: patriotic and proud about being an adopted Italian. In more honest moments, I realise that I might never quite be able to leave the country. That longing to leave, and the inability to pull yourself away from the *bel casino*, the 'fine mess', has been written about for centuries. Using the usual prostitution metaphor, one of the country's most important patriots, Massimo D'Azeglio, wrote: 'I can't live outside Italy, which is strange because I continually get angry with Italian ineptitude, envies, ignorance and laziness. I'm like one of the people who falls in love with a prostitute.' That, in fact, is precisely the feeling of living here: it is infuriating and endlessly irritating, but in the end it is almost impossible to pull yourself away. It's not just that everything is *troppo bello*, 'too beautiful', or that food and conversation are so good. It's that life seems less exciting outside Italy, the emotions seem muted. Stendhal wrote that the feeling one gets from living in Italy is 'akin to that of being in love', and it's easy to understand what he meant. There's the same kind of enchantment and serenity, occasionally insecurity and sadness. And writing about the country's sharp pangs of jealousy and paranoia, Stendhal knew that they exist precisely because the country's 'joys are far more intense and more lasting'. You can't have the one without the other.

I feel even more tied to Parma than to Italy. The city is one of the capitals of Italian culture, from cuisine to classical music. It is a place of such aggressive political opinions, coupled with incredible generosity, that I can't imagine wanting to live anywhere else. Giovanni Guareschi, the writer of the 'Don Camillo' stories, proudly wrote about his fellow *Parmigiani*:

Political passion often reaches a disturbing intensity, and yet these people are highly attractive and hospitable and generous and have a highly developed sense of humour. It must be the sun, a terrible sun which beats on their brains during the summer, or perhaps it is the fog, a heavy fog which oppresses them during the winter.[3]

That mention of humour reminds me that I spend large amounts of my days laughing. Wit, in the sense of both humour and intelligence, must be the defining characteristic of most *Parmigiani*. Never is there a dull moment because everyone is a natural raconteur. The humour is exceptionally surreal and intelligent, perhaps because everything that goes on is so incredibly complicated and byzantine.

Singing the words to that national anthem – 'we're ready for death' – I noticed that there's one, admittedly morbid, theme which touches all the aspects of Italy which have interested or infuriated me over the course of four years (the exquisite culture, the excruciating bureaucracy, all the style and the superstitions): *I Morti*. If you spend long enough in the country, you begin to notice that there's something very unique about death in Italy. I noticed it during my first few days in Italy. It was during a question about birthdays in a bar (the conversation, as it often is, was about horoscopes). Someone asked me when mine was, and I told him the date. In Britain, sharing a birthday with 'All Souls' had never raised eyebrows. Here, within seconds, everyone was frowning, backing off or else laughing, slapping me on the back and telling me I was a bit *sfigato*, 'jinxed'. My birthday, I was told, was the day of *I Morti*, 'the day of the dead'.

That initial wariness about a date of birth was, I supposed, the normal suspicion about ever mentioning death. To talk about future extinction is not the done thing, and is thought to bring 'the evil eye'. If you do venture in that direction, it's wise to 'make the horns' with index finger and pinky, pointing to the ground, as a sign of superstitious courtesy. In the south, many even wear an imitation chilli-pepper on bracelets or necklaces, the curling ends of the peppercorn producing those 'horns' which ward off evil spirits and therefore, for the time being, death. Given that wariness, someone born on the day of the dead is obviously thought to be a close cousin of the Grim Reaper and bound to bring bad luck.

Like the political mysteries and the Catholic miracles, when it comes to death there's still a sense of magical intervention: we don't know who's pulling the strings, but we know we're only puppets. A superstitious bracelet (or the vulgar version: touching the testicles) will ward off the bad luck in the same way mages and astrologers, the staple personalities of Italian television, will tell us which numbers to put down for the lottery. It might seem absurd to a modern rationalist, but there really is a belief in what Fellini called Italy's 'ancient cults'. It's half paganism, half Catholicism. I remember once going into the cathedral at Siena and seeing lines of motorbike helmets hung up on a wall. In front of them were candles, dutifully being lit by the sort of young men you don't normally see in churches: tough, tattooed, pierced. I asked one what he was doing, and he explained that the orange helmet on the top left of the collection was his. He had had a particularly gruesome crash a few weeks ago, and had come here to hang up his helmet in front of the Madonna with the rest. It was, he explained, a way of giving thanks for the fact that he had cheated death. It hung there like a modern, financial sacrifice to the deity in gratitude for his life.

When death does come, the rituals of mourning and commemoration are incredible: touching and communal in a way unthinkable elsewhere. I'm normally surprised by the collective amnesia, by the speed with which recent history is brushed under the carpet, but when it comes to *I Morti* the memory in Italy is a very long one. Every city or village feels like Shelley's 'widowed' Genoa where the 'moonlight spells ancestral epitaphs'. From every direction the faces of the dead stare back at you, either in sculptured busts or photographs. Every country, of course, has its memorials, but only in Italy is there such a sense that you're walking in someone else's footsteps. Perhaps it's because of the Catholic notion of purgatory, of companionship with and prayers for the dead; or else because, especially in the south, there's a kind of ancestor cult. Almost every alleyway seems to have its own plaque or memorial; I've often paused to look up at them, only for someone to stop and explain who the local dignitary was and explain the highs and lows of their lives. It's that communal, public side of death which is different. In Sicily especially, but all over the country, you see hand-written notices up on the street corners of parishes: 'The Gambino family thanks everyone who has been close to them in their time of mourning.'

If you open the back pages of Italy's oldest newspaper, the *Gazzetta di Parma*, dozens of faces stare back at you: these are *I Morti*, the dead. Some have passed away recently; others have had their photograph put there by relatives or friends on the anniversary of their death. In many other newspapers, national or local, the obituaries section runs on for as many pages as do the financial or sporting sections. When someone from the editorial team of a television channel or a newspaper dies, or even one of their relatives, there are often long threnodies for the following days and weeks.

Funerals themselves are spectacular. When there's a particularly famous passing-away, the funeral will always, without fail, be televised. Flags and fists are raised, huge crowds applaud coffins. It doesn't matter if the deceased is an actor or an anonymous victim of a sadly spectacular murder, the funeral is more than just a send-off, it's a pageant. Millions of viewers watch the catwalk of politicians who come to pay their respects. The coffin is open, the cameras rolling, microphones are placed near sobbing mothers. In more remote parts of Italy there's even someone called the *prefica*, the hired female mourner who guarantees that the wailing will be at a respectable pitch. The spectacle of death is especially marked in football. At every Roma home match, on the southern terrace of the stadium, there's a banner to supporters who have died that week, or even one to those who died on that day years ago. It's hard to imagine something so noble happening on the terraces at a British football ground. Many cemeteries are covered with football flags and scarves. 'W Parma' is often scrawled on the city walls (the 'W' being *viva*); or else 'M Juve' (*Morte* to Juventus).

But the dead aren't just seen, they are also 'heard'. The point about hearing the dead is that in Italy words are habitually put into the mouths of *I Morti*, as if there really were voices from the grave. It's part of the uncanny continuum that happens between Italy's life and death. In one cemetery in Naples, after the first, extraordinary championship won with Diego Maradona in the

1980s, someone wrote graffiti in the local dialect: *Guagliò, che ve site persi!* ('Kid, what you've missed!'). Legend has it that a few weeks later the reply from the cemetery, scrawled on another wall, arrived: 'I didn't miss a thing!'

It might simply have been an idle piece of graffiti, but 'voices from the grave' is Italians' favourite poetic genre. *The Spoon River Anthology* is, by a very long way, the best-selling poetry book in Italy. With its voices from the other side, the dead seem to be heard as they recount their simple, short lives. (When Pino Pinelli was finally laid to rest in 1980 – after his body had again been re-exhumed and examined for evidence – he was buried in the Anarchist section of the graveyard at Carrara, with an inscription from *Spoon River*.) *Spoon River* was also the cause of yet another nickname I had been given (to go alongside *Zio Tobia* and *Il Calvinista*). At the beginning of one academic year, a couple of students referred to me as *Il Suonatore*, the 'player' or 'musician'. They never explained why, and by the end of the year the whole class were happily giving me the bemusing epithet. It was eventually explained to me that Fabrizio De André, the plaintive Genovese singer, once issued an album of songs which were 'liberal' translations from the *Spoon River* anthology. The last song on the album is called *Il Suonatore Jones*:

> Libertà l'ho vista svegliarsi
> ogni volta che ho suonato,
> per un fruscio di ragazze
> a un ballo,
> per un compagno ubriaco.

(The English by comparison sounds rather dull: 'I've seen liberty wake up/ every time I have played/ for a rustle of girls/ at a dance/ for a drunken friend'.) His life finishes 'in nettled fields . . . with a broken flute and a raucous laugh and so many memories . . .' The fact that students (who all year had shown no inclination to read any poetry) had however devoured *Spoon River* and all its musical adaptations, said a lot about their aesthetic tastes.

Even Italy's fourth estate – its bureaucracy – has its own way of doing death. I've often heard stories of people who have mistakenly been 'killed' in the bureaucratic system. It's nothing sinister, simply the usual gremlins in the system. Since existence within the bureaucracy is often more important than being physically alive, it's actually quite useful (if you're behind on your income tax), but more serious if you're expecting to receive a pension. The alternative to bureaucratic elimination is to keep someone artificially, bureaucratically alive. It's a sort of resuscitation, in which if a relative is still alive in the bureaucratic sense, there can be all sorts of tax benefits for you (lower bills on the utilities depending on 'residence'; the number of houses you own and so on). For years I paid bills that were addressed to someone who had died years previously. The practice is vaguely morbid, but is very common. Because of the malfunctioning bureaucracy, until recently hundreds of thousands of dead Italians (the 'dead electors') were making their posthumous political opinions felt. Since they were still 'alive' in the annals, they could still (or their relatives could still) cast their vote.

The accommodation of *I Morti* has always been a major architectural event. Tombs and sepulchres and catacombs have always been ostentatious. They even became the country's top tourist attractions. The beginning of the Via Appia, the road which heads out of the capital towards Brindisi, used to be the chosen place of Romans for a Sunday stroll, there to enjoy and admire new mausolea which lined both sides of the road. A vital part of the Grand Tour was to search out the tombs of famous poets (despite the fact that many, including Virgil's and Nero's, were probably fakes). Dante's tomb at Ravenna is still an important stop-off for modern travellers, and the catacombs in Palermo are probably more visited than any other site in Sicily.

November 1, the day before *I Morti*, is another national holiday, the day on which it's traditional to visit ancestors in their cemeteries. (Towards the end of October bones suddenly start appearing in the Parma patisserie. The day of *I Morti* is an opportunity not just to mourn, of course; it's also culinary tradition. The bones, pastry-coated with garish cream, represent the bones of the dead.) As every Italian schoolchild knows from reading the country's most famous poem, 'The Sepulchres', Napoleonic law was responsible for Italy's breathtaking cemeteries. His *codici* decreed that burials had to take place outside the city walls. The result across Europe was the phenomenon of vast, out-of-town graveyards. Unlike Britain, where burial was more usually within church grounds, huge suburbs for the dead grew up outside Italian cities. They are the country's most beautiful, serene sites.

In Genoa, for example, the cemetery of Staglieno is built on a hill towards the north-east of the city. On November 1 I went along as a tourist. Since thousands of Genovese were visiting the cemetery, the florist outside must have made half his annual salary within a few hours. There were four trucks selling bouquets to the queues of mourners. The cemetery's centrepiece is an arcaded square which leads you to the pantheon. The inscription in Latin above the entrance reads: 'To the glory of God and to the memory of the illustrious *Genovesi*.' It's at Staglieno that Giuseppe Mazzini is buried, next to his mother, in a low, leafy temple. The inscriptions are political rather than religious. Today there are about two dozen fresh bouquets laid out. David Lloyd George, in 1922, left the inscription: 'To the champion of the oppressed people and the prophet of European brotherhood.' (The irony is that Mazzini, like Dante and many others now lauded as political or poetic heroes, died exiled from his city. He was, at the time of his death, living under the assumed name of John Brown in Pisa.) In the English part of the cemetery there's the gratitude of the Empire to Italians in the Great War: 'The British Empire will always remember, together with those of her children who have fallen for her, those of Italy who gave their lives during the Great War of 1914–1918.'

Genoa is a grandiose example. The following year I went to one of the smaller rural cemeteries outside Parma. Because it was for less illustrious souls, it appeared like a complex of giant filing cabinets. *I Morti* are slotted into place, and then rotated according to age and rent in deep walls that are often three or four metres high.

The funeral itself involves plasterers sealing off the end of the opening to the file, called the *loculo*, the 'niche'. It might sound soulless, but it isn't: the dead can still be visited, you know where to find them. Almost all the headstones (in reality, the edge of the filing cabinet) carry photographs. On the day of *I Morti* you go and visit your ancestors, and can even look at your own slot, already booked in the family's allocated space. The point is that the dead are on display. Even in death, there's a careful presentation, and even the rigid hierarchies of Italian society survive. The more grand the family, the greater the burial space. Not content with a filing cabinet spot, some build their own temples or shrine. It's the ultimate in posthumous one-upmanship: 'Look what I built before I died.' The cost of marble slabs, arranged to form a temple about the size of a garden shed, often mean that people save for decades just to have the appropriately grand resting place. Silvio Berlusconi has even built his own mausoleum in the grounds of his Arcore estate. It's designed along the lines of an Etruscan necropolis. Inside are 36 burial slots, reserved for members of his family and his business and political partners.

Before Italy became, for foreigners, a symbol of the vitality of life (the Edwardian stereotype), it was a symbol of the opposite: the land of the dead or the dying. Henry James had called Venice 'the most beautiful of tombs'. 'Nowhere else,' he wrote, 'has the past been laid to rest with such tenderness, such a sadness of resignation and remembrance . . .' The other-worldly quality of the floating ghost-town of Venice meant that James saw it as a kind of Avalon, a place where bodies were carried in gondolas to their resting place:

. . . the little closed cabin of this perfect vehicle, the movement, the darkness and the plash, the indistinguishable swerves and twists, all the things you see and all the things you do feel – each dim recognition and obscure arrest is a possible throb of your sense of being floated to your doom . . . [4]

Italy's 'old age' made it the natural place for mourning writers to visit during and after the First World War. For Modernists it became imagined as a metaphoric mausoleum, a place where they could come to examine what it meant to be old and to die. James Joyce wrote 'The Dead' in Trieste. Thomas Mann's *Death in Venice*, in which 'the pale and lovely summoner' smiles and beckons man to his death, was just the most obvious example of the genre.

Given its civil wars, though, death in Italy is often more divisive than communal, and memorials and mourners are sometimes acutely politicised. On one of the walls in the main square in Bologna there's a collage of all the partisans from the city who died in the 1943–45 civil war. It's like looking at an auditorium of the fallen: a wall of hundreds of black and white faces watching you, almost defying you to challenge their political creed. There are often little vases of flowers left there, or else candles are lit. That in itself is enough to tell you where the political loyalties of the city lie. In fact, the odium between right and left, which became militarist in the 1970s, now finds its most acute expression in the bickering over the wording of memorials. A mile away, outside the station in Bologna, the clock is permanently stopped at 10.25. There was a move by the railway authorities recently to get the clock working again, but the plan was shelved because of a local outcry. 10.25 was the time at which the bomb ripped through the waiting room of the station in 1980, killing 85 people. A little later, revisionists wanted to etch the word 'Fascist' from the memorial to those who died; the move – either a worthy attempt to heal wounds, or else a rude attempt to whitewash history – was blocked by the city's (*Forza Italia*) mayor. It's like that monument in Pisa: 'Anarchist killed by police at an anti-Fascist rally': provocative as much as it is conciliatory.

Connected to the politicisation of death is its aestheticisation. Death in Italy has frequently had its aesthetic edge, especially in the country's terrorism. Non-Italian writers had hinted at the mesmerising quality of violence and terror – Yeats wrote of the 'terrible beauty'; Shelley about the 'tempestuous loveliness of terror' – but it was Umberto Eco who really analysed the politics of death, and thereby gave a political dimension to the ways in which Italian death and terrorism had become attractive and almost longed-for.

He discerned not only that death had become aestheticised and adored; he identified the necrophilia as profoundly Fascist:

> ... it's very elusive ... but there is one component by which Fascism is recognisable in its purest form, wherever it shows itself, knowing with absolute certainty that such a premise will bring The Fascism: it is the cult of death.[5]

The taste for killings and martyrs was, for Eco, Fascism in its purest form. The beautification of terrorism in Italy, perceived by generations of writers, was for him more telling than any professed political dimension. Fascism meant adoring and serving death, be it as the slayer or as the slain:

> To love death necrophilically is to say that it's beautiful to receive it and risk it, and that the most beautiful and saintly love is to distribute it ... This stench of death, this putrid need of death, one feels today in Italy [1981]. If that's what terrorism (in its deep, ancestrally 'squadrista' soul) wanted, it's got it ... [6]

Fascism, for Eco, was political nihilism: a desire for martyrdom, a servitude to death.

Related to that aestheticisation of death is the notion of a *bella morte*, of a 'beautiful death'. It's surely unique to Italy and certainly a strange adjective to use. We might say 'peaceful' or 'painful' death, but in Italy it would be 'beautiful' or 'ugly'. If you're arguing amongst southerners, one of the most brutal insults is to talk about their *mortacci*, their 'ugly dead'.

It is only now that I realise that 'beauty' as it's understood in Italy simply doesn't exist in English. A *bella morte* is a moral as much as aesthetic judgement: it implies that someone died in an elegant, righteous way, probably neither in poverty nor in pain. It doesn't, clearly, imply that the corpse was particularly attractive. Only now do I realise how wrong I have been. I used to think, when I first arrived here, that the Italian obsession with beauty was the negation of morality; that the beautification of everything and everyone was so obsessive that good and bad got left behind. Now, thinking about *bella morte*, I finally understand that the notion of beauty in Italy is a conflation of aesthetics and ethics. I finally understand that Burckhardt quotation, suggesting that Italians have 'outgrown the limits of morality and religion'. The beauty syndrome isn't the vanity and superficiality I thought it was; it's a means, much more nuanced than the moralising of northern Europe, to identify who someone is.

To say someone is ugly isn't only a physical judgement, it's a moral one. Ugliness implies in Italian repulsion, which isn't only an analysis of visual presentation. It's an analysis also of someone's worth, their 'goodness'. A *bell'uomo* isn't only a good-looker (literally a 'beautiful man'), he's also a 'good man', someone who is attractive as a person. Because the words 'good' and 'bad' are so rarely used, beauty is the litmus paper by which everyone is judged. It's more sophisticated than morality because, in some strange way, it is more comprehensive. A description of beauty covers more ground than goodness, it includes more characteristics; not just righteousness, but civility, dignity, stature and so on. *Bellissimo* isn't used just for appearances, but for *il gesto*, the 'gesture'. Someone doesn't do a 'good' deed, they do a 'beautiful' one. It's like the old Greek idea of *kaloskagathos*: beauty and goodness are, rather than mutually excluding opposites, actually the same thing.

Talking about immorality is thus irrelevant in Italy, because it sounds preachy and prescriptive. Every time left-wing politicians, foreign journalists and the public in general accuse Berlusconi of immorality his popularity ratings with the other half of the country soar off the scale. He actually benefits from shrill attacks and immoderate language about immorality. The funny thing is, though, that no one has ever accused him of being a *bell'uomo* – despite the fact that, for his age, he is looking suspiciously good. That in itself gives the true measure of Italian beauty: it contains a moral message.

Postscript

At the time of writing, many developments have already overtaken the events described in these pages. Pino Rauti has resigned as secretary of the Tricolour Flame neo-Fascist party. The new leader immediately pledged support to Berlusconi's Pole of Liberties. All those sentenced for the Piazza Fontana bomb remain at liberty, pending extradition and appeals. The Slaughter Commission has concluded its thirteen years of research and controversy-stoking.

Adriano Sofri remains in prison. His accomplice to the murder of Luigi Calabresi was re-arrested in spring 2002 once his anorexia was deemed cured, and then released when his illness deteriorated once more.

The riddle of television ownership is still unsolved. Rather than sell his own channels, Berlusconi has suggested the sell-off of RAI, effectively its privatisation. By now, every news programme on every channel will run two or three long, admiring items on *Il Presidente*. No critical voice can be heard.

The Pole of Liberties government has proposed the creation of a 'Clean Hands Commission' (a right-wing version of the Slaughter Commission) in order to establish the truth about *Tangentopoli*.

Padre Pio was made a saint in June 2002. A film about Roberto Calvi and P2, starring Rutger Hauer, was released and immediately banned on the grounds that it was libellous. The director declared: "We live in a country of blind, deaf mutes. I am bitter, disappointed, I'm almost ashamed to be Italian."

The Italian royal family, the Savoia (following a vote in the Senate of 235 votes to 19 in favour of their return) are on the brink of re-entering Italian territory.

Berlusconi's Minister of the Interior has been forced to resign after calling Marco Biagi, the murdered government advisor, a *rompicoglioni*, a 'pain in the arse'. The Bossi-Fini Act has become law, meaning that all foreigners seeking work now have to be finger-printed. Another new law, called 'legitimate suspicion' means court cases can be moved elsewhere and begun from scratch if there's a 'suspicion' that the judge isn't sufficiently sympathetic to the accused.

In 2002 Parma football club, for the third year in four, reached the final of the *Coppa Italia*. The opposition was, obviously, the 'Old Lady' of Italian football, Juventus. Parma, the 'Cinderella' of the 'seven sisters', somehow won. After the game, I walked with thousands of delirious fans from the stadium towards Piazza Garibaldi under torrential rain, listening to songs about how vulgar the mothers of Juventus fans are. Everyone was carrying a blue-and-yellow flag or else letting off smoke flares; the out-riders for the procession had belts wrapped around their fists in case they saw anyone dressed in the Juventus black-and-white. At one point, a dozen of them raced down a narrow side alley, and a crowd sprinted over to watch the fight. In the main square, under the arches, four Bavarian men in shorts were playing Amazing Grace on three-metre long horns. It was all, as I was warned at the very outset, one *bel casino*. And standing there, drenched by the rain, I realised that I didn't want to live, couldn't even imagine living, anywhere else.

References

1 *Parole, Parole, Parole*

1 James T. Boulton, ed. *The Letters of D. H. Lawrence*, vol. 1 (Cambridge, 1979)
2 Carlo Levi, *Christ Stopped at Eboli* (London, 1947)
3 Marco Rogari, *Burocrazia Fuorilegge* (Milan, 2001)
4 Corrado Stajano, *L'Italia nichilista* (Milan, 1982)
5 Jacob Burckhardt, *The Civilization of the Renaissance in Italy* (London, 1990)
6 Luigi Barzini, *The Italians* (London, 1964)
7 Ernesto Galli della Loggia, *L'identità italiana* (Bologna, 1998)
8 Dante, *The Divine Comedy* (trans. Peter Dale, London, 1996)
9 Carlo Ginzburg, *The Judge and the Historian* (London, 1999)
10 Luigi Pirandello, "So It Is (If You Think So)" in *Six Characters in Search of an Author and Other Plays* (trans. Mark Musa, London, 1995)
11 Maurizio Dianese and Gianfranco Bettin, *La Strage* (Milan, 1999)
12 Pier Paolo Pasolini, *Lettere Luterane* (Turin, 1976)
13 Leonardo Sciascia, *L'Affaire Moro* (Milan, 1994)
14 Umberto Eco, *Sette anni di desiderio* (Milan, 1983)
15 Donald Sassoon, *Contemporary Italy* (New York, 1997)
16 Carlo Levi, *Le mille patrie* (Rome, 2000)

2 'The Mother of All Slaughters'

1 Giovanni Fasanella, Claudio Sestieri, Giovanni Pellegrino, *Segreto di Stato* (Turin, 2000)
2 Leonard Weinberg and William Lee Eubank, *The Rise and Fall of Italian Terrorism* (Boulder, 1987)
3 Claudio Pavone, *Una Guerra Civile* (Turin, 1992)
4 Leonard Weinberg and William Lee Eubank, *The Rise and Fall of Italian Terrorism* (Boulder, 1987)
5 Franco Ferraresi, *Minacce alla Democrazia* (Milan, 1995)
6 Robert Putnam, 'Atteggiamenti politici dell'alta burocrazia nell'Europa occidentale' (Rivista Italiana di Scienza Politica 3, no 1, 1973)
7 Sergio Zavoli, *La Notte della Repubblica* (Milan, 1992)
8 Alessandro Silj, *Never Again Without a Rifle* (New York, 1979)
9 Ibid
10 Maurizio Dianese and Gianfranco Bettin, *La Strage* (Milan, 1999)
11 *Corriere della Sera* (13 December 1969)
12 Maurizio Dianese and Gianfranco Bettin, *La Strage* (Milan, 1999)
13 Ibid
14 Giorgio Bocca, *Il Filo Nero* (Milan, 1995)

15 Ernesto Galli della Loggia, *L'identità italiana* (Bologna, 1998)

3 Penalties and Impunity

1 Alan Friedman, *Agnelli and the Network of Italian Power* (London,1988)

4 'The Sofri Case'

1 Dario Fo, *Accidental Death of an Anarchist*, trans Ed Emery (London, 1992)
2 Adriano Sofri, *Memoria* (Bari, 1990)
3 Daniele Biacchessi, *Il Caso Sofri* (Rome, 1998)
4 Giorgio Bocca in *La Repubblica* (21 July 1982)
5 Franco Ferraroti, *L'ipnosi della violenza* (Milan, 1980)
6 Maurizio Dianese and Gianfranco Bettin, *La Strage* (Milan, 1999)
7 Giovanni Fasanella, Claudio Sestieri, Giovanni Pellegrino, *Segreto di Stato* (Turin, 2000)

5 The Means of Seduction

1 Italo Calvino, *La speculazione edilizia* (Milan, 1994)
2 Quoted in Edward Murray, *Fellini the Artist* (New York, 1976)
3 Pier Paolo Pasolini, *Lettere Luterane* (Turin, 1976)
4 Italo Calvino, *La speculazione edilizia* (Milan, 1994)
5 Quoted in Ernesto Galli Della Loggia, *L'identità italiana* (Bologna, 1998)
6 *The Economist* (April 24 May 4 2001)

6 Clean Hands

1 Eurostat, *Enterprises in Europe* (Brussels, 1996)
2 Quoted in *The New York Review of Books* (October 18, 2001)
3 Carlo Pirovano ed., *Italia moderna: la difficile democrazia* (Milan, 1985)
4 Ibid
5 *Corriere della Sera* (3 May 1992)
6 Paul Ginsborg, *L'Italia del tempo presente* (Turin, 1998)
7 *Corriere della Sera* (29 May 1992)
8 *Il Giornale* (27 January 1994)

7 Miracles and Mysteries

1 Quoted in John Cornwell, *Breaking Faith* (London, 2001)
2 *Henry James Letters. 4 Volumes.* Ed. by Leon Edel (Cambridge USA, 1984)
3 Charles Dickens, *Pictures from Italy*, Ed. by Kate Flint (London, 1998)
4 *Espresso* (number 40, 1981)
5 Paul Ginsborg, *Italy and Its Discontents* (London, 2001)
6 Tina Anselmi, *Commissione Parlamentare d'Inchiesta sulla Loggia Massonica P2* (Rome, 1984)

8 An Italian Story

1 Alexander Stille, *Excellent Cadavers* (London, 1995)

10 *I Morti*

1 *Corriere della Sera*, (19 January 2002)
2 *La Repubblica*, (20 April 2002)
3 Giovanni Guareschi, *The Little World of Don Camillo* (New York, 1977)
4 Henry James, *Italian Hours* (London, 1995)
5 Umberto Eco, *Sette anni di desiderio* (Milan, 1983)
6 Ibid

Index